Indivisible by Four

A STRING QUARTET

IN PURSUIT OF

HARMONY

Arnold Steinhardt

FARRAR STRAUS GIROUX
NEW YORK

Farrar, Straus and Giroux
19 Union Square West, New York 10003

Copyright © 1998 by Arnold Steinhardt
Distributed in Canada by Douglas & McIntyre Ltd.
Printed in the United States of America
First edition, 1998
Third printing, 1999

Library of Congress Cataloging-in-Publication Data
Steinhardt, Arnold.
    Indivisible by four : a string quartet in pursuit of harmony / by
Arnold Steinhardt.
        p.   cm.
    ISBN 0-374-23670-4 (alk. paper)
    1. Guarneri Quartet.   I. Title.
ML398.G835   1998
785'.7194'0922–dc21
[b]   98-7978

FOR DAVID, JOHN, AND MICHAEL

CONTENTS

Things should be made as simple as possible, but not any simpler.

— ALBERT EINSTEIN

INDIVISIBLE BY FOUR

Zone of Magic

Hmm. Not quite. Perhaps if I play the melody with a little more verve and abandon, with more suppleness, it will come alive. But not too much abandon! Otherwise, John will have trouble following me. We two violins have to be perfectly together, like twins in matching outfits. And don't forget Michael. His viola part, with the underlying rhythmic pulse, is a running commentary on the violins' conversation, and if we dawdle, we'll be out of synch with him. Try it again. No, no. Out of tune. That wouldn't sound pretty over Dave's sustained cello line.

The row of naked dressing-room lightbulbs casts a clinical glare on my music. Why isn't this getting any easier? We have played this piece, the Smetana String Quartet "From My Life," literally hundreds of times, and before each performance I grapple with the same melody, a love song, really, trying to capture its youthful ardor. Am I simply treading water as a musician or are my expectations growing with each year that we—the guys, as I call us, or, more formally, the Guarneri String Quartet—have been together? One might expect that after this long, Smetana's emotive music would have settled comfortably into the muscles, tendons, even the synapses of the brain, and play itself.

I continue my pre-concert ablutions—warm-up exercises and a final check of the first violin's most vexing passages in the music for this evening. The three string quartets on tonight's program—Haydn Opus 74, no. 3, in G minor, Janáček no. 2, and Smetana's "From My Life"—are all powerful works that place large demands on the wit, hands, and hearts of their four performers.

As concert time approaches, the nerve endings in my body begin to feel large and oversensitized. It is the same odd sensation I experienced as a six-year-old performing for the very first time at a student concert. The glass of water I was trying to drink beforehand slipped from my little hand and broke. These days, I seem to handle my water better, but the feeling persists, a hint of a performance about to begin. The ingredients in this pre-concert recipe remain constant— anticipation, excitement, and a bit of anxiety. But the proportions change depending on the music, how I feel, and, for want of a better description, on how the planets have lined up at that particular hour. Do the others have these sensations? You'd think I would know by now.

My reverie is broken by the stage manager's ten-minute call. Why is he speaking with an accent? Oh yes, this is Buenos Aires. Hard to keep track when you play in a different city almost every night. Time for a final inventory: violin (tuned), bow (rosined), music (don't forget the encore we decided on—that little Mozart fugue), brush stray hairs off the shoulders, make sure bow tie is straight. Ready.

I hear crosscurrents of cello, viola, and violin sounds intermingling and drifting through my half-open door, a delicious cacophony, as David, Michael, and John warm up in adjacent dressing rooms. Their individual styles are profoundly familiar to me. After all these years, I would recognize their playing anywhere, instantly. The rising and falling of a phrase, the little quirks of their vibrato, the very favorite way each man has of soaring from one note to another almost vocally—these are the unmistakable individual and personal expressions of musicians who have thought long and hard about what they do.

Eight minutes before concert time Michael is practicing a lyrical viola solo in the Janáček, emphasizing its climax by intensifying his vibrato. David works on a brilliant cello passage in the Haydn first movement, playing ever so slowly before letting the phrase go at full gallop. And John has either mastered tonight's program or given up on it entirely. He is playing a fugue from one of the solo Bach violin sonatas, the chords ringing out cleanly and incisively. No, keep the doors closed. Their musical identity is as recognizable as their faces.

Buenos Aires is the last concert of the season before our self-imposed summer vacation begins, and frankly, I feel a schoolboy elation at the thought of being finally let out of Guarneri U. Nine months of pressure-cooker activity in which all four of us are rehearsing, playing, traveling, attending business meetings and parties, and teaching is enough togetherness for one year. Enough of "us." It is time for "me."

Something else, too, has slowly and cumulatively begun to creep into the equation. As one year blends into the next, there is a sense of astonishment at the improbability of the same four men still being together in one performing unit. Given the unpredictable and often short life of a string quartet, it is remarkable that the four of us have not only stuck it out but actually loved the ride. And what a long ride! With this particular concert, at the end of a South American tour, the Guarneri String Quartet finishes its thirty-second year together and plans for the thirty-third next fall. The firm and measured cadence of our life as a quartet seems to mimic the inevitability of the seasons' coming and going. These days, I have taken to wondering before each concert, which one is this? Could Buenos Aires be number 2,983? The statistic is impressive.

What witch's brew did the Guarneri Quartet concoct to stay together for so long, while most other chamber-music groups have weathered turnovers or self-destructed entirely? It is a question asked by everyone—listeners out of mild curiosity, interviewers on assignment, and musicians shaking their heads in wonder. Any more than for a team climbing Mount Everest or a manned space mission, not everyone is temperamentally suited for this line of work. Many musicians cannot take the strain of going *mano a mano* with the same three people year after year. When a quartet player leaves a group, the reason is rarely made public, but on the musical grapevine one hears whispers: he was always too loud, she picked on me incessantly, I should have been playing first violin, they made life on tour too difficult. Walking offstage at the close of a concert several years ago, a violinist in a well-known quartet lunged at the cellist. "I'm going to cut your heart out for playing so loud," he snarled. The fellow had to be restrained, and although no blood was spilled, needless to say the cellist soon left the quartet, perhaps under a variation of the witness-protection program. Some of our best-known quartets have had enough turnovers to be properly called octets or nonettes. The Budapest Quartet, named by its four Hungarian founding members, ended with four Russians; and with the retirement in 1997 of the Juilliard String Quartet's first violinist, Robert Mann, who had been the only remaining founding member, the new second violinist, Ronald Copes, became its tenth member.

Not unlike any other group with serious ambitions, the Guarneri Quartet was founded on a bedrock of love for the string-quartet literature, and on a belief that the four of us had enough in common to allow an enterprise to take root. But in every quartet's evolution, either a player will develop an allergic reaction to his colleagues and the profession's demands or the sharp edges of personal difference will soften into a good working atmosphere. The Guarneri Quartet might have gone either way. David Soyer is blunt and highly opinionated, John Dalley is sparing in his comments and often reserved, Michael Tree is an efficient problem-solver with an ebullient manner, and (please don't tell the others) I am a voice of reason and accommodation. "I never thought you four would make it as a quartet," our good friend the violinist and instrument dealer Charles Avsharian confessed to me years ago. "You're all too different." But, contrary to the dire prophecies, we have come to enjoy our differences more than they make us uncomfortable, and—call this the luck of good chemistry—these interlocking disparities in temperament, style, and artistic impulse have even served us well. Instead of generating the explosions some people expected from our mismatched personalities, we have created a kind of hodgepodge of checks and balances. When, for example, I burst the classical mold with a phrase of excessive romanticism in the middle of a Mozart quartet, my colleagues are always on hand to save me from myself.

But it is the string-quartet feast itself, easily two hundred works strong, that has nourished us year after year, and this minimizes all the personal difficulties. There is simply nothing better than playing string quartets and performing them in public. Almost all the giants of music are there: Haydn, Mozart, Beethoven, Schubert, Brahms, Schumann, Mendelssohn, Dvořák, Bartók. And every year brings new adventures. There are still pockets of the standard repertoire that we have missed, forgotten or ignored treasures of the past to ferret out and reintroduce to the public, and new music to learn. Hans Werner Henze recently wrote a piano quintet for us and Peter Serkin; and in the near future Richard Danielpour will write a string-quartet concerto for us and the National Symphony Orchestra. Adding to the endless conjecture about what the composers of the past really wanted for their music, we work with live, breathing ones who have very specific instructions. Composers are eager for performers' advice on both instrumental and musical matters, and that gives us the excitement of having a small hand in the creative process. What must it have been like to be a member of the Schuppanzigh Quartet working with Beethoven or the Kolisch Quartet with Bartók!

The stage manager's five-minute call interrupts my thoughts. We gather in the backstage half-light for a final tuning and for our last-minute warm-up rituals. I play a dozen notes up and down my violin for reassurance that my fingers are still attached to my body and are actually in working order. David tunes his cello brusquely, confidently, without further warm-up. Is he saying, "Que sera, sera"? John is more dispassionate. He not only tunes his violin but checks his strings for true intervals at the fifth, sometimes shaking his head when a perfectly new string doesn't behave as he expected. And Michael is an opera singer who makes sure he has those gorgeous viola notes ready for the public, by trying out a few on himself. Even these insignificant roulades are deeply familiar. These men are very well known to me, I can say quite smugly—their tastes, their quirks, their turns of mind. I can even tell you silly things about them that no one may have the slightest interest in hearing. Dave loves Twinkies, Michael dislikes olives, John prefers heavy cream in his coffee. They in turn know, I assume, that I don't care for anchovies. And I know other things—about the beauty of their playing and the power of their communication in the concert hall. These are the qualities that elicit the mutual respect at the heart of a successful string quartet.

The sheer body of knowledge both significant and trifling that we have about one another, these quasi-CIA files, embarrasses me slightly. Meeting by chance in a hotel lobby or at an airport gate, we exchange greetings that can hardly begin to express the sum total of our thousands of hours of experience together. With that "hello" there is sometimes a lowering of the eyes, a slight awkwardness, a mock formality, as if to cover over a not quite natural act. After all, should we be spending more time with each other than with our wives and children? Yet often we must.

Those of us who choose to live and work in this little chamber-music capsule have a stronger need than most to guard our personal lives and keep them private. We draw the curtain somewhat on our families' goings-on, our joys, our sorrows. If I sit with David in an airplane that is carrying us at 35,000 feet to the next concert, we do talk about quartet playing, about the President, about the poor, and about last night's linguini with white clam sauce (overcooked, not enough garlic); but about things of a truly private nature we speak only very guardedly if at all. There is really no need for David to know that my wife and I had a spat the other day over who should take out the garbage.

We continue warming up. The concert is almost upon us.

It is at this moment that I often feel a reflexive regret: if only I had another day, another hour, or even another minute to practice tonight's three masterpieces. *Then* you would hear something! But time has run out, and a nagging question hangs over the performance about to take place: how well will it go? We have worked hard, individually and collectively, to fashion a cogent and convincing interpretation, but will we be inspired? If one of us decides spontaneously to fly with a new idea during the next two hours—a different coloration, an exotic phrasing detail—will the rest of us be quick enough to understand, respond, and take wing with him? In this pre-concert moment, the fragile connections among four very different people seem palpable. How truly dependent and vulnerable we are! It is not so different from the way rock climbers must feel, roped together, relying on each other to an equally high degree. I exaggerate. Nobody dies in chamber music (as opposed to opera). Nevertheless, as we are about to be joined together in making music, I sense that our relationship, however hard to define, goes far beyond the professional realm. David, John, Michael, and I are not types who look soulfully into one another's eyes and say how much we mean to each other, but we have shared too much experience in the almost three thousand concerts we have played together to be mere business partners or colleagues. Our early struggles for a quartet identity give us a certain war-buddy status. As chamber-music veterans, we occasionally reminisce about those early days, the memories of the hardships now wrapped comfortably in the knowledge of our ongoing survival and success.

But it is on the concert stage where the moments of true intimacy occur. When a performance is in progress, all four of us together enter a zone of magic somewhere between our music stands and become conduit, messenger, and missionary. In playing, say, the cavatina of Opus 130, we join hands to enter Beethoven's world, vividly aware of each other and our objective performance responsibilities, and yet, almost like sleepwalkers, we allow ourselves to slip into the music's spiritual realm. It is an experience too personal to talk about and yet it colors every aspect of our relationship, every good-natured musical confrontation, all the professional gossip, the latest viola joke.

From my position in the wings, I can see a portion of the lit stage. To label the stage a zone of magic sounds poetic, but it is also our work area. In the next two hours we will expend a significant amount of energy slaving over our instruments. And as people do in every workplace, we have our inside jokes and our private communications, a subtext to the story we spin out onstage. In the heat of performance, we send Morse code out in four directions—ensemble signals, significant glances, even smiles or lifted eyebrows as something goes especially well or perhaps not well at all. Michael rolls his eyes at me because David has not done the planned bowing, John and Michael lock glances as they play an inner-voice passage, second violin and viola in unison, or I look over my music stand at David, intent on following him as he deals with a difficult cello solo, his chin jutting forward with the effort. These visual exchanges are, like spices in a fine dish, necessary and energizing ingredients in our performances.

At the end of the concert, drained and exhausted from the heart-to-heart talk we have just had with an audience of strangers, we gratefully accept their return applause as a thank you. It is considered bad form for musicians to boast about their success or revel in the accolades—The audience went wild when I finished! They adored my playing! Why, I had to give three encores! and so forth. But when at the conclusion of the dazzling fugue that ends Beethoven's Opus 59, no. 3, the audience roars with approval, it is a very good feeling, and it never wears thin. We count our exits and entrances off and on stage as the applause continues. One, two, and, on a good night, three returns to the stage. That entitles the audience (in accordance with the Guarneri Quartet's rules of stage etiquette) to an encore. Another good feeling. David, our designated mouthpiece, announces the encore standing at his music stand, occasionally lacing the information with a well-placed joke or two. "We will play the scherzo from Mendelssohn's Quartet in E minor," he once told an audience that refused to stop clapping. "Wouldn't the slow movement be a better contrast to the Debussy we just played?" Michael whispered. "We'll be here all night with that andante," John muttered impatiently. "The scherzo is better." The conversation, which had started privately among us, gradually rose in volume. I put in my two cents. "Michael's right. The slow movement makes a better encore." By now our disagreement was public news. We were at an impasse and the audience began to buzz. Finally, someone in the back of the hall called out, "Play the scherzo." David wheeled around in the direction of this new entry into the conversation and shouted, "You keep out of this!"

On nights when the response is more tepid, Michael is the one who hopes for no encores at all as we wait in the wings. He just wants to rid himself of his concert shirt, soaked in sweat, and slip into something more comfortable. As the applause dribbles to a close, John has a different read on the situation. "Convenient, but ominous," he says cheerfully as the four of us amble back to our dressing rooms and pack up. Artur Schnabel once said that applause is a receipt for services rendered, not a bill for services due. Fine, but when you are bathed in applause after a good performance, it is hard to make that distinction. We are happy to play encores. And the bravos are a vote of confidence for us to go on to the next concert, and the next.

Backstage, fans, friends, and well-wishers regularly show up. We'll shake a few hands, sign a couple of CD jackets. "Wonderful concert," someone says, "but you must be tired of hearing that." Never. A woman told me several weeks ago that she cried during the slow movement of the Debussy quartet. "That bad!" I exclaimed, parrying her remark with a joke. Most musicians are awkward about accepting compliments, even though I know of no one who isn't pleased by them. I had been flustered by her comment because crying is about reaching the soul, and the woman's response to our playing and the music was beyond the realm of compliments. It went to the very heart of what music is about.

The stage manager calls for places. As we gather in the wings, we see the empty stage and four empty stands and chairs on the television monitor. "Where is the Guarneri Quartet, and why aren't they playing?" asks David, looking at the screen. John adds, "Does a quartet make a sound in the forest when no one is there?" Michael says nothing at first. The poor guy is sick with the flu and running a fever. He is valiantly playing the concert but has no excess energy for jokes. But then he does muster a remark. "Don't forget, the repeat in the Haydn is good."

"We'll do it," I counter, "but whether it's good is another story." "It's a good repeat," David says firmly. "Otherwise, the movement is unbalanced." John is quick to add his opinion. "Unnecessary and repetitious."

The stage manager eyes us with what appears to be a mix of curiosity and discomfort. I can see what he is thinking: these gentlemen are about to go onstage and they're still arguing! But that is the nature of a democracy, and a string quartet, remarkably, is just that, a true democracy. So much easier and faster to have a benevolent dictator who says to his three acolytes, Gentlemen, we will *not* make the repeat in the Haydn tonight.

With four strong and somewhat fearless personalities, our road was much longer, more stressful, and, in the great tradition of democracy, exhilarating. What tempo should the opening of Mozart's "Dissonant" Quartet be? Is it wise to place the Mendelssohn A minor Quartet, which finishes quietly, at the end of a program? Should we accept less than our established fee for a concert offered us in Des Moines, Iowa, on a free day between engagements already booked in Chicago and Detroit? Each question elicited discussion, disagreement, and even occasional lost tempers. In the early years, I would sometimes return from a rehearsal dazed and exhausted by the continual process of conflict and resolution. But as we began to understand our differing tastes and individual ways of thinking through problems, our little democracy became more benign. David, Michael, and John weren't the enemy—they were just different from me. If the process of reaching agreement was slow and the outcome uncertain, at least it pushed you to think clearly about the important issues. There was strength in this ambiguity. And at some point during the ongoing rehearsals, discussions, struggles, and performances, the individuals known as John Dalley, Michael Tree, David Soyer, and Arnold Steinhardt became the Guarneri String Quartet.

My line of sight through the slightly open door falls across the stage and onto the first row of seats. I glimpse a few expectant faces awaiting us and the music. El Teatro Coliseo is a Buenos Aires hall where we have played many times before. The audience's passionate devotion to string quartets seems to be in almost inverse proportion to the unremarkable appearance and insignificant size of this group of four.

"Gentlemen," the stage manager beckons with a sweeping, almost courtly gesture.

We walk onstage, David and I the six-footers, Michael and John of medium height. Each of us looks, walks, bows, and sits down differently. A music lover looking for visual signs that a fine quartet performance might take place will find nothing here. As the applause subsides, we open our music to the Haydn string quartet that begins the program. Four Americans trained by Russians, Armenians, an Austrian, a Catalan, and a Hungarian are about to play a work by an Austrian composer for a Latin American audience whose ancestry is largely Spanish and Italian. Perhaps we will find our zone of magic in this wildly cross-cultural stew.

Again, which concert is this? And how many more will the Guarneri String Quartet play before our saga comes to an end? I give a crisp lead to start the Haydn. It is time to finish our thirty-second season.

Diary. August 15, 1996. We have agreed to interrupt our vacation for a concert at Tanglewood, the music festival in the Berkshire Mountains. Our all-Beethoven program consists of two works, Opus 132 and Opus 59, no. 3 (one of the Razumovskys). I am oddly anxious about this concert in the middle of the summer. During the regular season, momentum builds up from the preliminary rehearsals through the many concerts that follow one after another. These Beethovens were part of last season's programs, but now, after only two months of lying dormant, they seem forbidding. We must reactivate the machinery of playing string quartets in a single afternoon.

The quartet meets backstage for a 3 p.m. rehearsal. We greet one another warmly but tentatively, intruding as we are on the sanctity of each man's vacation time. There is much to do. In the next three hours, we carefully go through the entire program, reestablishing connections with one another and reassuring ourselves that our familiarity with this exalted music has not disappeared into the summer air.

As we walk onto the stage of newly built Ozawa Hall, gracefully adorned in teak, I am more nervous than usual. The concert stage as well as the music we play can become quickly unfamiliar with disuse. The audience, which spills out onto the lawn beyond the hall, welcomes us enthusiastically and the performance goes well, even better than usual. Perhaps because this concert is disconnected from a comfortable berth in the regular season, we are especially alert. We play an encore. Now I can go home and weed my garden's arugula patch.

2

Soloist

IN ITS SUPREME WISDOM, the Curtis Institute of Music in Philadelphia required first-year students, along with studying their major instrument, to take courses in harmony, counterpoint, music history, piano, and something called chamber music. At the age of seventeen, I had only a vague idea of what it meant for musicians to play together in small groups. Why in a chamber, this music? I thought concerts were given in public halls, in auditoriums and theaters, not in chambers. If I thought about the word "chamber" at all, a torture chamber or chamber of horrors was what came to mind. Yet there under this curious heading "chamber music" on the school bulletin board I found my name along with three others listed one day. The notice had more or less the same effect on me as a summons to jury duty—it was something I knew I had to do but would rather have avoided. The group, the music, and even our first rehearsal had been invisibly programmed, like an arranged marriage, so to speak.

The four of us listed, all first-year students, had to seek each other out on our own, but in a school as small and intimate as Curtis this was not difficult. Passing through its front doors, one enters a world of oak-paneled walls and pillars, muted oil paintings adorning the walls, large lustrous Oriental carpets easing one's passage from one room into the next. Curtis has more the feel of a town house than of a school, and with good reason. Originally it had been the Drexel estate, one of many fine houses on Philadelphia's quietly dignified Rittenhouse Square. When Mary Curtis Bok decided in 1924 to create a small, elite, tuition-free music conservatory with her Curtis Publishing Company fortune, the Drexel place seemed well suited. As one of a mere 125 students enrolled in 1954, I had the feeling of being in an extended family or a privileged club more than in a music school. Indeed, when I entered the building for the first time during Wednesday's traditional afternoon tea, I thought I had died and gone to conservatory heaven.

Mary Curtis Bok Zimbalist, the school's founder, was presiding over the tea service in the patrician manner of someone raised in sustained wealth and culture. For each of the students and faculty dutifully attendant, she had the same words, delivered with a smile of unwavering propriety: Strong or weak, one sugar or two? My first view of heaven was very brief. Curtis, which had a jacket-and-tie dress code at that time, did not take kindly to the Hawaiian shirt I was sporting. Jack Cooper, one of the older boys, was assigned to escort me out of school and explain the facts of life to a Southern California kid who thought that formal meant a Hawaiian shirt with smaller pineapples on it.

When the four of us eventually located each other and met for our first rehearsal of Mozart's G major Quartet,

K 327, it was also the very first time I had ever played string-quartet music. As we exchanged pleasantries, I considered the setup: two violins paired together, facing the lower end of the tonal spectrum, viola and cello. Why two of us and only one of each of them? Why not one violin, one viola, and two cellos, say? Or four of us and none of them? And what will such a sparse collection of instruments sound like? In any case, the music would be an easy romp for me. I had looked over my assigned first-violin part beforehand, and there was nothing very difficult, compared to what my violin teacher, Ivan Galamian, demanded of me in my weekly lessons. After a kind of basic training for violinists at the beginning of the semester, Galamian had put me on a tough regimen of staples from the soloist's repertoire.

I was wading through the two dozen concertos for solo violin and orchestra that are a given in any fiddler's education. These exquisitely created works—by Bach, Mozart, Beethoven, Mendelssohn, Bruch, Wieniawski, Brahms, and more—were a showcase in which the violinist could excite, impress, dazzle, and inspire an audience. Then there were études by Dont, Gaviniès, Kreutzer, and Wieniawski, the equivalent of bodybuilding exercises at the local gym, designed to develop tone, strength, endurance, and agility; they culminated in the twenty-four caprices of Niccolò Paganini. Every conceivable difficulty was artfully employed in these dazzling and stylish pieces by the great nineteenth-century virtuoso: up- and down-bow staccato, left-hand pizzicato, double and triple stops, ricochet bowing, and whole handfuls of notes to be played at high velocity. These Paganini caprices, which I was currently grappling with, were not for the faint of heart. Tossing them off required a complete mastery of the instrument plus ample amounts of chutzpah. At a polar opposite, Galamian expected me to learn Johann Sebastian Bach's six sonatas and partitas for unaccompanied violin. Although now a staple of the repertoire, these were considered so dense and difficult by most violinists until the early twentieth century that they were used for little more than study purposes. Bach had taken an instrument that essentially plays one note at a time and composed music for it with two, three, and even four voices. The intrinsic difficulties were groundbreaking and enormous. Pity the poor violinist, a melody player all his life, having to juggle several independent voices at once for the first time.

My interest in the virtuoso violin repertoire had begun long before I entered the Curtis Institute. While other teenagers were turning the family car into a hot rod or trying to make the high-school football team, I was seeking out thrills as a fifteen-year-old trying to master some of the violin's most infamous killer pieces—Wieniawski's Scherzo Tarantelle, Sarasate's Gypsy Airs, Paganini's Perpetual Motion, and Lalo's Symphonie Espagnole, a movement of which I had played a year earlier at a Los Angeles Philharmonic Orchestra youth concert. It was fun to work the brilliant passages into shape and then play them at breakneck speed—something akin to running the hundred-yard dash or driving a race car. And then the slow parts! How delicious to pour my undefined but powerful adolescent feelings into a gypsy melody or a Spanish Habanera! Before school, I would practice an hour of scales and virtuoso pieces, standing on the floor heat register to thaw my toes and fingers in the damp cold of a California winter.

No, there was nothing daunting about the Mozart quartet we were about to rehearse: no daredevil runs at high speeds, no finger-twisters, just lyrical, pleasing music. Simple, I thought.

"Let's play it through," someone suggested. Heads nodded in approval, instruments and bows were raised, yet we sat mutely in place. We were an automobile without a starter. Marcia, our cellist, opened a small pocket score she had brought along and peered into it. "You have the first note alone, Arnold. You start," she suggested. Start I did, and the others joined in a very ragged play-through in which the ensemble was chaotic and we all missed cues. Where Mozart divided up a phrase and allotted a section of it to each player, we were at a loss as to how to connect the sections. A relay race was taking place in which each runner flubbed the passing of the baton. And if this was such easy music, why was I stumbling over notes, making a poor sound, and having such trouble with the simple rhythms? The first movement ended, and was followed by a black hole of silence. Our tongues seemed to have fallen out of our mouths.

Uncertainly, I spoke up: "Shall we play it again?" "Yes, yes, let's do it again!" said the others with relief. "Excellent idea. Yes, again."

The sad fact was that we had almost no idea how to approach this music. The first movement of the Mozart quartet is indeed good-natured and sunny, but it is certainly not simple. It is music with detail and imagination wrapped in innocent friendliness. The opening melody of sixty-nine notes, played principally by the first violin and accompanied by the other three voices, rises, falls, seems to pause, continues playfully, and finally comes to a gentle end. The performer may spend hours struggling to fashion those notes into something coherent, but he must never, never betray its difficulties to his listener. The sixty-nine notes should take wing and soar as if unimpeded by any technical or conceptual problem, a feat that all musicians seem to find exasperatingly difficult. After hearing a rehearsal of *The Abduction from the Seraglio*, the Emperor Joseph II said to Mozart, "My dear Mozart, that is too fine for my ears; there are too many notes." "I ask your Majesty's pardon," replied

Mozart, "there are just as many notes as there should be."
He might have said the same about his quartet's opening.

Throughout the two rehearsals that led up to our first
official chamber-music lesson, all four of us made timid suggestions. "Why not play the opening a little softer?" the
violist offered. "And can we use the same bowings?" added
our second violinist. But nothing we did seemed to bring us
nearer to the gentle beauty of Mozart's G major Quartet. We
needed help.

It was soon to arrive. The four of us filed into a large,
well-appointed third-floor room which looked out onto Rittenhouse Square. We were greeted by our chamber-music
coach, Jascha Brodsky, a slender, dapper man with a heavy
Russian accent. Brodsky was the first violinist of the Curtis
String Quartet, formed in the earliest days of the school.
(Originally, it had been called, curiously enough, the Swas-
tika Quartet, before this ancient word lost its innocence forever.) As we prepared to play, four great figures from
string-quartet history gazed down upon us. A large, framed
lithograph of the Joachim String Quartet on the wall de-
picted Joseph Joachim, reigning German violinist of his day
and friend and confidant of Brahms, rehearsing with his colleagues. On the stands before them, their music was clearly
seen opened to Beethoven's Quartet, Opus 59, no. 3.

As an outstanding violinist in a highly regarded quartet,
Brodsky was well equipped to lead us through the Mozart.
He settled into his chair and we started to play. We were
barely through the opening statement when Brodsky held
up his hand. "Look at what you have just played. Try to find
the hills and valleys, the dynamic ups and downs of the
phrase. Make a tentative plan. Don't worry if you are dis-
satisfied. Nothing is cut in stone; this is just a beginning."
As he chain-smoked, Brodsky continued to give us good,
basic suggestions. "The second theme contains four quick

sixteenth notes that you are playing very literally, as a metronome would. If you play them ever so slightly faster, just
tossing them off, they will sound stylish rather than la-
bored." With low expectations, we repeated the passage. It
unexpectedly sprang to life. This was a heady moment, as if
we had by alchemy transformed a stone into a lily.

We felt slightly more hopeful at our next rehearsal, Brodsky having given us advice and encouragement. But there
seemed to be more questions than answers. Simply to start
this four-cylinder motor was a problem. How does one give
a sign to begin? Having the first note of the piece, I was
presumably in charge, but my body language was too vague
for the others to decipher. We were not together. It took a
while for me to learn how to give a lead that was economical
in motion yet clear. Since solo lines occurred in all voices,
each of us had to develop this skill.

And just how does one actually play together? This subject was hardly touched upon in all my years of violin lessons
but now was an issue of utmost, constant concern. With
chamber music you had to learn how to be both soloist and
accompanist, often slipping quickly from one role to the
other. Most often, a solo line ruled, with the others dutifully
following it. But if, when accompanist, I merely listened to
the solo line, my violin voice would tend to lag behind. We
learned to watch carefully the motions of the solo voice's
fingers of both hands (and any other body language), as an
advance warning system for the sound that was to come.

Another question: How does one criticize without creating bad blood? "You've gotten behind every time we've
played those sixteenth notes," one of the group complained
to me, unable to keep the irritation out of his voice. It is
one thing for your teacher to give you hell during weekly
lessons, but when it came from the pipsqueak with acne
sitting across from me, I stiffened. Moments later, the slight

was forgotten as I informed our violist that he was out of tune. "I don't think I was," he said, trying not to sound defensive. "That's the way I've always played it." This was too big an issue for short-term solution. We bumbled along, trying bravely to accept the stings of criticism, which would thankfully cease when our transient group disbanded in a matter of weeks.

Another problem was the endless talking that went on. How could we ever get anything done if we talked all the time? Discussions were fine, but we couldn't bring them to a close easily or recognize when a solution to a problem was simply not yet available. Nevertheless, our Mozart inched forward by trial and error.

At the end of three or four lessons, Brodsky listened to a play-through of the entire piece and judged that our four-some and Mozart should part company. We knew that the very best groups were picked to perform in Curtis Hall, but Brodsky conferred no such honor on us. Just as well, I thought. Playing quartets was like being the Flying Wallendas: potentially breathtaking but never relaxing, and sometimes very stressful. Playing first violin in the string quartet had been a learning experience for me, but it certainly brought no epiphany. Still, I was very pleased to have worked with a musician of Brodsky's caliber—especially since, I reminded myself, a man of his advanced age wouldn't be around forever. That was 1955, and Jascha passed away in 1997 in his late eighties, teaching at Curtis to the very end. The old man I first played for must have been all of forty-five.

As my first year in Philadelphia progressed and I continued my violin studies, I began to pal around with my classmates. We ate together, went to concerts, movies, parties, museums, and ball games. In the process of exploring center-city Philadelphia, we became acquainted with most of the downtown restaurants: the Horn & Hardart Automat (where you inserted a few nickels in a slot and, lifting a glass door, you pulled out anything from chicken pot pie to cherry cobbler), the Harvey House (famous for its banana splits, which arrived with an American flag implanted in the vanilla scoop: first one a dollar, all that followed free), the South China restaurant (where we mastered the art of the chopstick), and Bain's Cafeteria with its elderly Jewish clientele (where Homer Lee, a gifted African-American clarinetist, tried out the Yiddish phrases we taught him, to the amazement of the old-timers).

And at some point we fell into the habit of playing chamber music together for the sheer fun of it. Curtis had no dormitories, so these sight-reading parties were held in the modest apartments all over town where the students lived. Volumes of music from the school library were piled up by the music stands. We would negotiate reading choices as if trading baseball cards: I'll play your Mendelssohn quartet if you'll do my Beethoven G major Trio afterward. The groups expanded and contracted, going from duos to octets and even nonettes. As time went on, a core group of students who were intensely interested in the chamber-music repertoire coalesced. I found myself drawn to this group—to the music, even to its challenges, and to the people who showed up at the gatherings, among the most thoughtful and interesting musicians in the school. Many would later have distinguished careers in music, particularly chamber music— the violinists Shmuel Ashkenasi and Jaime Laredo, the pianists Anton Kuerti and Lee Luvisi, and two others named John Dalley and Michael Tree.

We kidded the cellists about having to play their instruments upside down and nailed to the floor, but for us violinists there were several options. With many compositions requiring two violins, we could shuttle between playing first and second and, if no violist was present, even move over to that position. Curtis required violinists to study viola for a year, in my time with the Curtis Quartet's violist, Max Aronoff. I loved the viola immediately. Being long-armed, I found it relatively easy to handle the longer, broader instrument. Tuck the viola under your chin and, presto, you were a rich, deep-voiced mezzo-soprano. The viola's lower, deeper register is a balm to the ears of the violinist, whose fillings are constantly being rattled by a violin's high pitches. The viola requires wider distances between fingers, and different bow speeds and pressure, but the instrument was close enough to the violin for many to make the crossover successfully. Some were so bewitched by the viola's husky resonance that they never returned to its smaller cousin.

Our music parties were more than fun. They were a first glimpse of a new kind of treasure. Most of the music we read through at first were quartets: Haydn, Mozart, Beethoven, Schubert, and beyond. One masterwork after another came off the printed page and to life. As the first year faded into the second, the piles by our music stands shrank; we played on, intoxicated with each discovery, late into the night. The two or three dozen quartets we selected from Haydn's eighty-three alone provided enough material for many jam sessions. Violinists vied to play first violin, which has the lion's share of solo material and difficulty in most of the Haydns.

Eventually, we ventured into the quintet literature, first the three celebrated ones with piano by Schumann, Brahms, and Dvořák, and then on to string quintets. Looming large among these was Schubert's Two Cello Quintet, written only two months before his death in 1828. This work of luminous sonority, epic, unhurried grandeur, and "heavenly length" (as Robert Schumann described Schubert's C major symphony) is inevitably on everyone's list of most beloved chamber pieces. It demanded more of us than our sight-reading parties could give. With Jascha Brodsky coaching us, we plunged into genuine rehearsals.

There were dividends to this team endeavor: lively discussions, boisterous spirits. Each of us would present his ideas on how the quintet should be played, and disagreements inevitably followed. Another set of ideas always seemed to be waiting in the wings. What a departure from my violin studies, in which I spent long hours working in complete solitude! With repeated rehearsals, each of us began to develop our musical credo and a certain skill in packaging and selling our opinions. Our discussions sometimes reminded me of debates among politicians, with each player trying to state his point of view convincingly enough to win a congressional majority, in this case the House of Schubert.

Rehearsals were now a far cry from those of two years before, when four novices had dipped their toes with trepidation into a Mozart quartet. The experience we had gathered from our weekly lessons and from Curtis's required music courses certainly contributed to rapidly increasing confidence. Something else, though, made the Schubert quintet easier: it wasn't a quartet. In picking the works we might study and truly perform from among all the compositions we played at those sight-reading sessions, we instinctively steered away from quartets: they were too hard, too fussy, too much work. Add a fifth instrument—in this case, the deeply resonant cello—and a richer, more voluptuous sound came forth. If one violin hesitated and lagged slightly, if the cellist played a note too roughly, or if the violist had a slightly different bow stroke, the wash of sound created by five instruments covered and forgave many small imperfections. For me, our performance of the Two Cello Quintet six weeks later in Curtis Hall was a scary but ultimately joyous event. I was rapidly developing a double life: by day my violin studies with Galamian, by night this newfound world of collaborative magic in our chamber-music bashes. It occurred to me that even though I wanted a solo career, chamber music might be a glorious avocation.

◦

To DEMONSTRATE my unswerving allegiance to my dream of becoming a violin soloist, I signed up for Meadowmount, Ivan Galamian's summer camp for string players. Meadowmount is situated near Elizabethtown, New York, in lovely rolling farmland that runs up against the Adirondack Mountains. The slave-labor atmosphere established by Galamian contrasted sharply with our location. It was like a prison camp in a national park. Six to eight hours of daily practice was the norm, and slouchers were simply expelled. Up at seven, breakfast, four hours of practice, lunch, more practice, and only then came summer-type things such as Ping-Pong and swimming. Sometimes during the morning labor we could expect a visit from Galamian himself. He would amble down the hallways, snapping his fingers loudly, ever on the lookout for those who played badly or—God forbid—not at all. As we looked out over the peaceful vista from our practice cells, hundreds of thousands of notes were being stroked, coaxed, cajoled, and tortured out of violins, violas, and cellos. In this string player's penitentiary no license plates were made, but I imagined that farmer Coonrod across the road must think we were developing some top-secret weapon against the Russians (it being the height of the cold war), along with germ warfare and the neutron bomb. The dormitories droned like giant beehives as we fiddled our days away.

One afternoon, a loud knock came at my door. Our taskmaster Galamian, I feared—but no, it was only the student next door. "I couldn't help hearing you as I was rosining my bow," he said, "and in my estimation you are the third greatest violinist in the world." I was flattered, I was intrigued. And who might numbers one and two be? "Jascha Heifetz is first and everybody else is tied for second," he replied, shutting the door in my face.

Ivan Galamian was at that time the world's reigning violin teacher, and with good reason. Literally hundreds of excellent violinists had come out of his studio. It was said of Galamian that he could teach a table to play the violin. Step by step, he would slowly but inexorably lead the student through the basics of violin playing. Middle-aged, with dark, curly hair and a swarthy complexion, Galamian had eyes that you remembered—dark, intense, penetrating— long after the lesson was over. When I had first played for him at Curtis, Galamian had shaken his head sadly. "You play the violin well, but I don't know how," he said in a thickly accented but barely audible voice. "Your bow arm needs work." He then gave me a series of exercises to do before a mirror. "What music would you like me to play, Mr. Galamian," I asked. "No music," he answered. "Well, then, what études?" "No études." "Scales?" "No scales." I stood there, perplexed. Then Galamian explained that he wanted me to concentrate on the finger motions of the bow hand by doing them without the violin. I was living with a family friend at the time, a former pianist. When for days on end no sound came out of my room, she demanded to know how I planned to become a musician without practicing.

It is hard to play the violin—the bow held above the strings in the right hand, as if you were a magician about to pull a rabbit out of a hat; the left arm, holding the violin, twisted unnaturally to the side so that the fingers are in the correct position. My twenty-year-old son recently asked me to show him how to hold the instrument. When I guided his flexible young limbs into place, he said, "Ouch! That hurts." And there are so many ways to sound bad during those first years—to play out of tune, to scratch, to force, to squeeze, choke, and strangle the violin. For family, friends, and neighbors in close proximity to a beginning violin student, his practicing can be a form of exquisite torture. No wonder so few have truly mastered the instrument.

The dazzling example of success we had directly before us at Meadowmount was the violinist Michael Rabin. At nineteen he already had a huge career as a soloist. Michael had studied with Galamian at the Juilliard School of Music in New York and for many summers at Meadowmount. Michael had something else going for him. Both of his parents were musicians—his father a violinist in the New York Philharmonic Orchestra, his mother a pianist. She was the driving force behind his success, everyone said.

There was no question about Michael's great ability, but it was Mrs. Rabin who made him practice scales and exercises from kindergarten on. It was she who called out from the kitchen where she was cooking for him to do that passage in the Mendelssohn concerto over and over again, first slowly and then in different rhythms, until it emerged in its final brilliant form. Mixed in with the many jokes at camp about old domineering Mrs. Rabin was a trace of envy. Perhaps none of us would have wanted her as a mother, but, then again, none of us had Michael Rabin's career, did we? When the great Russian violinist Toscha Seidel (one of my first teachers) was asked whether his own teacher, Leopold Auer, could be called truly great, he responded with a story that reflects on the Rabin phenomenon. "One day I arrived for my weekly lesson with Professor Auer. When I came to the staccato passage of the Wieniawski Polonaise Brilliante in A major, I was unable to do it. 'How dare you play for me without a staccato!' Auer screamed. He threw me out. When

I returned home, Mama asked me why I was home so early. When I told her, she beat me and sent me to my room. Then Papa came home and saw that Mama was unhappy. When he found out why, he beat me. Next week at my lesson with Auer, I had a perfect staccato, and in answer to your question, yes, he was a great teacher." This kind of parent was the engine that drove kids like Toscha and Michael to early mastery of the violin. Galamian knew all too well what the demands of the violin and the concert world are. In effect, he had created a camp that served as a Mrs. Rabin, and the funny thing was that all of us fought for the privilege of doing slave labor there.

My own parents were not the ogres of such stories. They were music lovers with a special affection for the violin. When the brothers George and Ira Gershwin wrote a song, "Mischa, Jascha, Toscha, Sascha," spoofing the reigning violinists of their day, they were referring to the performers of half of my parents' record collection. The first violin sound I can recall was the Beethoven concerto from one of those records, and it pierced this five-year-old's heart to the core.

Not long after, Mr. Singer, my elementary-school music teacher, called to inquire whether I would like to join the school orchestra. The school had all the necessary instruments on hand, and Singer, the little orchestra's conductor, also taught the rudimentary skills for each of them. At the age of six, I knew I wanted to play the violin. For a two-dollar deposit, the California public-school system provided me with an instrument, and at the end of that school year my parents saw enough musical talent in me to give back the violin (two-dollar deposit returned), buy me my own, and find a good private teacher.

Once I began playing the violin, my parents had a simple formula for me to follow. They were happy to pay their hard-earned money for lessons, but only if I practiced. With the best of intentions I promised, but a disciplined child is an oxymoron. It was more fun to play outdoor games with the neighborhood kids, pausing to eat fresh figs from the trees that grew wild on the vacant lots nearby, surprisingly close to downtown Los Angeles. When I returned home bruised, tired, and happy, my parents were waiting. It was dinnertime and I had not practiced. Tears were followed by more promises. I did want to play the violin. When I listened to Mischa Elman, Jascha Heifetz, or Fritz Kreisler playing on one of our records, my emotions were stirred. Elman was melancholy, Kreisler made me smile, and with Heifetz, my pulse raced and my palms sweated.

My new teacher, Mr. Moldrem, had a way with children. When I played well at my lesson, I received a silver star on my music. When I played especially well, an infrequent occurrence, a gold star was placed next to, say, "Long, Long Ago," one simple melody I remember mastering. A gold star was pure ecstasy. Mr. Moldrem knew how to explain things in a way that children could readily grasp. Learning different rhythms, for example—the concept of dividing a unit of time in two, three, or four parts (quarter, eighth, triplet, and sixteenth notes)—was difficult for me as a seven-year-old, but Moldrem simply told me to think pear, apple, pineapple, watermelon. Instant understanding.

As much as I disliked practicing, I loved performing for people, and our own house often served as an unlikely concert hall. My parents and their circle of immigrant friends were born and raised in an early-twentieth-century Europe without television or even radio. Entertainment and "the creative spirit" tended to be self-generated. So when friends gathered at the house, Isaac Malinsky did tricks, Duvid Raichelson sang folk songs, and Shloime Bock recited his poetry. Inevitably, at a certain point in the evening, there were calls for the "young geniuses" to play, first me and later my younger brother, Victor. I would show off my latest wares, a salon piece to touch the heart, or a virtuoso work that dazzled and impressed. Oohs, ahs, and smothering hugs were the rewards.

Nevertheless, earthly pleasures again and again seduced me away from the scales, exercises, and simple melodies that Mr. Moldrem prescribed. Things came to a head after Mother demanded one time too many that I practice. In a child's rage, I broke the violin over the corner of our dining-room table. There we stood, facing each other, in shock over what I had done. The violin hung limply by its strings, still attached to the neck I held in my trembling hand. Whenever I think of this domestic scene that took place over fifty years ago, I am filled with a warm and deeply satisfying glow. Why should an act of violence give me such pleasure? Not long ago, I asked Mother whether she remembered the dining-table incident. Of course she did. But I had gotten it wrong. *She* had broken the violin. We began to argue, each claiming to be the perpetrator of this dastardly crime, and it became quickly apparent that Mother had as much invested in her version of the story as I in mine. And the truth? Ask our dining-room table.

The violin was somehow glued back into working order, after I promised, yet again, to improve my practice habits. Mr. Moldrem assigned me "Son of Puszta," a work based, as I recall, on Hungarian folk elements. Dad loved the tunes and would sing along with me. After a certain amount of improvement, he deemed it time to call the Tafts—relatives far enough up the food chain to own a recording machine, no small achievement in 1948. The large floor model, state of the art for that time, occupied a place of honor in their living room. For my dad, it was an opportunity to record my playing for posterity on this exotic machine and also to show off for the relatives what his eleven-year-old genius could do. When Irving Taft turned the machine on, lowered the needle onto the spinning record surface, and pointed for me to begin, I already had an uncertain feeling. Perhaps I hadn't taken "Son of Puszta" seriously enough, and furthermore, an audience I hadn't planned on had gathered: Irving and Bela Taft, their two sons, Mom and Dad, and my five-year-old brother, Victor, himself about to start piano lessons. "Son of Puszta" did not go well. As I finished the last note, Dad could contain his aggravation no longer. "Aach, you made a mess of it," he said, raising his hand in disgust, before Irving could lift the needle from the record. My performance and Dad's critique are enshrined forever. Once in a while I come across the old record, which I keep to this day as a kind of talisman. The odd but not unpleasant odor of the record's acetate wafts up to me as I pull it out of the sleeve, along with Dad's critique: "Aach, you made a mess of it."

My parents hoped I would become a concert violinist. My father loved the violin, had heard all the great ones live. He had even invited Mother on one of their first dates to hear the child prodigy Yehudi Menuhin in Carnegie Hall, playing Brahms and Beethoven concertos in short pants. It was Dad with his fine but untrained ear who had tuned my beginner's violin for me, and it was he who coaxed me as I practiced: "That trill should be faster, like Fritz Kreisler's." Or, when I played roughly: "More like Mischa Elman—now that was a tone."

But it was Heifetz whom my parents invoked again and again as the standard on which all violinists should be judged, Jascha Heifetz, arguably the greatest violinist of the twentieth century. "Practice hard and you could become the next Heifetz," they would tell me; or, at a student performance, I would hear, "He's good, but no Heifetz." As I improved and gradually acquired a sense of my own worth, the constant comparison with Heifetz began to grate. "I guess you'll never be a Heifetz," Dad said ruefully while I was home on vacation from Curtis. That was the last straw. "Look," I threw back at him, "I may not be a Heifetz, but Heifetz is no Steinhardt." There was a shocked silence. He was unprepared for such a remark, and a look of accusation came over his face. I knew the words before they came. "Look who thinks he's better than Heifetz."

∽

IRONICALLY, IT WAS AT Meadowmount, the great training ground for soloists, that another stone was laid down in the path that would lead me to the string quartet. Along with Galamian and the great cellist Leonard Rose, the camp boasted another master performer, the violinist Josef Gingold, concertmaster of the Cleveland Orchestra but during the summers a teacher of chamber music. Gingold loved music but he adored the violin. We would try to fool him with some arcane morsel from the literature. "Joe, do you know Arensky's Violin Concerto, Opus 53?" "Opus 54," he would reply in his singsong, gravelly voice, which almost every one of the eighty violinists at camp loved to mimic. The truth was, we all worshipped him. Lessons with Gingold were like love-ins. He loved the music, he loved our playing, and he loved the stories connected with each piece and each performance he had heard. And Gingold himself had played in the renowned Primrose Quartet during his days with Arturo Toscanini and the NBC Orchestra. You could check your self-doubts at the door. "You will play this wonderfully," he growled as we began the Ravel string quartet. Then came the Smetana quartet and even the wildly difficult Beethoven Quartet in F major, Opus 59, no. 1, one of the Razumovskys. Gingold would demonstrate on the violin with that sweet, silken tone of his, tell a story or two to divert us from the perils we were about to face, and then hoodwink us into playing far above our powers. "Yeees," he croaked, his face bathed in a beatific smile, as the last notes of the Beethoven faded away. We had just managed a respectable play-through of the first movement's arching melodies, the clockwork ensemble demands of the second, the sublime melancholy of the third, and the headlong virtuosity of the last movement. If we could play Opus 59, no. 1, what couldn't we play? The string quartet had lost some of its power to frighten.

When Meadowmount ended, I took the train from Elizabethtown to New York's Grand Central Station along with many other campers. Watching the Adirondacks glide by, I thought with satisfaction about my work with Mr. G., as we called him. But string quartets with Joe—that wasn't work, that was pure nectar. Something about that combination of instruments intrigued me. String quartets had gained a toehold in my musical consciousness.

·◇·

A FOURTH YEAR of study at Curtis would normally have been my last, but at the first lesson of that school year Galamian confirmed what I suspected: my playing was simply not secure enough and I would not be ready to graduate in May. He recommended a fifth year at the school. I had just gone through an enormous growth spurt—ten inches in four years. My muscles had to catch up to my bones, and now my brain was trying to adjust to this new, larger house. So was my playing. Though I didn't discuss it, there was another advantage to taking an extra year. I had no clear idea of life and work after graduation. It was a fine idea to be a concert violinist, but how did one go about it? I had no eager, well-to-do sponsors standing in the wings ready to launch me into a solo orbit. If I had played a certain number of successful concerts, a manager might have taken me on, but how was getting concerts possible without a manager? It was a classic "catch 22" predicament years before Joseph Heller coined the expression.

The only avenue that seemed open to me was a prestigious violin competition: win one of these and you were given concerts, even money, and a certain amount of publicity. But it was an awful business. You were a nag in a horse race with a number on your back. There's nothing wrong with a real horse race—the first one across the finish line wins—but how does one judge a musical entrant in a competition? By how fast he plays, how few mistakes he makes? How does one grade beauty, after all? "Steinhardt comes around the far turn leading the pack with the fastest Tchaikowsky concerto but, yeegads, he just stumbled over that sixteenth-note passage and has been overtaken by three other violinists, one playing faster, one playing louder, and one tossing his hair more convincingly." No wonder musicians are wary of competitions. The winners often triumph because of what they didn't do: they didn't play out of tune, they didn't play wrong notes, they didn't scratch, they didn't do anything offensive. Contestants who commit these sins are quickly voted out, but they may be the ones to turn a beautiful phrase and play with great abandon, the ones who reach out to the listener's heart and mind. The competition winner has a reputation for being a safe, solid, but not always exciting player. At worst, competitions cultivate the idea of playing against other violinists rather than playing for the music. I didn't like this circus-like atmosphere, but what were the alternatives?

I had tried my hand at the Philadelphia Orchestra Youth Competition the year before—a contest whose winners performed a concerto with the orchestra—but I hadn't gotten past the semifinals. This year was different. The countless times Galamian had badgered me to use every last inch of the bow's hair as it glided across the strings, to dig into the string for a more focused and forceful sound, and to loosen up the motion in both my arms, had been done with a specific goal in mind: he wanted to build a violinist who sounded good not only in the practice studio but also in the last row of a three-thousand-seat auditorium. Finally, my playing was beginning to coalesce. As I auditioned on the stage of Philadelphia's Academy of Music, my nervousness fell away, and this time I played well. I was one of the winners.

Performing with the Philadelphia Orchestra several months later was like riding in a Cadillac. The orchestra's opulent sound bathed the senses, and Eugene Ormandy, then its director, who prided himself on being able to follow a soloist's every whim, provided an accompaniment that fit like a soft glove. Standing before the orchestra, I gazed up at tier after tier of listeners rising to the heavens, it seemed, in the Academy's splendor. So this was what it was like to be a soloist! Only beforehand had I felt a little awkwardness between conductor and soloist as we prepared to make our way onstage. "I want you to pay no attention to me as you take your bows, young man. You are too tall and I plan to be nowhere in sight," Ormandy whispered in my ear. "I may be short, but you make me look like a midget."

This prize whetted my appetite for a more ambitious project. I made plans to enter the Leventritt International Violin Competition the next fall. At the time, it was the most distinguished competition in the United States, and winning gave you appearances with six major symphony orchestras— New York, Cleveland, Pittsburgh, Detroit, Buffalo, and Denver. The winner would be taking an important step toward a career, I reasoned. I planned my repertoire and started practicing. Competitions might be horse races, but they had to be mapped out like military encounters.

At the same time that I was plotting the first steps toward a solo career, our chamber-music marathons continued. Gathering our courage, my fellow students and I started reading through the late Beethoven string quartets, and one evening the second of the five quartets, Opus 130 in B flat major, had its turn. This was the quartet that even we young musicians knew about. Beethoven's publisher had deemed its last movement, the Great Fugue, so harsh and indecipherable to the general public that he begged the great man to write another movement in its place. To everyone's surprise, perhaps Beethoven's included, he acquiesced. That evening, we chose to read the work in its original version, with the Great Fugue. We looked forward to another complex and thorny work in four movements, following on the heels of the first of his late quartets, but Beethoven defied our expectations in every way except one—we were overwhelmed.

Opus 130's curtain raiser, a slow, atmospheric introduction, soon breaks into the quickly paced main body of the first movement. A fanfare-like call—long, long, short, short, long—is followed by the lyrical second theme, which fragments into oddly scurrying groups of sixteenth notes. The introduction, however, refuses to be dismissed out of hand, periodically reasserting itself throughout the movement and even providing its ending. The second movement, lightning-quick and quirky, finishes almost before it has begun, a perverse and teasing punctuation to the musings of the first movement. The third movement is lyrical, mixing singing melodies with rhythms that are like the inner workings of a watch; its atmosphere is one of lilting delicacy. The fourth movement, a rustic country dance, is set like a refreshing oasis between what has passed and what will follow—two of the most remarkable movements in the quartet literature. The fifth movement, a cavatina, starts with a deeply moving four-part hymn that eventually leads to a middle section in which the first violin's anarchic line hardly corresponds to the slowly repeating notes of the other voices—a lost, disoriented, and desperate soul groping to find a way out of chaos. Then the hymn returns, closing with sonorous, deeply peaceful chords.

Thayer, in his biography of Beethoven, reports that Karl Holz, a good friend of Beethoven's and the second violinist in the Schuppanzigh Quartet (which gave the first performance of this work), remembered the great man's response to a performance of the cavatina. It "cost the composer tears in writing and brought out the confession that nothing he had written had so moved him; in fact, that merely to revive it afterward in his thoughts and feelings brought forth renewed tributes of tears" all the more remarkable in that he was stone-deaf at the time. Perhaps Beethoven was uncomfortable with the sublime creation he had brought forth. After all, divine beauty is the exclusive domain of the gods. The aura that lingers after the last pulsating chords of the cavatina have died away is shattered by a powerful chord announcing the beginning of the sixth and final movement, the Great Fugue. Its theme, first whispered strangely by the first violin and then shouted one by one by each of the other instruments, hurtles the listener against jagged shards of dissonance. The Great Fugue's violently contrasting moods intimidate, shock, and excite. This isn't so much a musical composition as a full-scale storm, an act of nature.

To the four of us who had just encountered Opus 130 that evening, it was irresistible. We decided to learn the work and perform it as a school project. John Dalley and I were, respectively, first and second violins; Jerome Rosen (later both violinist and pianist with the Boston Symphony) played viola; and Michael Grebanier (future principal cellist of the San Francisco Symphony) was the cellist.

Why did we choose this quartet to study, from among the hundred-plus masterpieces in the literature? It was a great work, a visionary work, we said to ourselves, but as with all sublime creations, its magic eluded description. What we could say, however, was that all four of us were transfixed by Beethoven's daring, his breathtaking originality, the dramatic placement of each succeeding movement, and the unusual number of movements themselves. Gathering for our first rehearsal, we all felt the anticipation and excitement that a climbing team experiences when planning the roped ascent of an alpine peak. This was the Eiger North Face of the string quartet.

The very first phrase of the first movement put us on notice—four hushed, descending notes in octaves and unison that blossom into a full chord and then recede quietly in a two-note resolution. Our rehearsal began something like this:

JOHN: Not together.

JERRY: Not together again.

ARNOLD: Also out of tune.

MICHAEL: It sounds so draggy.

JERRY: That's because we're worried about playing together and waiting for each other.

JOHN: Start again.

ARNOLD: *Still* not together.

JERRY: Let's try for the atmosphere. Never mind if it's not together.

MICHAEL: Too loud. We're all playing the same notes. Let it whisper.

JOHN: Better.

ARNOLD: Why don't you use a smaller motion for your leads, John? All that movement breaks the spell of the opening.

JOHN: Then it won't be together.

JERRY: We'll get used to your lead and follow you.

MICHAEL: You are using more vibrato than we are, Arnold. Why don't we start without any, a white sound, and add the vibrato gradually with the crescendo?

ARNOLD: I spend all my life learning to vibrate and now you don't want me to use it?

MICHAEL: Yes.

JERRY: Come on, guys. Coffee break is over. Start again.

It took us fifteen minutes to work through the first ten seconds of Opus 130 and several months to bring the entire work to performance level. As I remember our labors, I think the mountain-climbing analogy holds. We worked intensely to negotiate Opus 130's dangerous twists and turns, its difficult unison passages, its sudden tempo changes. The opening sequence of notes, however, signaled something else as well. It was to be a voyage of a spiritual nature. If we were alpinists climbing the Matterhorn, we were also monks in a religious order probing into states of mind and spirit, with Ludwig van Beethoven as our guru. In that Curtis Hall performance later that year, I was swept away.

In the hushed and reverential Meno mosso e moderato that follows the initial cataclysmic announcement of the Great Fugue, things were going well, I thought to myself. I looked up at the others to bond with them in our great endeavor. The consequence has made me forever after superstitious of self-congratulation during a performance, for when I looked back down at the music, a sea of notes, one indistinguishable from the next, greeted me. I was lost, with no obvious landmarks in the sparse landscape to help me get my bearings. The others kept going, and eventually, after what seemed like an eternity, I did find my place. The movement proceeded and then roared to its life-affirming end.

In that moment on the stage of Curtis Hall, my connection to the string quartet changed forever. I may not have viewed it yet as a life's work, but I thought something of the highest value had been set forth in the lean but effective vocabulary of four single string voices. To play in a quartet was to engage in a meditation with three like-minded companions—"a discourse among four reasonable people," as Goethe said.

·◇·

IN THAT FOURTH YEAR of school, like so many of my friends with similar solo ambitions, I continued to play chamber music whenever possible. I played with Michael Tree, who already had had a successful solo debut at Carnegie Hall; with Jaime Laredo, who was preparing for the Queen Elisabeth Violin Competition (which he won the next year); and with a variety of players all scheming for debuts, concerts, managers, and careers. It was a two-tiered existence, working toward a soloist's life while indulging in the chamber-music performances that gave us such pleasure.

We thought little about how chamber music would affect our lives, but in fact a sea change was about to take place in the United States. Before the 1960s, being a professional chamber musician smacked of being a failed soloist. Indeed, managers often discouraged soloists from having anything to do with chamber music. Like sex, chamber music in the privacy of your home was your business, but on the concert stage, what would people think? Although real music lovers knew better, an invisible class system was in place whose prejudices were only slowly beginning to crumble. At that moment, I can recall no instance when the subject of chamber music crossed the lips of any of my four teachers. Only a few quartets earned a living in America from concerts alone—the Budapest, the Juilliard, the New Music (in which David Soyer was the cellist) come to mind. Assuredly, many other great quartets flourished in the United States of that era, among them the Hollywood, the Curtis, the Gordon, the Fine Arts, the Griller, the Paganini, the LaSalle, the Pro Arte, the Hungarian, the Lenox, but their members did a variety of other work to make a living. The string quartet was a precious elixir to be enjoyed when a break from the more mundane demands of life allowed it. Things were only slightly better in Europe, where the string quartet had been firmly woven into musical life for more than two centuries. A quartet career had been barely possible before the Second World War. The Budapest Quartet, after all, had started in Europe, but to make a living from quartets exclusively in the United States seemed an almost impossible task.

Soon, however, more and more musicians and listeners were kindling an interest in chamber music. A whole industry of professional string quartets was about to move into production. Soloists began to come out of the closet and admit they had always loved chamber music. We listened to Pablo Casals and Isaac Stern making memorable music with their colleagues on records—Schubert's Two Cello Quintet, for one—giving the field a new cachet. Truly great musicians seemed regularly to cross the boundaries to chamber music—artists like Casals, Stern, and the pianist Rudolf Serkin, head of the Marlboro Music Festival, which I very much hoped to attend the following summer.

As the year passed, a call came into school for one last violist for the Casals Festival Orchestra in Puerto Rico that spring. The auditions were to be held in the New York City apartment of Alexander Schneider. At that point in my life I knew Schneider only as second violin of the Budapest Quartet, but I also knew that Sascha, as he was called, had single-handedly cajoled Casals out of retirement and created a festival for him. Two of us from Curtis made the bus trip from Philadelphia to New York, trudged up several flights of stairs, and found ourselves out of breath in a dimly lit hall in front of a nondescript door. Odd, I thought to myself, that a distinguished musician should live in such modest circumstances. The door was opened by a small, compact man, and behind him appeared a world for which we could not have been more unprepared. Paintings of every shape and size and description on the walls, immense Oriental rugs on the floor, antique furniture—some serious, some extremely tongue-in-cheek—filled this oversized room. It was not what one would call beautiful, but like Sascha Schneider himself, it was breathtaking, theatrical, excessive. "Vell, kum een, my dirrs," he said in the thickest of Russian accents.

Sascha was personable, but he got down to business quickly. My friend started first, but howls, exclamations, supplications, and outbursts of anger kept interrupting his playing. "Ya, vibrate. More bow. Noooo. More phrasing." Basically, Sascha heard playing that was small in both volume and conception. It was black and white on a small screen, and what he wanted was an interpretation on the biggest of screens, in three dimensions, and in full color. Forewarned, I tried to infuse extra excitement into my playing when my turn came, but the man intimidated as much as he inspired. Sascha coaxed, yelled, sang, and raged as I desperately attempted to heed his advice while sight-reading the scores placed before me. "Don't play orchestra," he hollered. This was one of Sascha's most frequent admonitions, as I was to find out, a not so flattering reference to the indifferent attitude of some orchestra players. On the bus back to Philadelphia, both of us were glassy-eyed and dazed—

victims of this tornado of a man; but somehow I had gotten the position. Two months later, I was sitting in the last chair of the viola section of an orchestra composed of the most splendid musicians from around the world. Casals had suffered a heart attack the year before, but he was able to make a surprise appearance conducting us. For me, it was the start of a long and treasured association with Casals: playing for him both in the Casals Festival Orchestra and at Marlboro, privately in master classes, in chamber music, and having him as the Guarneri Quartet's mentor.

∿

THE NEXT SUMMER, chamber music was set aside as I again willingly submitted myself to Galamian's gulag at Meadowmount in preparation for the Leventritt Competition. Requirements for the competition included an unaccompanied work by Bach, two concertos, a twentieth-century composition, Paganini caprices, and a brilliant showpiece. The hours of daily practice were no longer aimed at an abstract goal. I needed every minute of that time to bring these works to performance level, and Meadowmount was the perfect setting. Furthermore, at the camp's regular concerts, repertoire could be tried out in front of the most critical audience in the world, one's fellow violinists, who tended to regard everyone else's performance as a smelly cheese—questionable until proven otherwise.

When Meadowmount finished in the middle of August, I moved back to Philadelphia, into a furnished room with a bed, a table, a chair, and a hot plate. It seemed a suitable monk-like cell for what I had to do in the month before the Leventritt. Curtis wouldn't start for several weeks, and most of my friends had not returned to distract me. I practiced all day, every day, stopping now and then to rest, grab a snack, or divert myself awhile.

There is a certain time in life for this kind of daily regimen—when one is young, but only when one is young. It builds muscles and establishes the connections between brain and hand movements that make the mechanics of playing as automatic as tying a shoelace. An instrumentalist will draw on this for the rest of his life. But as in Aesop's fable about the ants and the grasshoppers, there is no Play Now, Pay Later. Attempting to build this foundation as one gets older is a perpetual act of catching up, aiming for something that is elusively just out of reach, and dangerous punishment to an aging body. Certainly, by the age of twenty-five, the musculature, the hand and arm positions, are pretty much set for life. The cake is baked. It perplexed and disappointed me when Galamian had refused to work on some of the great sonata literature with me. "Do that later on," he had advised. "Play Bach and the established concerto repertoire, but before it's too late, you must study Paganini, Wieniawski, Vieuxtemps"—referring to some of the most maddeningly difficult music a violinist can negotiate. Now, fiddling the hours away in my little room on Philadelphia's St. James Place, I was very grateful for the years of étude drudgery I had put in. One has to train practicing six hours a day in order to practice six hours a day.

The Leventritt Competition took place that September on the stage of New York's Town Hall. Backstage, the air was heavy with an odd mixture of nervous excitement, camaraderie, and competitiveness. Many of the violinists I was up against were fellow students, friends, and chamber-music partners. We had played chess, gin rummy, and Ping-Pong together, talked about music, and compared notes on aspects of violin technique over beer and pretzels. It was not right to be pitted against each other, each of us hoping for good fortune and, therefore, the misfortune of the rest.

Town Hall was not equipped to handle the dozens of violinists in the competition, each in a last-minute panic to practice the most difficult passages one last time. Violinists could be found fiddling in the small warm-up rooms, on the stairs, in the wings, and even in the bathroom. I was extremely nervous but as well prepared as I knew how. I was called to the stage. As I tuned, the judges sat impassively in a row halfway back in an otherwise empty hall. I waited for instructions, my heart thumping insistently. "Isn't he the last-chair violist from the Casals Festival?" I heard in a stage whisper. It was Alexander Schneider's unmistakable voice. The Bach B minor Partita and Mozart's Fifth Concerto went well enough to put me into the finals, where I was to play Prokofiev's Second Concerto in G minor. At that point, a little bit of luck came my way. One contestant playing before me also performed the Prokofiev, and quite by accident I heard one of the judges, Georg Szell, conductor of the Cleveland Orchestra, shout from the hall for him to play the coda of the last movement. This seemed mean-spirited. The coda is a long, running passage of quick notes with similar but always changing patterns, notoriously difficult to memorize. It's hard enough to play it as the culmination of an entire concerto when you're on a roll. The coda by itself, cold, was Szell's way of testing whether the poor fellow would fall on his face. I didn't wait around to see what happened with him, but rushed to my little warm-up cubicle for a last-minute check. When my turn came, the judges' requests ended with samplings from the Prokofiev. Muted snippets of conversation floated up to me onstage. The judges were consulting. Finally, it seemed that my audition might be over without my having to play the coda after all. Then I heard a loud, clear voice with a distinctly German accent: "We would like to hear the coda, please." I don't know whether Szell was happy or disappointed when I slipped on no banana peels and made no mistakes.

The competition was over. All that remained was to phone in several hours later for the results. As I dialed the Leventritt number, there seemed to me no realistic possibility that I might have won the prize. I had worked myself into a high pitch of reverse denial. In my mind, all the other contestants had excelled, whereas I was covered in sores and blemishes. "Congratulations," said Mrs. Leventritt over the phone. "You are the newest Leventritt winner. Come meet the judges and celebrate with a glass of champagne." Somewhere in midtown Manhattan, I stood staring blankly at the pay phone that had just served up these words. Two years of work and planning had actually achieved their goal! In shock, I glided through traffic toward Mrs. Leventritt's Park Avenue apartment. Six appearances with major American orchestras! To think about it made me giddy.

Mrs. Leventritt introduced me to the judges one by one. Then I was shaking Georg Szell's hand. Without relaxing his grip, Szell pulled me into an adjoining room for a talk. In every action and word he was brilliant, knowledgeable, dedicated, disciplined—an enormous, rather frightening presence. He immediately began to quiz me: What did I know about the grace notes of the Mozart concerto I had just played? Was I aware that the original manuscript rested in the Library of Congress in Washington, D.C.? (Not many months later, at Szell's prompting, I actually held this manuscript in my hands. Turning the pages very, very gingerly, with a uniformed guard standing observantly in the background, I found that Mozart's clear and almost flawless script was in small but important ways different from the edition I had been using.) Leaving Mrs. Leventritt's apartment to board the bus back to Philadelphia that evening, I was in a state of high excitement. This was a foot in the door to a concert career; my appearance with the New York Philharmonic in Carnegie Hall was only months away.

Carnegie Hall. Even the taxi drivers know the joke. Get into a cab and say, "Carnegie Hall, please, Fifty-seventh and Seventh Avenue," and more likely than not the driver will turn and ask slyly, "Know how to get to Carnegie Hall? Practice!" The oldest, lamest joke in the musical world. But potentially true. Practice hard and long enough and you just might perform on the stage of a hall that has entered our cultural mythology as the symbol for music in America. Carnegie Hall for an American musician is like the Vatican for a Roman Catholic, and playing as soloist in Carnegie with Thomas Schippers conducting the New York Philharmonic was going to be the major event in my musical life to that point. I came down with a full-blown case of anxiety, tossing and turning for two nights before the performance of Wieniawski's Second Violin Concerto. Of course, my parents were there, and so was my teacher, Ivan Galamian. Friends from school, acquaintances, my aunt and uncle, cousins once and twice removed, all flocked to Carnegie Hall.

The doors swung open and I walked out onstage, the layered horseshoe tiers ascending dizzyingly upward, beckoning, cajoling, and challenging me: Do your best, your absolute, ultimate best. When the first notes of the orchestra tutti wafted into the hall, there was a resonance, a bloom to the sound that seemed to burnish the music with the golden glow of candlelight. Before a well-informed and passionate public in one of the world's great cities, I responded to Carnegie's invitation, losing myself in the solo voice and playing with more focus and inspiration than I thought possible. My great-aunt Rivke Raisel, who had never before been at a concert and who still spoke mainly Yiddish after sixty years in America, turned to her son: "He sounds wonderful, but tell me, is that a violin or a fiddle he's playing?"

When the concerto blazed to its virtuoso finish, I was both relieved and happy. I had jumped through all of Wieniawski's hoops creditably and was now looking forward to the five other orchestra appearances in the coming season. With greater conviction than ever, I resolved to do whatever it took to join Mischa, Jascha, Toscha, and Sascha in the pantheon of great concert violinists.

Diary. September 7, 1996. I arrive last for our first rehearsal of the new season. Nancy, John's wife, and Kirsten, one of their daughters, greet me warmly in the kitchen. We talk about the summer and how quickly it has gone by. John, Michael, and David hardly acknowledge me. They are immersed in discussion about details and potential problems in our first tour of the season. We have two concerts in Southern California followed by one near San Francisco only to return to Southern California for a concert in Pasadena one day later. All agree that managers should be required to go on tour with us as punishment for their transgressions.

By now, we are seated with our instruments in hand, but both David and Michael remind themselves of jokes they are bursting to tell. The jokes are, thankfully, new ones. Then John tells of a dream he had about Michael. We laugh.

Finally, the rehearsal gets under way with the Fauré String Quartet, Opus 121, one of our oldest friends. I notice that we have become gentler with the dynamics, less aggressive, and more subtle about ritards everywhere. We proceed to another old friend, Mozart's Quartet in F major, K 168. The rehearsal is friendly and good-natured. Kirsten complains later that we sounded as if we were having fun, not working. What a long way to have come in thirty-two years!

3

The Heart of the Matter

THE CROWD of family, friends, and well-wishers gathered backstage to help celebrate my Carnegie Hall debut parted respectfully, allowing a single person to come forward. It was my teacher, Ivan Galamian, who congratulated me on a fine performance and on the progress I had made in the last few years. He was not a man of many words or, for that matter, of ill-considered compliments, so those few sentences of praise meant a great deal. "I will see you on Wednesday at three for your lesson," he added. Lesson? In the afterglow of a successful performance in Carnegie, I had momentarily forgotten that I was still a student. Two days later I was back in Philadelphia attending classes at Curtis, living in my one-room apartment and weighing the choices for dinner: canned spaghetti with tomato sauce or canned spaghetti with meatballs. There was one difference, however. I was now a professional musician with a string of Leventritt appearances to work toward in the coming season.

William Steinberg called to ask whether I would play the Stravinsky Violin Concerto with him and the Pittsburgh Symphony Orchestra. I accepted impulsively, without considering the difficulty of learning a work I had never even heard before. It would be an adventure and a challenge, I thought. Only later, while I was visiting family and friends in Los Angeles, did the daunting nature of my task begin to sink in. I was unfamiliar not only with the concerto but with Stravinsky's tonal language.

I ran into Sylvia Kunin, a great supporter of young musicians in the Southern California area, and asked her if she knew anybody familiar enough with the Stravinsky to help me. "As a matter of fact, I may," she answered. "I'll call you this afternoon and give you his number." I was greatly relieved and not altogether surprised. Hollywood had drawn many fine musicians to the Los Angeles area. Probably a dozen outstanding studio violinists knew the Stravinsky and would be able to offer me valuable pointers.

True to her word, Sylvia called. "Here's the number I promised you. The man's name is Igor Stravinsky. He should be able to help you with the concerto." The phone almost slipped from my grasp. "Sylvia, you've got to be joking. I can't call Igor Stravinsky. He's the most renowned living composer in the world. He's too busy to have anything to do with a kid not yet out of school." A trace of irritation crept into Sylvia's voice. "Look, I just spoke to Stravinsky. He says he'll talk to you; so talk to him."

I hung up and stared at the phone. It was hard for me to believe that Igor Stravinsky had a telephone number, just like the rest of us. God didn't have a phone number. Why should Stravinsky? Nevertheless, my trembling hand reached out and dialed his number, which, I noted with astonishment, had the same number of digits as those of ordinary mortals.

"Hahloh," a voice spoke into my ear. "Uh, could I, could I possibly speak to, uh, Mr. Stravinsky?" I managed to croak. "Oh, you must be the young man who is playing my concerto. I have no time for old works, you know. Everybody thinks I stopped composing after I wrote the Firebird Suite, but never mind. Come over to the house now. I have a record of my concerto that might be useful and I'll lend it to you." Fifteen minutes later, I was ringing Igor Stravinsky's doorbell. He answered the door himself and ushered me in. His diminutive frame, baggy tweed trousers, and deeply resonant voice combined to form an impression of urbane and casual elegance. "You can keep it as long as you want," he said, handing the record album to me. "But you must give it back. It's my only copy."

I left Stravinsky's house in a daze. The great man was so decent, so generous, so accessible! "Accessible" was not a word I would have used to describe his violin concerto, I thought, as I rushed home to listen to the record. In addition to being instrumentally awkward, the concerto seemed to break all the laws of musical syntax and harmony known in my limited musical universe. But as I listened repeatedly to the record, with Stravinsky conducting and Samuel Dushkin the violin soloist, its radical elements began to coalesce into an understandable mixture of classical form and quirky modernism—"architectonic and anecdotal," as Stravinsky himself once described his ballet *Rite of Spring*.

Two weeks later, I called to return the record. Again, Stravinsky himself answered the phone. Again, Stravinsky was the one who cordially greeted me at his door. In the brief conversation we had about the concerto, he offered no magic key to its interpretation. He seemed a practical kind of man, in manner and deed, and the recorded performance, brisk and straightforward, reflected this. I thanked him too quickly for his help and left, overwhelmed by his stature as a musician. I didn't even have the presence of mind to ask him to sign the music of his Suite Italienne for violin and piano that he gave me, but I came away with a close-up view of the man and a growing appreciation of Stravinsky's compositions.

Within a month of the Stravinsky performance, I was to play the Mendelssohn Violin Concerto with Paul Paray and the Detroit Symphony Orchestra. This worried me much less than the Stravinsky. Every violinist who calls himself a violinist has studied the Mendelssohn. I was eleven when it was first given to me by my teacher Peter Meremblum, himself a former student of Leopold Auer. Our neighbors put up a for-sale sign in front of their house shortly after my daily practice on the Mendelssohn commenced, and the sign remained for the two months that I worked on the concerto. At the moment when Meremblum decided that I'd done my best and assigned me another piece, the for-sale sign next door disappeared. Mother congratulated Mrs. Zigmond over the back fence for having sold her house. "We haven't sold the house, Mrs. Steinhardt. My husband and I decided that since Arnie was able to learn the Mendelssohn Concerto, we wouldn't move." Meremblum must have agreed with the Zigmonds, for he arranged for me to play it on the radio the next year, and it was the Mendelssohn again that Ivan Galamian chose for me to perform as a beginning student at the Curtis Institute of Music several years later.

Despite my long relationship with the Mendelssohn concerto, it seemed, mysteriously, to get more and more difficult as the Detroit concert approached. Mendelssohn composed it while on summer holiday, only two years before his death. "I'm lying under apple trees and big oaks," he wrote to a friend. "I have strawberries for coffee, lunch, and dinner. I

drink spring water, get up at six, and still sleep nine hours."
The transparent and delicate beauty of the music emanating
from those summer days was receding from my grasp. If the
mighty Beethoven Concerto can be considered the king of
violin concertos, then the Mendelssohn's sweet melancholy
makes it rightfully the queen. Years later, after I compli-
mented Pinchas Zukerman on his moving performance of
the concerto recorded with Leonard Bernstein and the New
York Philharmonic Orchestra, he said to me, "Ah, I did that
before I knew how difficult it was."

All my Leventritt concerto appearances that year, including my New York debut and even the dreaded Stravinsky,
went well, and the reviews were consistently good to excellent, but the Mendelssohn performance exemplified a certain
musical malaise I was experiencing. There was nothing glar-
ingly wrong with the Detroit concert. My performance was
both respectful and respectable, and I even enjoyed the experience. Jack Benny, the comedian, had stuck his head into
my warm-up room before the rehearsal and demanded to
know whether I was pleased with his humiliation. He, too,
was rehearsing the Mendelssohn for a pension-fund concert
and he complained that I was making him look bad. But
somehow I felt personally and musically unfinished. I was
twenty-one years old, and in a perfect world it would probably have been better to be playing these engagements five
years down the road, when my musical convictions were
more fully formed. Like most competition winners, I also
came to realize that a prize is a stepping-stone to a career,
but not a career itself. There was certainly no frenzy at my
door to sign me up for next season's concerts.

As my five years at Curtis came to a close, two unanswered
questions hung over me. What plans should I be making,
and what should I do about military service? Like most single, healthy males graduating from school in 1959, I was

ripe to be plucked by the armed services. The fact that we Curtis students were musicians, artists, if you will, and cultural emissaries of our country, impressed Uncle Sam not one whit. I had the choice of being drafted or signing up for one of several programs that would give me a certain control over my military future.

Georg Szell provided an answer of sorts to both questions. He invited me to become assistant concertmaster of the Cleveland Orchestra. My career plans had not included sitting in the violin section of an orchestra, even the front row, but this was no ordinary orchestra or conductor. The Cleveland with Szell had a reputation for precise ensemble and music making on the highest level. Szell proposed that I join the orchestra, learn the repertoire sitting next to Josef Gingold, my mentor from Meadowmount days, perform at least one concerto each year, and study at Szell's expense with the great Hungarian violinist Josef Szigeti. As assistant concertmaster, I would lead the violin section and serve as a liaison between orchestra and conductor when Gingold was not there. This position was already known as a launching pad: the three violinists who preceded me had all gone on to careers as either soloists or concertmasters of major orchestras.

A crossroad was before me. I could continue to pursue a solo career, but then what about chamber music, which consumed more and more of my time? Marlboro had invited me to its festival in southern Vermont the next summer. A conductor's baton waving in my face had been the last thing in my mind, but playing in the Cleveland and working with Szell, Gingold, and Szigeti, I finally decided, might be a sublime sort of graduate school. I accepted, but there was still one big obstacle. Joining the orchestra depended on my getting into the Ohio National Guard to fulfill my military obligation; otherwise, I would be drafted. Szell, wanting to take no chances, personally drove me to the Guard armory and then to the doctor's office for my physical. Homburg hat in hand, he sat impassively in the waiting room while the doctor looked me over. Everything appeared to be fine, but a urine specimen was still required. As I walked past the great man to the bathroom, jar in hand, his eyes never left me. This is not really happening, I thought: an aspiring twenty-one-year-old musician does not have to promenade before one of the great conductors of our time carrying a jar of his urine. We might have been characters in an Edward Albee play: this was true Theater of the Absurd. But as I emerged from the bathroom clutching my container of steaming liquid, Szell continued to scrutinize me. The warm amber liquid sloshed in its jar as I walked past him with as much dignity as I could muster. I reached the door, and I heard Szell's voice, with its clipped German accent: "Imported or domestic?"

Word finally came that I had passed the physical. Next season I would be assistant concertmaster of the Cleveland Orchestra and glockenspiel and bass drummer in the 122nd Army Band. That would be in September, but Curtis graduation took place in late spring, and I could look no further than the Marlboro Festival I would attend that summer.

It is hard to know whether Marlboro stoked the fires of the growing chamber-music boom or vice versa. Probably both. The school and festival had been founded in 1951 by Adolf Busch with his brother Hermann, Adolf's son-in-law the pianist Rudolf Serkin, and Busch's colleagues Marcel, Louis, and Blanche Moyse. Busch conceived of an artistic community that would come together each summer to exchange ideas and explore the great chamber-music repertoire. By the time I arrived in 1959, Marlboro had grown into a large musical family. In the 1960s the list of Marlboro musicians included Serkin, Pablo Casals, the flutist Marcel

Moyse, the violinist Felix Galimir, and three members of the Budapest String Quartet—violinist Alexander Schneider, cellist Mischa Schneider, and violist Boris Kroyt. Serkin's spirit loomed over the place: his performances had a rare coupling of scholarly seriousness and manic intensity, and his artistic standards spread invisibly but palpably throughout Marlboro. The devotional way in which Serkin listened to music at the concerts, almost all of which he attended, was revealing. He would lower his head, sometimes partially covering his eyes with one hand, seemingly to shield himself from the outside world, the better to look inward into the music's essence.

At the same time, Serkin was a gregarious man with a penchant for practical jokes. I was an eager, willing collaborator. Musicians at the festival were required to serve for one week on the kitchen and dining-room crew. As I cleared away the main course one evening, I placed a round, smooth boiled potato on a dessert plate instead of the planned scoop of vanilla ice cream, and poured chocolate sauce over it. Serkin was animatedly talking to his neighbors as I served the concoction to him. This was the latest round in a practical-joke war that had been going on between us all summer long—cherry bombs, fake worms hanging from nostrils, etc. From the side of the dining hall I watched for Serkin's reaction. Without a pause in the conversation or a flicker of acknowledgment either then or at any time after, he polished off the *pomme de terre au chocolat*. Whose practical joke had it been, after all?

Not more than minutes into my first summer at Marlboro, I felt the presence of Alexander Schneider. He came for me, looking like a reprint of the old U.S. Army recruiting poster of Uncle Sam pointing his finger. "I vant *you*," Sascha said. He gathered three of us—me, Les Malowany viola, and Leslie Parnas cello—and told us that in four days we were to perform the second of Béla Bartók's six string quartets. We gasped. None of us had played the Bartók, a work of constantly changing meter and complex rhythms, with an ending of starkly bleak harmonies. But he turned away all protests. Force of nature that he was, Sascha had no "no" in his vocabulary.

Rehearsals started almost immediately, with Sascha using his second-violin seat as a command post. He knew the work inside out, having performed and recorded it with the Budapest Quartet. The learning process that would have taken us weeks if not months was dispensed with in a few internal rehearsals, because Sascha knew where the thorny passages were and how to resolve them. As he raved, ranted, and coaxed, he gave us shortcuts and tips and instructed us in the optimum tempos. On July 10 and 12, 1959, we gave what I remember as two very good performances of the Bartók Second String Quartet. Sascha had put us in orbit. As with Beethoven's Opus 130, I was overwhelmed with the music I had just come to know. Something about the string-quartet form itself, I realized, ignited powerful creative fires in a composer.

When the Marlboro Festival came to an end in mid-August, I was reluctant to leave Vermont. Many of us lingered to explore the countryside, crossing old abandoned logging roads, occasionally stumbling across cellar holes and forgotten graveyards whose tombstones dated from the eighteenth century. But finally I could procrastinate no longer, and I headed west in my 1947 Studebaker for full-time professional employment in Cleveland.

Several hours into my trip, the exit sign for Buffalo appeared. This was Mischa Schneider's hometown. On a whim, I pulled off the highway and called him from a roadside pay phone. Mischa, Sascha's older brother, was cellist of the Budapest Quartet, which had an affiliation with the University of Buffalo at that time. The two of them looked unquestionably like brothers, but from there on, the resemblance was evident only occasionally. Where Sascha was boisterous, theatrical, and often outrageous, Mischa was soft-spoken, endearing, and thoughtful. Yet, when they were together either onstage or in company, one sensed a loving bond, as if their differences fit together to form a larger, familial Schneider. There were, of course, the significant similarities—a passion for music, highly opinionated views, and full-blown Russian accents. "I vill make offer *eem*possible to refuse," he said on the phone. Mischa proposed dinner at his house and a ticket to the Budapest's first all-Beethoven concert that very night. Of course I couldn't resist the chance to see Mischa, whom I loved, and hear a Budapest concert.

As its name suggests, the Budapest String Quartet was founded by four Hungarians, but over the years they had been gradually replaced by other players. There is a riddle attributed to Jascha Heifetz: What is one Russian? A nihilist. Two Russians? A chess game. Three Russians? A revolution. And what is four Russians? The Budapest String Quartet.

Over dinner with Mischa and his wife, June, I asked whether he wouldn't have to leave early for rehearsal. It was, after all, the quartet's first concert of the season. But no rehearsal was planned, even though they had not been together for the entire summer. Later that evening, the four Russians—Joseph Roisman, first violin; Boris Kroyt, viola; and Alexander and Mischa Schneider, second violin and cello, respectively—made their way onto the stage in measured steps, exactly equidistant from one another, and sat down. I was nervous for them. The late Quartet in E flat, Opus 127, opened the program, a large-scale masterwork with an obstacle course of difficulties. What kind of madness was an unrehearsed performance? It was the kind of thing

we would do in music school on a dare. But the Budapest
was playing for an audience of chamber-music aficionados
who were reverently attending a Beethoven cycle—all sixteen quartets in six concerts. They were going to church.

The first violinist usually leads the opening chords, but
Roisman, a study in suavity, merely put his bow on the
string and began to play. By some act of telepathy, the others
knew exactly when to join him in perfectly interlocking harmony. Beethoven's stentorian chords rang out grandly as an
announcement of the very special things to come. There were
the inevitable lapses in a performance that drew only on their
extensive experience, but I will remember forever the sweep
and stylishness of the Budapest's playing.

Something else struck me forcibly. Roisman seemed to
avoid the old, traditional first violinist's role as group leader.
All the quartet's voices seemed equal, each one shining forth
when necessary and then receding into the texture. I asked
Mischa about this over tea and cookies when we returned
to his home later that night. "The Budapest is the first
democratic quartet. Our style of working is very Jewish.
Everyone talks at once." Mischa laughed, still tickled by
the quartet's modus operandi. A quartet without leaders or
followers? I mused. Was this democracy, Communism, or
utopia?

∾

LESS THAN a week later I was in the seat next to Josef Gingold, awaiting my first rehearsal with the Cleveland Orchestra. I had asked Gingold what to expect and in reply he
told me a story. Several years earlier, the city's baseball team,
the Cleveland Indians, had won the World Series just before
the season's opening rehearsal, and the orchestra decided to
have some fun with Szell. He gave the downbeat for Schubert's Unfinished Symphony and out came "Take Me Out

to the Ball Game." "What is going on here?" demanded Szell as he pounded on the podium for quiet. Gingold rose from his chair and explained to him that Cleveland had won the World Series and what the song meant. "The boys wanted to play a little joke on you, Dr. Szell," he said, chuckling. Szell considered this for a moment. "Ha ha ha. Very funny. Schubert's Unfinished, please."

Even in my excitement, I couldn't but notice the heaviness in the Severance Hall air as we awaited Szell's arrival. Before a summer storm, one often feels this kind of atmosphere, which seems to press in on the senses. At 10 a.m. sharp the maestro entered stage left and mounted the podium with a "Good morning, ladies and gentlemen. Brahms' First." There had been no stragglers and very little talk beforehand. The troops were awaiting the general's inspection.

In that first rehearsal, Szell conducted an immaculate and polished read-through of the Brahms symphony. The orchestra sounded phenomenal to me, but Szell was not happy. He set about realigning principal and accompanying voices so that all the instruments could be heard according to their true importance in the musical texture. He was willing to take a great deal of rehearsal time to achieve these goals. One might expect this to be the aim of a string quartet, where clarity and balance are all-important, but in an orchestra, with the huge wash of sound created by a hundred people playing a hundred instruments, many conductors consider it too difficult and too time-consuming. Not Szell. In a Szell performance the listener had the feeling that by magic the musical score had opened up and simply played itself for him, all instruments in perfect balance and ensemble. That perfection had its darker side: at worst, his performances could sound unyielding and clinical, but when the spirit moved him, audiences heard detailed and wonderfully nuanced interpretations.

In joining the orchestra, I had given up the soloist's individual voice and the communal pleasures of chamber music to become just one of some thirty violinists. I was a single stalk of grain in a field of wheat, but what a field! When the ambrosial theme of Brahms' last movement was played by the entire first-violin section in that first rehearsal, all other career thoughts were pushed out of my mind by the sweeping conception of our conductor and the flair and precision of his great orchestra.

Finally, it was intermission at the first rehearsal. The Brahms had come to an end, and I remained rooted to my seat in a near-trance. Several musicians rose from their seats and headed toward me. At twenty-two, I was the youngest player in the orchestra. How nice, I thought, a welcoming committee. In truth, however, Sam Salkin, first violin, tried to sell me a watch; Ed Matey, second violin, offered me mutual funds; Irv Nathanson, double bass, wondered if I needed instrument insurance; and Angie Angelucci, French horn, tried to sell me a Plymouth. The Cleveland Orchestra's slim thirty-two-week season allowed me, as a bachelor, the luxury of spending my summers in Marlboro, but most of the orchestra, with families to feed, did what they had to to make a living. I didn't buy the watch, I did buy mutual funds and insurance, I did not buy the Plymouth. Two out of four wasn't bad.

A long series of unforgettable performances filled the following years. Being at an orchestra concert is a celebration of the aural palette, but being *in* the orchestra is like riding a giant wave. When Ravel's Second Daphnis and Chloé Suite approached its end, with the entire orchestra at full tilt around me, I felt I was on that wave, being swept along by an overpowering storm. When Szell loosened the reins of control just enough to allow the orchestra to broaden as it crested the great climax of the first movement of Beethoven's

"Eroica" Symphony, the feeling was oceanic—what Sigmund Freud described in another context as "a feeling of an indissoluble bond, of being one with the external world as a whole." And the eighty minutes of Mahler's Ninth Symphony seemed to pass in the wink of an eye, as if Mahler had managed to bedevil the passage of time itself. Walking up the stairs that led to the stage for the final performance of the Ninth, I found Szell at the top, eyeing me closely. "Well," he said as I reached his level, "have you brought supplies, provisions, a sleeping bag?" It took me an instant to realize that the great man was displaying his sense of humor.

⌒

DURING MY YEARS in the orchestra, I was soloist in the Wieniawski Second, the Mozart Fourth and Fifth, the Glazunov, the Bartók Second, and, ultimately, the Beethoven violin concertos. With the exception of Bartók and Glazunov, I performed all of them with Szell. Off the podium he became a somewhat different man, warmer, less doctrinaire, more relaxed. Once he teased me about my rendition of the Mozart cadenzas I played for him before the general rehearsal of the A major Concerto. "Must you be so serious?" he asked, after I had played a little bridge between two themes in the last movement. He sat down at the piano and demonstrated what the joke in this little cadenza was and how to deliver the punch line. His playing was stylish, even witty—a side of him that we in the orchestra saw only rarely—but he had made his point.

When the rehearsal was over, Szell asked me how I was enjoying Cleveland. The truth came out of my mouth before I could censor my tongue. As a young man of twenty-two looking for adventure, romance, and any conceivable kind of excitement, I found Cleveland livable but also stolid and boring. Indeed, there was a joke making the rounds at the time. Question: What's the difference between Cleveland and the *Titanic*? Answer: Cleveland has a better orchestra. Szell, who had clearly taken a fatherly interest in me, became angry. "How dare you allow yourself to be bored here? Across from Severance Hall is the Cleveland Museum of Art, one of the great museums of the world. When you leave here, visit it, look at the art, stimulate yourself, educate yourself! Then go home and read a good book."

Szell's knowledge and understanding of the classical and romantic Central European repertoire was complete. He could sit down at the piano and read a complex Richard Strauss score and transpose it into other keys at will. And he knew chamber music. When the orchestra went on tour, Szell and Gingold would often play a musical game together. A pocket score of the complete Mozart string quartets was opened and one measure of one voice of a quartet was offered up for each to identify. Gingold told me that Szell was always able to identify any passage from any quartet, and always won.

Szell was the guiding spirit that propelled me in 1962 away from what was now a customary summer at Marlboro to study in Switzerland with the Hungarian violinist Josef Szigeti. Szell had suggested, arranged, and paid for the trip because he felt it would be valuable for my ongoing musical education. "I want to emphasize that this is not a Swiss vacation for Arnold," he had written Szigeti before my arrival. "Make sure he works. I am paying for it, you know." Szigeti made sure.

Szigeti had been a great violinist. Stated differently, he was a great musician who happened to play the violin. A friend of mine, the cellist Daniel Saidenberg, heard Szigeti at his American debut in the 1920s. He was taken to the concert by his chamber-music teacher Felix Salmond. Saidenberg had been thrilled by Szigeti's sensitive playing, but during the performance Salmond turned and whispered to him, "Szigeti will never make a great career here. He is too fine a musician." But he did have a highly distinguished career worldwide, and now, in retirement from the concert stage and with more time for himself, he was teaching selected pupils.

For Szigeti, a musical composition always had connections—to other works, to its historical context, and to the existing tradition of performance. "What instruments of the orchestra do you hear in this passage of the Bartók Rhapsody?" he asked me as we walked in a Swiss alpine meadow near Riederalp and the Aletsch Glacier. He was trying to stimulate my sensitivity to the minute shadings of different notes in a particular phrase. Szigeti had worked and performed the First Rhapsody with Bartók himself: I felt as if one of the prophets were illuminating the Bible for me. That summer Szigeti had just turned seventy. He was tall and slender, with a high, domed forehead—a refined man, frail in body but incessantly active in mind. He tinkered endlessly with violin fingerings, putting them at the service of the music rather than the convenience of the player. All forms of classical music interested Szigeti—solo, chamber music, orchestral, opera. He was the only teacher of mine who ever talked at length about the joys and intricacies of the string quartet. Szigeti's daughter, Irène Magaloff, told me recently that he once went so far as to form a quartet to be financed by a Swiss banker. They did play some house concerts for the financier, but the project remained on the drawing board because of Szigeti's busy solo schedule.

More than thirty-five years later, the summer spent with Szigeti still nourishes me. His shaky handwriting adorns the music I studied with him and still use. "Art, not scholarship," Szigeti wrote across the front page of my copy of the First Rhapsody, which Bartók, incidentally, dedicated to him. "Tender," "expansive," "keep triumphant," "Chopin dialogue," "breathless," and "stormy" are scrawled over passages of Fauré's First Violin Sonata.

It was time to return home. I shook Szigeti's hand for the last time, but this still passionately involved musician was more interested in our ongoing discussions about music than in saying goodbye. "You are making good progress with Mozart's Fifth Violin Concerto, but your task will be made simpler if you study his string quartets," he observed. My orientation to music had moved several degrees in that direction.

When I returned to Cleveland for the beginning of the 1962–63 season, I knew it was time to think about moving on. Ironically, Szell's sponsorship of my studies with Szigeti became a major factor in my decision to leave his orchestra. Szigeti had focused on the most personal elements in music. It was that quality in Szigeti's playing that had so moved me, even at the end of his performing career, when his physical capabilities had begun to fail him. When Szigeti spun a phrase with a vibrato unlike any I had ever heard before and when his bow glided almost too quickly across the strings, the wispy, tremulous sound he produced went directly to the heart. My musical voice was different from Szigeti's, but it was exactly that quality I yearned for in my own playing. As great as the Cleveland Orchestra was, the voice I had begun to cultivate was again about to disappear in a sea of violin sound created to Georg Szell's specifications. That was the heart of the matter.

Diary. September 15, 1996. Rehearsal before our first concert of the season at South Mountain, Massachusetts. Program: Mendelssohn D major, Opus 44, no. 1; Fauré E minor, Opus 121; and Schubert's "Death and the Maiden." We work on the Fauré. There is a discussion about the opening viola solo. David suggests that Michael present it in a more declamatory manner, as a contrast to the first violin's quieter answer. Michael, doubtful, tries it that way. I am pleased, but John objects. He contends that we are putting more into the music than Fauré really wanted. More discussion follows, without a resolution. Michael will have to decide for himself at the concert. The moment of truth arrives and Michael plays the opening viola solo as if it were an announcement for the new millennium. David, uncharacteristically, misses his entrance completely. We walk offstage at the end of the work and David comes close to congratulating Michael. "My idea was good. It was just the way I like it. So much so that I forgot to come in."

[4]

Birth Announcement

THE GREAT MUSICIANS seem to have wide-ranging interests
that cover much more of the musical spectrum than simply
the solo works for their own instruments. Szigeti, Casals,
Szell, Stern were such men. So was Rudolf Serkin, who performed as soloist throughout the world during most of the
year and presided over Marlboro during the summer. For a
renowned soloist to commit an entire three months to chamber music was rare. With this act he put an official stamp
of approval on the genre and served notice to music lovers,
managers, and the musicians themselves that it was all right
for soloists to associate with chamber music—even to *be*
chamber musicians. As far as I was concerned, I no longer
needed to make a choice between solo and chamber music:
I could do both.

In the ten summers I spent in southern Vermont learning
repertoire and cross-pollinating with other musicians, Marl-

boro served as a giant laboratory for us. Where else could we come together for as long as needed to study a work in depth? The purity and value of Adolf Busch's idea attracted people from all over. Two of my friends from Curtis, John Dalley and Michael Tree, resurfaced there. In the summer of 1962, Michael and I worked together on a performance of Bartók's Sixth and last String Quartet—he played first violin; Herbert Sorkin, second; I played viola; and Leslie Parnas, cello. When the pizzicato cello chords signaled the end of this quartet, the mood of anguish and utter resignation made it difficult for the audience to applaud or for us to rise from our seats. We had absorbed yet another masterpiece. Deeply affected by the experience, Michael and I began to talk after sets of tennis or over meals about playing quartets seriously. It had been fun being serious with Michael in the Bartók. He was one part musician, one part cutup. No matter how intense rehearsals became, with a joke or some buffoonery Michael would always keep us from taking ourselves too seriously.

That same summer I met David Soyer at Marlboro. We studied a Brahms piano trio together with the pianist Constance Keene. It was an inauspicious beginning, since the group never got past the rehearsal stage, but David made an impression on me. He was stimulating and candidly direct— in his behavior toward others, in rehearsal, and in his playing. This could be slightly unnerving, but it was also his charm. During that summer David and Michael played the Fauré Piano Trio with the very young Peter Serkin (son of Rudolf). John Dalley and I also played together in the Schumann E flat Piano Quintet with Rudolf Serkin piano, John first violin, I second, Samuel Rhodes viola, and Hermann Busch cello. John was a no-nonsense sort of guy who always came to rehearsals beautifully prepared. He was affable if not overly talkative, until something pushed him across an invisible line. At that quite unpredictable moment, a madcap free-association humor would erupt in John that threatened to bring rehearsals to a grinding halt. In the summers when David, John, Michael, and I were all at Marlboro—1962, '63, '64—our paths crossed more and more often. In 1962 and 1963 alone, the four of us played together ten times in various combinations. We were like planets being caught in a gravitational field.

With all this focus on chamber music, my interest in a solo career began to flag. I had already had a taste of the soloist's life: over the years in Cleveland I had performed with six major orchestras and, along the way, with many smaller ones as well. The average concertgoer might think that a soloist can express, unfettered, his true artistic impulses in the concerto literature, but I found in these concerts that an orchestra, even the best of orchestras, is a very large creature that speeds up, slows down, and makes cumbersome twists and turns. Playing with Szell and the Cleveland had spoiled me, for they somehow made the elephant seem more like a gazelle. Elsewhere, I often had to follow rather than lead, and many times such a gulf opened up between the conductor's and the soloist's conceptions that the one or, at maximum, two allotted rehearsals hardly seemed sufficient to work out a satisfying interpretation. How different in chamber music, where you had some control over the people you played with and the amount of rehearsal needed! In a quartet one could, for better or worse, be totally responsible for the artistic results.

And I began to relish more and more the stimulation and camaraderie of chamber music. Practicing the solo repertoire hours a day in the confines of my room felt insular and lonely. In stark contrast, string-quartet rehearsals were taken up by many different seductive social transactions—lively discussions, good-natured ribbing, provocative disagreements, and the ever-present potential to be both student and teacher. The high-profile life of a soloist would be gone, of course: standing in front of an orchestra or alone as a recitalist, the spotlight focused intensely on me, my artistry, personality, and ego. Sitting in a quartet, I would appear in a more diffuse light—light divided, as with everything else, in four. There certainly was a trade-off here, individual versus group, me versus us, the ramifications of which were still hazy in my mind. But the artistic rewards were clear-cut. Playing a Beethoven quartet with three like-minded musicians was no less inspiring than playing his concerto with a great orchestra. Gradually but inexorably, forming a string quartet became my fervent wish.

Even with the creation of a quartet specifically in mind, how did one go about it? You couldn't stand on a street corner with a sign or put an ad in the paper. *Strictly Personal*: Young violinist seeks string-quartet companions. Must have high level of instrumental ability and chamber-music experience. Must be willing to rehearse without guarantee of concerts or money, accept unrelenting criticism, travel endlessly, be joined hours on end with the same three people; and enjoy life. (Photo optional.) The ad skirts the essential paradox that an excellent quartet player must have the convictions of a fully developed artist and the malleability and open-mindedness of a labor negotiator. Doesn't flexibility fly in the face of the lifelong quest each of us has to cultivate our own uniqueness? When player A and player B arrive at a certain level of artistry, they are by definition different. In matching players, should you look for powerful musical personalities who may often be at odds or for ones as similar as possible? Is there an ideal person who, while different, shares a common musical comfort zone with you, a place where you can meet, as at the United Nations, to deal with points of view and shades of meaning? As David, John, Michael, and I had our first tentative conversations about starting a quartet, these were the issues we faced.

Since John, Michael, and I had been at Curtis together, we had a long and warm shared history. We were known items to each other. But I had never met David until Marlboro, and it was a while before I came to know him and his pedigree.

John was born into a musical family. His mother, Gretchen, was a cellist and teacher. His father, Orien, was a conductor, an educator, a violinist, and one of the original faculty at the Interlochen National Music Camp in Michigan. Before the age of four, John knew he wanted to play the violin. And during his formative years, his father held a variety of positions in different parts of the country, exposing the young violinist to many musical influences. His first teacher was Virgil Person, in Emporia, Kansas. John made very rapid progress with Person, who, he assumed, had a wealth of experience teaching children. Years later, he learned he had been Person's very first beginning pupil. In Wichita, Kansas, a city blessed with a commitment to music in the public schools, he played in his junior-high-school orchestra and continued his violin lessons. He was already playing string quartets every Saturday, sometimes with his father. In Tuscaloosa, Alabama, he studied both violin and chamber music with Ottokar Čadek, who had been first violinist of the New York String Quartet in the 1920s. John entered the Curtis Institute at the age of eighteen, where he studied with Efrem Zimbalist, then director of the school and one of the world-renowned pupils of Leopold Auer. After graduation, John joined the faculty of Oberlin Conservatory and played second violin in the resident string quartet, all the while performing regularly in recital and as soloist with orchestra. Eventually, John moved to New York City, where he freelanced and then joined the short-lived American String Quartet with David.

Michael received his first violin lessons at the age of five from his father, Samuel Applebaum, a well-known violin teacher and pedagogue. Together with his wife, Sada, Applebaum had written a number of books on music and musicians. While growing up in Newark and then in Maplewood, New Jersey, Michael heard string quartets regularly at home: his father played with diverse musicians—some world-renowned, some his students, who were often amateurs. In an Applebaum chamber-music evening, it was not uncommon for a doctor to be called away in the middle of a Haydn quartet in order to deliver a baby and then to return an hour or two later for Brahms or Dvořák. By the age of eight, Michael was already sitting in on these sessions and at twelve he was accepted at Curtis, where he studied violin first with Lea Luboschutz and Veda Reynolds, then with Efrem Zimbalist. During the summers, both John and Michael continued their studies with Zimbalist in Maine, where the Zimbalists and many of the Curtis faculty had summer homes. After graduation, Michael made his debut at Carnegie Hall and gave another recital there two years later; subsequently, he performed both as soloist and in chamber music. He formed the Marlboro Piano Trio with David and Anton Kuerti in 1958.

When David was ten years old, he was taken to a Philadelphia Orchestra concert, during which he pointed to one of the cellos and said, "I want to play *that*." So David's parents bought him a cello and arranged for him to study with Emmet Sargent, who played in the Philadelphia Orchestra. At thirteen he won a scholarship sponsored by the New York Philharmonic to study with its assistant first cellist, Joseph Emonts. The scholarship included chamber-music lessons with Imre Poganyi, then leader of the Philharmonic's second-violin section but earlier the original second violinist of the Budapest String Quartet. From that moment on, chamber music fascinated him. He subsequently studied with Diran Alexanian and later with Emanuel Feuermann, while continuing his chamber-music education with Adolfo Betti, first violinist of the Flonzaley String Quartet. David won the Philadelphia Youth Competition in 1941 and performed Ernest Bloch's Schelomo with Eugene Ormandy and the Philadelphia; when the United States entered the war, he enlisted in the Navy Band. After the war, he made his debut at Town Hall, followed by recitals in Carnegie Hall and again in Town Hall; he began freelancing around New York City, for a time was staff musician at CBS, played in the NBC Symphony under Arturo Toscanini, was a member of the Guilet and New Music String quartets, and eventually studied with Pablo Casals.

Our shared interest and experience in both solo and chamber-music literature was potentially a powerful binding agent, but there were so many intangibles. We came from different backgrounds, even different parts of the country. How would my balmy Southern California, John's Midwestern prairie, and David and Michael's more structured and formal East Coast mesh?

I was the youngest of the group, John and Michael two and three years older, respectively. David was somewhat older than the rest of us. Was that an issue, I wondered. He was hardly old enough to be our father, but in the mind of this twenty-six-year-old, the fourteen-year age difference between us was something to ponder. Was a forty-year-old's perspective in synch with our not-yet-thirty minds? And I asked myself whether we would age at the same rate, like four cheeses on a shelf. As it turned out, David has the physical constitution of an ox, and his experience in rehearsal, performance, business, travel, and general overview was to be invaluable.

No matter how much theorizing went on, we would know the truth about another's acceptability only after many seasons of concerts and rehearsals. That didn't bother us unduly. Scary as the idea of a union was, all of us were unhesitatingly committed to playing quartets, and we seemed to get along in the groups that brought us together in twos and threes. At least, no one had stomped off in a huff when disagreements arose. All too often at Marlboro I saw what happened when people's chemistry simply did not work: the first rehearsal often was the last. "Impossible to work with him!" was the explanation overheard at the scheduling office.

Toward the end of the summer of 1963, with the encouragement of Rudolf Serkin and Alexander Schneider, the four of us began talking seriously about forming a string quartet. Our prospects looked good on paper. David, Michael, and John already had distinguished chamber-music careers, and although unable myself to boast of such a background, I had considerable experience in chamber-music performances at Marlboro and elsewhere.

If we were to become a string quartet, David would be the cellist, of course, but who would play the other bases on this team? John, Michael, and I could play all three positions. There would have to be one former violinist. Michael, showing a natural affinity for the viola, unhesitatingly staked his claim. David counseled that John play second violin, given his great experience in that position, and I play first. We both consented. Violinists tend initially to be attracted to the glitter of the first part, with its frequent solos and higher voice, and I was no exception. What about the alleged stigma of "playing second violin to someone"? Robert Schumann said, "If all were determined to play the first violin, we should never have complete orchestras." The same is of course true of string quartets, whose members are equal if sometimes different. Still, while the second violin may have fewer melodies to play, it is often the engine that drives the quartet, laying down a contrasting rhythm and leading the rest of the group while the first violin is off whistling his tune. John was that rarer breed, a violinist who would play the other violin but certainly not second violin. To further emphasize our basic equality, we decided that whenever a piece with only one violin was to be performed, John would have right of first refusal.

The quartet had been formed. We had no concerts scheduled, no manager, not even a name, but we now constituted a string quartet. Serkin and Schneider helped us celebrate. Rudi brought a bottle of champagne and Sascha lots of advice. "Don't socialize together, spouses shouldn't mix into quartet business, no postmortems after concerts," he sermonized with a wicked grin. A good-humored but fragile atmosphere pervaded the room as we lifted our glasses to toast an endeavor we all knew could sputter out after a month or grow into a long-lived career. The four of us would return to our present lives until next summer, I in the Cleveland Orchestra and the others in their various groups in New York City.

But we couldn't really finish the celebration without playing. On that late-summer afternoon, as the leaves in southern Vermont were just beginning to turn, the four of us sat down quite alone in a small practice studio and opened the volume of collected Mozart string quartets to the D minor, K 427. As David's gentle descending line, John and Michael's pulsating figures, and the sweet sadness of my overlaid melody poured out, I had the feeling of arriving home, of absolute rightness.

Mozart's wife, Constanze, talked about this quartet in her memoirs. She and Mozart were in the same room when she went into labor with their first child, Raimund Leopold. Mozart was composing at his desk and at the piano. When she would have a contraction, he would interrupt his work and come to the bed to comfort her, and as soon as the contraction was over, he would return to his work. This went on for several hours, during which he composed (or wrote out) a significant part of the D minor Quartet. If Mozart thought of the quartet as an announcement of his first child's birth, then some two hundred years later our playing of his quartet was another kind of birth announcement.

Diary. September 25, 1996. London airport. I run into David. He is pushing his luggage cart, I mine. I ask him what he is thinking. "I'm thinking I don't want to be here, I want to be home," he says mournfully. This is only partially true, at best. Dave loves the concertizing, he is interested in the places we go, and remembers much about the cities, their museums, their people, their food. But grousing does him good—all of us, for that matter.

Today we will fly to Berlin, check into a hotel, have lunch, and then rehearse for tonight's concert in the Philharmonie. It will be a long day. Dave is right. I also wish to be home and not in Heathrow.

I see Michael in front of the flight-announcement board. He has a cart loaded down with viola and carry-on luggage. He is lost in thought, a pocket calculator in his hand. I imagine that Michael is trying to figure out how much money to change into German marks. Our carts meet in front of the duty-free shop, and we examine waist pouches, watches, and cameras together. "Tchotchkes," Michael mutters dismissively.

I have no intention of buying anything, but I like to play a little game with myself in these stores. Of all the things for sale, none of which interest me, I have to buy one object. Which one should I pick? I look at porcelain cups, perfume, liquors, silk scarves, and ties, carefully weighing one item of bad taste or uselessness against another. Finally, I pick something mundane but, considering the choices, not half bad—a bottle of single-malt scotch whisky.

At heart, I am a shopper. Over the years on the road, I have bought shoes, socks, underwear, shirts, slacks, sports jackets, belts, ties, pottery, watches, chess sets, books, folk and fine art, Oriental rugs, music, violin and viola bows, antique furniture, and a didgeridoo.

[5]

Fifty Bucks a Concert

"WHY WOULD ANYONE want to play string quartets?" This
question was posed to me over lunch at the Plaza Hotel by
Eugene Ormandy. During the winter he had invited me to
be concertmaster of the Philadelphia Orchestra, and when I
informed him of my quartet plans he insisted on a face-to-
face meeting.

"Your fee will have to be split ten ways, you know."

"Ten ways," I repeated uncomprehendingly.

"Yes," Ormandy continued with relish. "The four of you,
your manager, and all your wives and mistresses." I hadn't
thought of this. If I'd been more quick-witted while declin-
ing this plum of an offer, I might have pointed out that as
a member of his orchestra I would receive only one-
hundredth of the fee, not even counting spouses, with the
lion's share going to Mr. Ormandy himself.

Still, it raised a legitimate issue. Would we be able to

make a living, forever dividing the pot four ways? I had asked David Soyer this question shortly after we decided to form our quartet. As senior statesman of our group and a former member of two professional string quartets, he would know. "Expect fifty bucks a concert and all the crap you can put up with," he volunteered cheerfully. I suspected there might be some truth to Dave's little joke, one that he used regularly when asked about quartet life, but I laughed it off. For Michael and me, both single at the time, slicing the pie in four presented no particular hardship. There would simply be a little more pizza, a little less steak au poivre in our lives. But John and David had families; each had wives and children in various stages of development. Looking back on this time, I realize that their decision to be part of a quartet was an act of courage as well as love. Unless they had been hiding things from me, neither was wealthy. They were forgoing the steady paycheck that a university position, an orchestra job, or freelance work would provide for a deeply uncertain future. I assume that each had a little nest egg put away, but anyone who has lived in New York City, our planned home base, knows how quickly money slips through one's fingers. John and David, encumbered with all the expenses that family life entails, were making major life changes— and we had no concerts, no manager, no recording contract, not even a teaching position on the horizon. If our quartet had applied for a loan, the bank officer would have laughed in our faces.

As if things weren't insecure enough, we decided as a general policy to accept no additional work that would interfere with the quartet. No outside chamber music, solo concerts, or other professional activities would impede our progress on the long, arduous road ahead of us. It was David who was insistent on this point. He had seen too many quartets fall by the wayside when diverted by other interests and the not insignificant concerns about money. Resisting other temptations seemed like good, solid reasoning—until an attractive solo concert prospect arrived at my doorstep. What would be the harm, I asked myself, in accepting the recital date offered me? It would be a change of pace and there would be a good fee. But it entailed two days of rehearsal before the concert plus two more days flying to the West Coast and back, five days in which the other three would sit idly by, unable even to rehearse. I declined. Only engagements that met our strict policy of non-interference slipped through. Previous commitments would be honored, however: I was to tour with a chamber orchestra playing Mozart concertos; David and Michael had concerts with their Marlboro Trio; and John had his own promised performances. But our eyes were focused on the quartet. There was something almost devotional about our abstinence. We were taking vows. Like a biblical commandment, it had been written, "Thou shalt not commit performance with others."

With an uncertain future ahead, we may have seemed like lemmings falling into the sea, but healthy optimism reigned. We were young enough, good enough, and after several thousand hours of diligent work, we would be experienced enough. If some group was bound to be the next great string quartet, why not us? And word was beginning to spread about our untried outfit. "Take my advice. Don't play a note," said Mischa Schneider, shaking his head. "There has been such talk about how good you will be that any performance is bound to disappoint. Please. Quit while you're ahead."

Word of our quartet spread all the way to Binghamton, New York. During a Cleveland Orchestra rehearsal in the spring of 1964, a man named Philip Nelson from Harpur College called to request a meeting. None of us had heard of him or Harpur College, and I knew only vaguely the whereabouts of Binghamton. Two weeks later in Cleveland, I was shaking hands with a man who looked more like a golf pro than the music-department chairman he claimed to be. In reality, Nelson, with his crew cut and his wing-tip shoes, was both an outstanding golfer and a man with high ambitions for his fledgling department. Having heard about us from Jascha Brodsky, he made an offer that we found difficult to accept and equally difficult to refuse: to coach some of Harpur College's advanced students, rehearse before faculty and students, and play fifteen concerts during the year. Oh, about the salary. For the year's work there was only $10,000 left in the budget, not individually, mind you, but for all four of us. Even in 1964 dollars, this was a paltry sum. My share, $2,500, might just pay for the rent in the Manhattan bachelor apartment I would have to move into next September. On the other hand, nobody seemed to be knocking down doors to hire us. As a matter of record, the total number of offers we had received was one: this one. The position grew more attractive as we mulled it over. We could live in New York City and commute to Binghamton, earn a little money, and with an average of three compositions in each of the fifteen concerts, we would have the Herculean task of learning forty-five different works in that one year. It was slave labor hovering at around minimum wage, but it just might be a valuable experience. We accepted.

⌀

A SUNDAY-AFTERNOON PERFORMANCE of Verdi's Requiem conducted by Robert Shaw ended my last season with the Cleveland Orchestra. Requiems can be gloomy affairs, but Verdi's has lightness and buoyancy to it. It was to be my personal and almost joyful requiem for the Cleveland experience. The years with Szell, his splendid orchestra, and the orchestra's many extraordinary musicians had been far more than a graduate school. Marc Lifschey's haunting oboe solos in the great Schubert C major Symphony, the noble French horn melody of Tchaikowsky's Fifth Symphony in the hands of Myron Bloom, Josef Gingold's shimmering concertmaster solos in Brahms' First Symphony, Jules Eskin's emotive cello aria in Brahms' B flat Piano Concerto, the aura that Robert Marcellus created in the opening clarinet solo of Tchaikowsky's *Francesca da Rimini* Overture—these moments and many, many others were engraved in my memory.

With the uplifting vocal lines of Verdi's Requiem resonating in me, I felt no regrets about the years spent in Cleveland. But no more orchestra! For all its glorious sound, the orchestra was much like a feudal kingdom. Szell was the ruler of an empire composed of the nobility (the section heads), and vassals and serfs (section string players, second woodwind and brass players). At least, that is the way Szell seemed to view himself and the rest of us. As assistant concertmaster I was one of the so-called aristocracy, but in the end everyone answered to the king. Any player who desired creative personal expression, especially any string player buried in the section, found precious little of it in the orchestra, and especially in this one, where the leader exerted an iron rule over his subjects, down to the last detail. It was said that Szell even checked to see that the cleaning people were providing an adequate supply of toilet paper in Severance Hall's bathrooms.

I was impatient to join Michael, David, and John in our new life together, and happy to make the transition from large to small. Others might see it differently, though. The Southwestern painter R. C. Gorman once remarked in reference to the way he lived: "Why play string quartets when you can have the whole orchestra?" I would take issue with Mr. Gorman. True, I was leaving an immense and varied orchestral instrument for a group of four like-sounding stringed and bowed instruments. Some would call their sound scrawny, unvaried, uninteresting, but for me the string-quartet sound was compact, pure, and intimate.

Playing quartets was not exactly in the spirit of good old-fashioned American individualism. According to that script, I should have mounted my horse, slung my violin over my left shoulder, and ridden out of Severance Hall into the sunset, looking for solo concerts: tough, independent, self-sufficient. Instead, I was banding together with three others in a communal endeavor whose low-action plot played itself out slowly over years—not the stuff of movies. No, four unflashy guys in our line of work would be, if anything, the stuff of satire. Hollywood would present us as a New Age group—lighting candles, holding hands, and humming Ommmm before rehearsals.

Unspectacular as it might at first be imagined, our new work was in fact quite remarkable and dramatic. I was entering a social unit with no boss, no underlings, and certainly no conductor. What was one to call a group of four men who regarded each other equally, or as equal as they wanted to be? We had no formal laws or elected representatives. We had simply voted ourselves into office. This wasn't a corporation, either. No legal contract bound us together, and none of us could boast of deals guaranteeing a golden parachute upon retirement or be required to answer to stockholders. There were no leaders in this group—or were there four leaders? Perhaps we were democracy in its purest, most ideal form. The four of us had to search out each other's strengths and weaknesses to create a working organism that operated in complete freedom from layers of command. Why hadn't Karl Marx come up with this, instead of that Communism thing? And as for R. C. Gorman, he might see beautiful forms and colors, but as far as the attributes of the union we were about to create were concerned, he was blind.

In pursuit of this communal dream, I drove to Marlboro in early June of 1964. The four of us were to meet well before the festival started in order to get some serious preliminary work done. Rehearsals, which took place in a rustic cabin rented for the summer by David and his wife, Janet, continued while we participated full time in the festival. Nine months had elapsed since we had played the Mozart D minor Quartet in a cramped rehearsal studio just for ourselves. Each of us had had plenty of time over the winter to ponder a useful course of action. Our most immediate concern, however, was repertoire. Dozens of quartets were obviously required learning, but where should we start? We settled on a concept: lesser-known works of very well-known composers. The list we arrived at included works Mozart wrote as a teenager, K 159 and 160; Mendelssohn's A minor, Opus 13; Fauré's Opus 121; Berg's Opus 3; Schumann's F major; Dvořák's A flat, Opus 105; and Hindemith's Third String Quartet, Opus 22. This music would not place us in glaring comparison with established groups playing the top-ten chamber-music hits. It would give us a little breathing space to create our own style without both audiences and critics being tempted to say, "But the Budapest plays the introduction to Mozart's 'Dissonant' Quartet more slowly than you do." The lesser-known repertoire would also be a breath of fresh air for audiences tired of hearing the same old standards.

On the eve of our first rehearsal, the jokes about string quartets began to appear: jokes about fights, temper tantrums, vendettas, even physical violence, and all delivered with a knowing conspiratorial wink. A mean-spirited definition was served up: a string quartet was one good violinist, one bad violinist, one former violinist, and someone who doesn't even like the violin. We were given copies of an old *New Yorker* cartoon showing a quartet after a violent argument—hair and clothes in disarray, broken strings everywhere, and the cellist's head protruding from the splintered top of his instrument. The caption read: "Gentlemen, I believe this is the end of the Schwarzwalder Quartet."

Nothing of the kind happened in those first days of rehearsals. Mendelssohn's A minor and Hindemith's Third Quartets were put on the stands. I felt a giddy excitement as the four of us commenced work on the slow fugue which begins the Hindemith quartet. We commented, criticized, discussed, suggested. This was just what a string quartet was supposed to do. A great journey had begun.

Our plan was to rehearse at least three hours a day, every day, and with few exceptions that is what we did all year long. We produced a creditable quartet sound quite quickly. Dave is a natural cellist, with a virile, incisive sound. He has the economical moves of a fine athlete. Michael, a born violist, produces a rich, almost lamenting tone. The instrument's large size, a problem for many who attempt the switch from violin to viola, doesn't seem to bother him. John is a textbook violinist: his playing looks and sounds effortless. The cellist Madeline Foley once remarked after hearing us that John was a dangerously good second violinist. And I could also handle the violin well, even though, perhaps because of my long arms, the instrument tucked under my chin looked three-quarter size.

I admired other, more important qualities in my colleagues. When John sang with subtle lyricism, when David played with rugged abandon, or when Michael flew with almost gypsy-like verve, I was always engaged. These were some of the attributes that had originally drawn us together, but there was another vital quality that we shared and that seemed to connect us fundamentally. A listener hearing us individually would have to conclude that each of us prized suppleness above all; each of us tried to make music that was not like a hard object but more like clay still being sculpted, even like ocean waves moving constantly forward and back. The worst criticism we could hurl at a colleague in rehearsal was that his playing was stiff, square, or wooden.

Each of us had another necessary attribute: we were not shy about meting out criticism. Somebody more reluctant in this area might waste valuable time beating around the bush. "I just love the way you play that passage, but I wonder if you would mind, even though it sounded gorgeous, trying it a little differently. Your way is lovely but, now please don't take offense, could you just possibly play it, only if you're willing of course, a little . . . a little . . . softer?" In our group, an eavesdropper might have heard, "That's too loud. Play it softer!" David was unusually blunt, almost amusingly so. Michael was reasonable, rarely confrontational but vocal (even theatrical) when he had to be. John spoke succinctly when he had something to say, but he was unquestionably the man of fewest words. "Let the playing speak for itself" might have been his motto. Although not shy about speaking my mind, I was initially uncertain in what manner to criticize a colleague. There were so many approaches to choose from:

1. John, you play that melody differently from Michael.
2. John, could you make more crescendo at the beginning and more diminuendo at the end of your melody?
3. John, is there a way that you could energize that melody?
4. John, the way you play that melody is very boring.
5. John, that melody you just played? It sounds terrible.

Like a Newtonian law of physics in which every action produces an equal and opposite reaction, every act of criticism given had to be equally accepted. Or, rephrased: we could dish it out, but could we take it? It was too early to tell. We were on our honeymoon. In the glow of those first moments, what did we know of spats, serious blowups, or irreconcilable differences? At that point, we were no different from a pickup quartet that assembles for a single concert. It is immediately apparent to them that the program they have chosen from the standard repertoire shelf is wickedly difficult. They give a collective gasp. Doing this for a living, full time, whew! But can they truly imagine the long-term difficulties? A handful of rehearsals, one concert, and then these four people unclinch and go their separate ways. If the first violinist behaved like a prima donna, so what? Their time with him is finite. They make a mental note never ever to work with this diva again. But we were learning that in a professional quartet there is no such escape and that things big and small begin to fester. If John were to have the habit of, say, tapping with his index finger on the music stand every time he was about to criticize me (he doesn't), I might grow to hate that gesture after thirty years.

We began work on Mendelssohn's A minor Quartet, Opus 13, the work of a teenager touched with genius. Mendelssohn eagerly awaited each newly published work of Beethoven, studied it, and almost swallowed it whole, such was his reverence for the great master. That the A minor Quartet was clearly written in homage to Beethoven is apparent in its deep feeling and its almost verbatim quotations from Beethoven's quartets.

Along with the musical challenges that the Mendelssohn presented, I found myself running into unexpected problems. The quick, light, running notes of the third movement, the Intermezzo, were very difficult for me. I could play them up to tempo loudly, but when I attempted the passage lightly, as the composer intended, the notes came out unevenly. All the concerto playing in the world had not prepared me for this kind of bow stroke. It was a jeweler's work, the setting of small diamonds in a ring after one has been trained to set flagstones in a walkway. The others were having no such trouble. One by one their voices joined the sparkling texture until my entrance intruded, slightly unsure and sometimes downright wobbly. Why was I having such trouble? Perhaps because my arms are unusually long to be wrapped around a wisp of a violin, but the explanation for my problem mattered only insofar as it could help me find a solution. The fact was that for the moment I couldn't do the spiccato bowing with precision.

Inevitably, we made comparisons. Did John have a faster trill, David a richer sound, Michael quicker fingers, I surer intonation? It was discomfiting to sink into this comparative mode, and you could feel bad on either end. Perhaps John was uneasy that his trill outshone ours. In any case, I would leave these Mendelssohn rehearsals discouraged and also with a sense that I had let the others down. It was not as if David, John, and Michael were beating up on me. They wisely stuck to the issue. "Too loud." "Not together." "Try it again." Technically, I began to chip away by practice and experimentation at a bow stroke that would eventually improve enough to blend with the others. Playing quartets demanded the soloist's broad stroke and the delicacy of a miniaturist.

The Mendelssohn was put aside for Hindemith again. The first movement, slow and hypnotic, presented no real challenges for us, but issues arose that had to be dealt with:

ARNOLD: John, you're playing those notes up-bow. I'm playing them down-bow. Shouldn't we get together?
JOHN: I have to play up-bow because my next notes can only be done at the frog.
ARNOLD: But down-bow works better for me.
MICHAEL: Why can't each of you do a different bowing if that's what is comfortable?

ARNOLD: Won't it look odd, as if we haven't rehearsed?
DAVID: Who cares? As long as it sounds good.

David's cello was on the floor, not under his chin, and Michael faced away from the audience. It was John and I, violin twins sitting in a row, whose visual appearance was so connected. Wouldn't it be cute if our bows went up and down together like soldiers in a parade? Only, I was tall and slender, with long thin arms; John was medium-height, compact, with thick, muscular arms. The bow strokes he often favored at the base of the bow, where it is held, were best done by me at the other end, the tip. Here was a problem we solved with the best sound in mind rather than what was visually most soothing. It seemed like a good, practical solution to an issue that came up over and over again.

Others didn't always see it that way. Not long after the Guarneris began to concertize, a quartet first violinist came up to me after a performance and took me aside.

"Are things going all right in the group?" he asked in a lowered voice.

"They're going excellently. Why?" I responded.

"Well," he continued, looking around furtively, "your second violinist is not doing your bowings." For a brief moment I entertained the notion of sobbing out loud and confessing, "Yes! You're right. My second violinist is out of control and I don't know what to do about him." His seriousness could simply not be taken seriously. All this fuss over a bowing because of how it looked! I suspected he was one of those old-fashioned first-violin types who ruled the roost, in a quartet where the second violinist merely did the first's bidding—bowings and everything else.

A quartet led by the first violinist was the rule rather than the exception until well into this century. From the Schuppanzigh Quartet of Beethoven's time to the Busch Quartet of the 1930s, one strong personality was surrounded by three acolytes. You can hear the results in the recordings of the Busch Quartet. Not only is Adolf Busch consistently a little louder than everyone else; he is also the one whose powerful personality shines forth, leaving the others to be seen in his reflected light. Indeed, in England, the first violinist is called the leader and in German-speaking countries the Primarius. These terms seemed inappropriate to us when we later began to perform in these countries, but clearly they were more than mere words. As first violinist, I was the one most often asked about the seating arrangement onstage, the lighting, the dinner party afterward, and when the young lady brought a single bouquet of flowers onstage as we acknowledged the applause, to my chagrin and embarrassment it was I who was presented with it. What were John, Michael, and David—sauerkraut? We began to think after a while that people had a deep-seated need for a boss, a chief, a head honcho.

It was fine for our young group to profess equality, but did we secretly yearn for one person to take a strong hand? It didn't appear so. Suggestions were freely dispensed, usually followed by a chorus of strong objections. We relished flexing our musical muscles and being downright cantankerous with one another. With every note examined under the microscope and every idea given its day in court, the Hindemith and Mendelssohn quartets progressed, but very slowly.

Democratic impulses were reflected in our musical choices as well. It is easy to highlight a melody and have the accompanying voices recede respectfully into the background, like so many proverbial wallflowers. But the secondary voices, the inner voices, are important in and of themselves, and for the general texture or character of a work. We chose the less simple route of shading each voice accordingly. Dmitri

Shostakovich made an analogy drawn from the theater for pianists "who have only one character in the foreground— the melody—while all the rest is just a murky background, a swamp. But plays are usually written for several characters, and if only the hero speaks and the others don't reply, the play becomes nonsense and boring. All the characters must speak, so that we hear the question and the answer, and then following the course of the play's action becomes interesting."

Marlboro was in full swing as we rehearsed and reported now and again to Serkin. It was inevitable that sooner or later he would ask us to play at the festival concerts, and our acceptance of Serkin's invitation produced a small but significant change in our ongoing rehearsals. Things big and small continued to be discussed, but the nitpicking eased up and we focused much more on moving the work forward. If Dr. Johnson said there is nothing like the prospect of "being hanged in a week to concentrate the mind wonderfully," he must have performed quartets.

This is not to minimize or trivialize that rehearsal process. In addition to learning the Hindemith, Mendelssohn, and dozens of other quartets, we were engaged in several long-term evolutions. Each of us was undergoing a very personal interior struggle to develop as a musician and as a member of this particular quartet, even as the quartet itself was acquiring at a glacial pace its own identity. There were now hundreds of items on the docket for discussion. It was hard to know which required quick one-time solutions and which, with broader significance, deserved more measured responses.

In the second movement of the Hindemith, for example, we encountered our first unison and octave passages. As exciting as these sections might sound in performance, working on them is the musical equivalent of scrubbing the floor.

We slaved away cleaning up these exposed places, deciding to raise a pitch here, lower it there, and played two by two in order to isolate and repair rogue notes. The result, after an almost interminable and painful repetition, was that we improved the problem areas. But, in scrubbing Mr. Hindemith's floor, had we learned anything in the process about other composers' floors?

Now that the Mendelssohn and Hindemith quartets were to be performed, we had to resolve another lingering issue quickly. We needed a name.

"How about the New York String Quartet?"

"Too impersonal."

"How about the Manhattan String Quartet?"

"Already taken."

"How about the New Amsterdam String Quartet?"

"This is 1964, not 1664."

"How about the Arjonicher String Quartet?" This attempt to put our names together into a composite followed the pattern used by the members of the Albeneri Piano Trio: Alexander Schneider, Benar Heifetz, and Erich Itor Kahn.

"That sounds absolutely stupid."

"How about the Lotus Blossom String Quartet?"

"Why Lotus Blossom?"

"Why not?"

That was the trouble. All attempts to come up with a name deteriorated into jokes. Everyone had an opinion. One camp said it was important to exercise great care in finding a suitable name; the other maintained that it didn't matter. We would be known for our music-making, not our name—even the Lotus Blossom String Quartet would do if we played well enough.

The New World String Quartet was one of the few acceptable names on our short list when Boris Kroyt arrived to break the impasse. Between the two world wars and before joining the Budapest, he had been a member of a Guarneri String Quartet in Germany. When the group disbanded, the name had gone into cold storage. "Why not use the Guarneri name?" he offered. "I give it to you as a gift." Guarneri was, appropriately, the family name of some of the most famous string-instrument makers in the world. It also had a nice cadence to it. The fact that none of us had Guarneri instruments was ignored by all. We accepted the name with gratitude and a certain amount of relief that one more obstacle was behind us. Now that we were called the Guarneri String Quartet, all that remained for us was to become it.

On Sunday, August 2, 1964, at the Marlboro Music Festival, the new, green-around-the-ears Guarneri String Quartet performed for the very first time in Mendelssohn's A minor Quartet, Opus 13. For a brief moment beforehand, the bond among us that two months of toil had created gave way to another reality. There stood four men with different faces, body frames, playing characteristics, and souls. What kind of folly was the precise and deeply personal task we had set for ourselves? Then John, David, Michael, and I walked onto the Marlboro concert-hall stage. We had worked hard on the Mendelssohn but not at all on stage comportment. Michael emerged from the wings solemnly, as if he were the Pope. David followed, holding his cello in both hands and leaning forward against the stiff wind he was encountering. John entered matter-of-factly—was this a quartet concert or a bridge game? And I brought up the rear, chin jutting out and violin held in front of me as if I were presenting arms. All this I visualize clearly because for years afterward Sascha would do party imitations of our stage entrances that to this day have not changed.

Seated before a large Marlboro audience, we looked out onto a sea of familiar faces. This was not a random concert crowd. These were our friends, colleagues, mentors, people we had known and worked with for years. It was comforting to be playing our first concert here, but the slow, measured opening notes of the Mendelssohn were no easier for it. The constraints of playing string quartets are magnified onstage. It was hard to play together yet beautifully, but once we were into the main body of the first movement, the music's ardor swept us away. When the Mendelssohn finished, four movements later, I felt that a rite of passage had taken place. We *were* a string quartet. As we bowed and left the stage, Rudolf Serkin and Sascha Schneider were waiting backstage to congratulate us, and a crowd of well-wishers soon joined them.

There was little time for celebration of our debut. The Hindemith performance was fast approaching, and we were finding it difficult to get its character just right. The music has a dry wit, a little like telling jokes about water while trapped in the Sahara. It was hard to bring off a feeling that was so odd but very specific. We couldn't seem to get the ending of the last movement right, with its sometimes playful, sometimes menacing character. The cello slowly dies away and the piece pretends to finish quietly before one last defiant outburst from the four instruments.

DAVID: We're making too much of those last notes.

MICHAEL: How can one do too much? It's the end.

DAVID: But we've slowed down already. Playing the last statement still slower makes it ponderous.

MICHAEL: I don't know. I would feel foolish playing it in tempo.

JOHN: The ending has humor. It shouldn't sound heavy-handed. Why don't we try those last notes in a held tempo but without further ritard?

By this time rather weary from the many different ways the ending had been tried, to no one's satisfaction, we played it again reluctantly. Exclamations of approval burst forth. "That's it!" we all agreed, getting up from our chairs. The rehearsal was over and we were pleased to have found the solution for the Hindemith ending.

On Sunday, August 9, we made our second public appearance in Paul Hindemith's Third Quartet, Opus 22. We felt reasonably happy with the performance, but a shadow seemed to cross Michael's face and he shook his head as the applause and calls of Bravo! drifted into the wings where we stood.

"That ending doesn't work at all!" Michael groused.

"You liked it in rehearsal," David shouted so as to be heard above the din as we filed back onstage for another bow. Again, we returned to the wings.

"Well, it just doesn't work," Michael said, sniffing. There was no rejoinder from any of us—a tacit acknowledgment that he was right.

Assuming that we had played the ending basically the same way twenty-four hours earlier, what had changed? We had made a discovery about the act of performance itself. The practice studio is normal, real, everyday; the concert stage is colored more vividly, another state of mind, fabled. When a performance is under way and a connection is established between musician and listener, an understanding, a wisdom, a sense of deeply felt intuitive truth comes into play for the first time. Some of our pre-concert judgments were as unreliable as a three-day weather forecast.

This realization helped us enormously in the hundreds of disagreements we would have through the years that ended in a tie vote. In a piano trio there is never an impasse because of votes. The poor fellow whose brilliant idea is summarily dismissed may have his nose out of joint, but there is a blunt finality in two votes against one. The brute majority triumphs. Quartets, however, operate with the specter of a dreaded tie vote looming over them. What shall we do if John and David want a slower tempo in the Adagio cacciatore and Arnold and Michael yearn for a faster one? All the arguments for each position are laid out and examined every which way. No one budges. It wasn't like the Senate, where the Vice President can break a tie vote when all else fails. (The Budapest Quartet had a novel way of dealing with this problem. For each work they played, one member of the quartet was granted an additional composer's vote. When a tie occurred, the impasse was broken by the designated member's two votes as both composer and performer.)

The nature of our discussions under the cloud of an impasse changed with the understanding of the Law of Performance, the moment of truth that the concert stage gives to performances. "Let's do it Arnold's way tonight," David would say after we had a particularly spirited exchange. "Then you'll see how truly bad an idea it is." I accepted this. It was the right way to go about it. Everything would come out in the wash, so to speak, at the concert that night. The passage in question would be bathed in the light of truth, and somehow without egos being involved. Then everyone would know how rotten *David's* idea had been.

◇

MARLBORO AGAIN ASKED the Guarneri Quartet to perform at the festival's concerts, this time the Dvořák Piano Quintet. We had been working on the Dvořák with Peter Serkin, at the time an enormously gifted teenager. Perhaps you could say that the quartet in terms of ensemble age was barely pubescent itself. We were in our inaugural period of self-conscious musical discovery, and we used our rehearsals to squeeze every ounce of expression and significance out of Mr. Dvořák. Our performance of the quintet was hormonal and supercharged. I ran into Rudolf Serkin moments afterward. He had not come backstage to congratulate us this time, and no comment seemed to be forthcoming now. Still, I couldn't resist asking him what he had thought. He appraised me with a touch of a smile on his face. "You know, they used to play like that in Vienna when I was young." He smiled very sweetly. "That's why I left."

Someone must have liked the Guarneri String Quartet and Peter Serkin, for soon after, we were asked to play our first professional engagement on Nantucket Island, later that summer, and to include a piano quintet. The proposed concert was heady news for us. This wasn't just any engagement: it was to be our very *first* concert, an official Seal of Approval that stated we were a professional string quartet.

In late August 1964, we played at Nantucket's Unitarian Church. The program consisted of the only works in our repertoire: the Hindemith Third and Mendelssohn A minor quartets, and the Dvořák Piano Quintet with Peter Serkin. The bells, which pealed daily at exactly 9 p.m., had no sense of respect for the debut that was taking place. They could not be turned off. The program was arranged so that we would not be playing at the exact moment they began to toll. As we sat on stage waiting for the jangle of bells to stop, I preferred to believe that they were celebrating our arrival on the musical scene.

Diary. October 19, 1996. New York City. Metropolitan Museum. Grace Rainey Rogers Auditorium. This is the first in a series of six yearly concerts the quartet gives at the Met, where we have been playing since our beginning. A devoted audience attends our concerts here, but I am unprepared for what happens tonight. Early this evening, New York City is hit by a severe storm which causes massive flooding and traffic snarls. Getting into my tuxedo, I wait for the call from the museum canceling the concert—one of those acts of God included in every contract a musician signs. When no call comes, I make my way across town with difficulty and prepare for a public whose number may be no greater than ours in the quartet. The stage door swings open and there appears, astonishingly, a sold-out house that overflows onto the stage.

Some of the audience, friends and fans, come backstage afterward. There are the faithful who have attended our concerts from day one and have grown older with us, and the younger adults and music students who want to thank us and have a close-up look at real live musicians and glean some useful information from our chitchat.

The concert stage is also a magnet that draws people from the past who would normally be cut off from me. So I am not surprised when Ernest Schlesinger, whom I knew in elementary school, shows up in Tel Aviv, and Sue Newman, a chamber-music student of ours more than thirty years ago, appears backstage in Syracuse. Once in Los Angeles, where I was to play a concert, Mother handed me my high-school graduation-class photo. "I'm cleaning out the garage and I've kept this long enough. Either you take it or I throw it out." Being of an excessively sentimental nature, I did take it, but not wanting to bend the unusually wide photograph, I could only think to put it in the music cover of my violin case. That night, after the concert, my old high-school friend Danny Brodsley showed up with a pal. "You remember Bob, don't you," Danny asked. "He went to school with us." I didn't remember him, but suddenly I recalled the class photo. "Where are you here, Bob?" I asked, pulling a yard of graduating seniors out of my case. Bob recoiled slightly and regarded me with deep suspicion. What kind of a guy carries his graduation picture around thirty years after the fact?

6

Debut, or You owe me twenty-five cents

AFTER LABOR DAY, the quartet settled down in New York City and began work again. By now, the newness and glitter of our endeavor had worn off and we were faced with the unglamorous task of learning a huge body of repertoire. As a young quartet, we would have had this task in any case, but our first concerts at Harpur College were fast approaching.

We settled into a routine of daily rehearsals at David's Manhattan apartment on the Upper West Side. In the living room where we regularly worked, a harp set to one side presided regally over the proceedings. David's wife, Janet, was one of New York's most sought-after professional harpists. They had actually met at a recording date several years earlier.

Janet was a gracious host, offering us snacks when we took rehearsal breaks, but Michael and I often reverted to adolescence, making pests of ourselves in the kitchen and pilfering food from the refrigerator behind her back. Occasionally we were caught in the act, in which case Janet would announce sternly that the hospitality phase of our relationship was over. David and John heartily endorsed Janet's decision, decrying us as scoundrels and freeloaders, but at the next rehearsal she would usually relent, a kindly soul through and through.

During those rehearsals I began to get an inkling of the enormity of what we had undertaken. There seemed to be no limit to the amount of time needed to bring a work to completion. We could discuss a single upbeat in a Haydn quartet for five minutes. Should it be short or long? *If* short, just how short? How should the beginning of the note be articulated? How loud, how soft? Each of us seemed to have a strong opinion. Whatever was the longest distance between points A and B, the Guarneri Quartet had a knack for discovering it.

None of us was trying to sabotage rehearsals, mind you; we were just disagreeing. After a lifetime in music—and each of us had had one—a person is bound to develop powerful convictions. Note after note, phrase after phrase, the modest decisions one makes, some seemingly insignificant, slowly gather into something that can be called a predilection, and finally a fully evolved set of personal laws, a kind of Constitution of Performance. At each rehearsal, these four conglomerations of opinion collided. I suggested that the last two chords of the Haydn G major Quartet, Opus 76, no. 1, be slower, to give a sense of finality to the work. David made a face. "That's so *fussy*-sounding," he countered. "It should be straightforward and in tempo." The provisions having to do with endings in David's and Arnold's bylaws apparently did not agree. Frankly, I couldn't imagine the Haydn end without a ritard. It seemed so right, so obvious.

Why couldn't David see it my way? In the discussion that followed, we each tried to justify our opinion. "Without a ritard, the listener will have no idea the piece is over," I explained. David shook his head unhappily. "But slowing down at the end is so, so . . . affected!"

Michael and John also had their basic differences. As so-called inner voices, the second violin and the viola often play similar figures together or one after the other. John's playing tends toward a classic reserve; Michael's is more emotive. David and I would have to smile as we listened to them alternate a three-note figure in the slow movement of another Haydn quartet, Opus 20, no. 4, thoroughly convincing and well played by each, but very different. David sometimes editorialized by singing along. "He's Jew-ish," he would intone as Michael played; "He's Gen-tile," when it was John's turn. Midwestern or Mediterranean? John and Michael would each have to alter his favorite way of playing those three notes and meet somewhere in the middle, John a little more free, Michael slightly more sober.

In those early rehearsals, I found it hard to give in to an opposing idea, and not just because I was used to having my own way. If my convictions were worth anything, why shouldn't I fight for them? It might be construed as a sign of weakness if I rolled over at the first sign of disagreement. A person could lose his soul if he wasn't careful. The four of us often fought tenaciously for each note, each dynamic, each tempo, giving in only reluctantly to the will of the majority.

The ego. Does one have to give it up to play quartets? The definition of a professional string quartet might be "a never-ending succession of unsuccessful attacks on the individual's ego by an ever-stronger and more cohesive ensemble." Chamber-music history is littered with the bodies of those who felt their souls were being undermined by constant criticism and the bludgeoning effects of the group's majority vote. The symptoms of "quartet syndrome" can be anxiety, a feeling of worthlessness, and paranoia. The constant carping, close quarters, lack of personal control, and sheer difficulty of working in an inescapable foursome are good reasons why the large majority of quartet players have ultimately gone on to graze in different pastures.

There is a positive spin to the ego issue. If my ideas are constantly being challenged, doesn't this force me to clarify my position in my own mind in order to defend it valorously? And what is necessarily bad about having three other healthy egos, three strong sets of convictions, to learn from? If the criticism doesn't kill me, it will make me stronger, goes the cliché. Besides, playing in a quartet is presumably not about "me" but about "us." There is an ego satisfaction in contributing to a group and watching it improve. If one approaches quartet playing with the idea that each person has something valuable and different to offer, it can operate, ideally, like a self-cleaning oven.

The sometimes agonizingly slow rehearsal process had one benefit: it gave us ample time to study a quartet in depth as we assessed each note for weight, size, and texture. During the long incubation, we found our opinions evolving and changing. We worked on the Haydn G major for an entire week, for example. The idea John had suggested on day two concerning the trio section of the minuet seemed excessive at first. He thought the running notes called for a swaying, dance-like character rather than the straitlaced manner in which I played them. I was not so sure. They should sound supple, but not gypsy-like, I thought. But on day four, when we repeated the movement, his idea felt organic and right. It was not only fun to be a gypsy violinist, but in keeping with the music's character. Even David's opinion about playing the end of the Haydn in tempo, which I had initially dismissed, became more palatable with time. Some kind of invisible fermentation process was at work, which we could see only through our changing ideas.

Those early rehearsals were stimulating but exhausting. Michael and I, the two bachelors, would often seek relief afterward in lunch at Steinberg's Kosher Dairy Restaurant on upper Broadway, scarcely a block from David and Janet's apartment. After three hours of intense confrontation, it was curious that we willingly submitted ourselves to *more* abuse—this time from Steinberg's surly waiters. The food was mouthwateringly good, but the waiters must have learned their serving skills from a prison warden.

"What'll you have?"

"I'd like the kasha varnishkas, please."

"Don't have the varnishkas. The cheese blintzes are better."

"But I wanted the kasha varnishkas."

"Look, would I steer you wrong? I'm bringing the blintzes."

As Michael and I finished our entrées, I had to admit that the cheese blintzes slathered in sour cream were sensational. Secretly, we enjoyed these skirmishes with the waiters. It was part of the anti-charm of Steinberg's. The waiter would begin clearing away the empty plates.

"How about some Jell-O?"

"No, thanks."

"It comes with the meal."

"No, thanks. I don't care for Jell-O."

"Don't be stupid. You're paying for the Jell-O. I'm bringing you the Jell-O." And the waiter would bring a dish of strawberry Jell-O and then stand behind me to make sure I ate it.

"Was it good?"

"Yes, it was absolutely wonderful. Really."

For an instant, I thought of bringing him to future sessions as my mouthpiece.

Along with rehearsals, we began to schedule reading sessions for possible additions to the Guarneri's repertoire, in which each of us contributed quartets we knew or had heard recommended. Our disagreements over the candidates were just as strenuous as our fights over ritards. John brought in the Sibelius String Quartet. The rest of us were only dimly aware of this piece in five movements. Sibelius is known for his great orchestral scores, among them symphonies, tone poems, and a violin concerto, whose grandeur and intensity lie just below a sparse and cool Scandinavian surface. The quartet called "Intimate Voices," is dwarfed by these giants and generally unknown or ignored. It certainly sounded like Sibelius as we read one movement after another, but in my estimation something seemed missing. Was it the large orchestral scale that we knew and loved, or had Sibelius simply come up with inferior material?

"John, it's really not a very strong work," said Michael in the gentlest voice he could muster. We all knew that John's father had gone to Finland to study with Sibelius in the late 1930s.

"I love Sibelius, but this is weak music," David said.

"It's such an odd piece. Not very successful," I added, putting the final nail in the coffin. I felt sorry for John as we handed the parts back to him. He returned the music to his violin case. "You're overlooking a masterpiece," he said quietly.

That's the way it was in the Guarneri Quartet; the majority always ruled. Well, almost always. We felt compelled to make an exception to its armor-clad finality, which we might have called our "misery" clause. If, for example, David and I had gushed over the Sibelius quartet John brought in, but Michael still broke out in hives at the mere mention of it, he would have gotten to veto the majority opinion. The quartet hoped to soften the majority vote's potential tyranny with this escape hatch. It was invoked many times and in surprising ways over the years when one of us felt strongly enough not to cross a picket line to play a concert, not to perform in a country with a repressive regime, not to travel to a region threatened by terrorist attack, or, of course, not to play a work he couldn't bear.

⌐∾·

WE WERE FAR from resolving all our differences on the handful of quartets in our repertory when the time came for our first visit to Harpur College in Binghamton, New York, on the other side of the Catskill Mountains. Philip Nelson, music-department head, had included open rehearsals for students, faculty, and townspeople as part of our duties. Delving into the intimacies of the music, discussing points of interpretation, and criticizing each other in front of complete strangers felt like disrobing in public. But we couldn't afford to make these show rehearsals; the Guarneri Quartet had some forty-five different works to prepare for our impending concerts and we needed the time. Before long, we had forgotten about the onlookers and were being our usual prickly, highly critical selves. The process must have been interesting, because with every session our audience grew. Were they coming to witness a rehearsal or a contact sport?

A question-and-answer period was held at the end of each open rehearsal. In one of these, a young lady in the audience divulged a very special talent: she was able to make contact with the dead. What does one say to people who claim to see aliens, levitate, or speak with ghosts? Her statement brought conversation momentarily to a halt, but when no one seemed capable of responding to this breathtaking information, we moved on to other questions.

At the very next open rehearsal, the Guarneris became embroiled in a fierce debate about the meaning of slurs or legato marks over the closing notes of Beethoven's cavatina. This has been a running argument ever since Beethoven placed these ambiguous indications in a variety of compositions, including the Cello and Piano Sonata Opus 69, the Piano Sonata Opus 110, and the String Quartets Opera 74, 130, 132, and 133, the Great Fugue. Should the slurred notes be seamlessly connected, separate, or pulsating? Did the fingerings written by Beethoven himself over certain passages in both the Cello and the Piano Sonatas suggest a certain separation? The argument raged unresolved at our rehearsal. Suddenly, we could see a lightbulb go on in David's head. He pointed to the woman who could speak to dead people. "Cynthia," he said, "would you speak to Beethoven?"

"Of course," she replied, as if the request had been to borrow an egg from a neighbor.

"Then ask him how we should do the slurs at the end of the cavatina."

A month passed before our next visit to Harpur College. At the open rehearsal, David didn't hesitate.

"Well, did you speak to Beethoven?" he demanded of Cynthia.

"Yes, I did," she said matter-of-factly. I could hear an audible gasp in the audience. She went on, "He says that any way you'd like to play the slurs is fine with him."

The Guarneri Quartet began its series of concerts at Harpur College. As we all knew by then, nothing in the rehearsal process completely prepares you for a performance. A small space is replaced with a large hall, the cozy familiarity of a furnished room gives way to the formal concert stage, and, most important, live human beings rather than blank walls are waiting to receive your special musical message.

On September 20, the Guarneri Quartet played its first concert at Harpur College, followed by two more, on September 28 and October 3. "There ought to be a law against first performances," someone said as we walked offstage after the last of the three concerts. In the space of two weeks, we had played nine works, seven of which were new to us. For us, the Binghamton concerts were low-profile first performances away from the eyes and ears of the big city cognoscenti and New York's musical grapevine. Here, without undue stress, we could acquire onstage experience with the half-dozen quartets we had learned and, at the same time, begin to gather impressions of who we were in front of an audience. Would our interpretations be delicate, wildly bravura, or reflective? The answer would come out slowly during repeated performances. Until a performance simulator is devised, there is no substitute for the onstage experience that Harpur College provided us.

We were a young group filled with energy and enthusiasm, and our early concerts were muscular, high-testosterone affairs. Our fortissimos shook the rafters, accented notes had the same effect as a double espresso, and the prestos made heads spin. In our effort not to be boring, we often overplayed. A rustic Haydn minuet, for example, became highly intense in our hands, and Fauré's gentle and reflective String Quartet, completed by the seventy-eight-year-old composer only a month before his death, acquired a more dramatic character in our eagerness to play with a full dynamic range. Still, the audiences responded enthusiastically. They felt a certain proprietary claim as they listened and watched our growing pains. We were the local mascots.

When the Guarneri Quartet's association with Harpur College came to an end four years later, the audio engineer gave me tapes of all our performances as a souvenir. I held them in my hand—now a bit of history—wondering whether they were really worth hearing, but curiosity got the better of me and I picked one at random from the earliest concerts. Our quartet was first-rate, I thought, but sounded somewhat frenetic, as if we didn't trust the audience to get the point if delivered subtly. In the course of a very short time, our playing had moved somewhat from these high-contrast dynamics to a more textured approach, and from consistently intense phrasing to occasional moments of quiet reflection. We no longer always felt a compulsion to *do* something with every single note. You could be attentive to the music without pawing it to death, to play it lovingly and organically; ideally, it should sound as if we were spontaneously composing the music the very moment we played it.

I put the tapes on the top shelf of my clothes closet, where they have remained. It would be unthinkable to throw them out, but on the other hand I have never had the courage to listen to them again. I am afraid of the youthful excesses the tapes contain. They remain in my closet buried behind old sweaters, like so many canisters of radioactive material.

~

WITH AN EVER-INCREASING REPERTOIRE and some solid performing experience under our belts, it was time to think about a coming-out concert so that the public, critics, and potential managers could look the Guarneri Quartet over. A manager was definitely the next order of business. It was hard enough to create a string quartet. We had neither the time nor the gift of salesmanship necessary to hawk our wares to the concert circuit. Luckily, Harold Schonberg, critic for *The New York Times*, had written favorably about us at our first Marlboro performance the summer before, so we had one clipping to show and hoped our name was not totally unknown.

We approached our mentor and friend Alexander Schneider. Sascha had created a concert series at the New School for Social Research in New York City, and he proposed a pair of debut concerts for us there in early 1965. We were ecstatic. New York has always been the bigger-than-life stage on which every aspiring musician must eventually appear. Playing well here could coax open the doors to the music business. Managers, record producers, and tastemakers all seemed to live in or around New York City.

If playing well in a debut concert was important, so was the choice of repertoire. We decided to continue our theme of lesser-known works of the masters: Alban Berg Opus 3, Mendelssohn A minor Opus 13, Schumann F major, Mozart K 171, Fauré Opus 121, and Dvořák A flat major Opus 105. We wanted to play to our strengths and also give the public fresh material.

Our first concert was scheduled for February 28, and as the date approached, I felt an odd discomfort. Unlike Mischa Schneider, who told of the terror that gripped him as a young man before any solo performance and how stage fright seemed to drop away with the support of three others in a string quartet, I had never been afflicted with anything more than garden-variety nerves before a solo appearance. In any case, the spotlight would not be on me in this debut concert, but on us. But whereas, before, my concert fortunes rose and fell solely on the quality of my own playing, I was now connected with and dependent on David, John, and Michael for a good performance. How strange! If I played out of tune, we played out of tune; if they stumbled, so did I; and if I managed to play beautifully, we would all share the credit. The responsibility pressed in on me. My future was their future; theirs was mine.

A case of nerves can unhinge a performance—with lack of concentration, shaking hands, and missteps you never imagined in rehearsal. But a little fear is a good thing: it can supply the adrenaline and focus needed to coax the very best out of a performer, and even some extra magic. Just before that first New School concert, it was hard for me to know if the others were nervous, too. It was always easier to discern this in the heat of performance. My bow arm and Michael's sometimes quivered a bit, and David tended to groan (as his teacher Casals had done). John's playing, on the other hand, seemed impervious to nerves. He was like a rock. Nothing fazed him. I envied his cool, and I also depended on it. John was the navigational system you could always count on for sure intonation, steady rhythm, and crisp articulation.

There were the usual jokes and good spirits as we warmed up together in a tiny room just offstage. Then Sascha made an appearance. "You no-good ganovim [thieves, in Hebrew]. You think you're big shots playing in New York. Ya, ya," he threw at us in mock anger. Then his face softened. "Vell, good lock, my dirrs." Moments later we were onstage, playing our debut program.

If the Guarneri Quartet was nervous, this propelled us forward. It seemed to me that we played well and with true emotional engagement. The hymn-like closing strains of the Mendelssohn A minor Quartet brought the concert to an end. It was the same material with which the quartet had begun, recast from the romantic little song "Ist es wahr?" (Is it true?), which the eighteen-year-old Mendelssohn wrote only months earlier. As lovely as the opening is, its reincarnation four movements later, now remembered and cherished by the listener, is deeply felt. The audience, reluctant to break the silence as the last pulsating chords died way,

clapped diffidently at first and then crescendoed into an enthusiastic reception.

Unbeknownst to us, two men sitting together among the
listeners had a more than casual interest in the quartet—
Fritz Steinway and Max Wilcox. Steinway, a member of the
great piano-making family, had recently joined forces with
three others, Harry Beall, Ruth O'Neill, and Arthur Judson,
to form a new concert management. There was nothing new
about the concert business for Judson. He had been one of
its most powerful players for almost half a century. A brief
fling at retirement had been a disaster and he had decided
to reenter the field, muttering, "Only God would allow a
fool to start a new company at eighty-two." Judson instructed O'Neill, Beall, and Steinway: "I'll pay the bills, you
do the work."

Max Wilcox, the man sitting next to Steinway, was a
record producer for RCA. He was the all-important liaison
between the musicians and the recording engineer during
recording sessions and also during the sorting-out process
afterward. Wilcox played the piano himself, had a highly
developed musical ear, and as a record producer was sought
after by the finest musicians in the world. For many years
he produced all of Arthur Rubinstein's records. Both Steinway and Wilcox had learned of the Guarneri Quartet's existence through the Marlboro Music Festival's grapevine that
summer. When the concert ended, Max turned to Fritz and
said, "You should manage them; we should record them."
The Guarneri String Quartet was launched.

Another event of significance took place during that concert. Immersed in the music we were playing, I was only
dimly aware that Michael kept looking into the audience
between movements. A young woman in the first row had
caught his attention, and, as Michael told me much later, a

conviction had gradually come over him during the evening: I am going to marry that woman one day. Jani, the object of his interest, was an eighteen-year-old from Austria who had recently moved to New York City with her family. When she recounted the story of that evening to me recently, she conceded that she'd thought, what was the harm in returning his gaze, even flirting a little? The protective space dividing performer from listener made the little exchange safe and harmless. But Hannah Busoni, the daughter-in-law of the pianist and composer Ferruccio Busoni and a friend of both Jani and the quartet, altered the situation unexpectedly at the concert's end. "Let's go out and have a piece of strudel and a cup of coffee, but first I want to congratulate the guys," she said, sweeping Jani backstage. Michael made a beeline for her. Three years later, they were married.

The few concert bookings we had garnered for ourselves for the rest of the 1964–65 season included some away from New York City. John, Michael, and David, who had all been in professional chamber-music groups before, knew what to expect from the traveling life, but I was a novice. I imagined airports, hotels, and concert halls shrouded in veils of glamour. What should I wear on these trips, I wondered. It was the unbuttoned 1960s, so suits and ties were out, bell-bottoms and double knits in. Perhaps slacks, a beautiful psychedelic shirt, and matching sports jacket. My mother had the same idealized view of life on the road. She had accompanied the quartet on one of our trips to Harpur College, where we had always stayed at a local Holiday Inn flanked on one side by an ugly commercial highway and on the other by a garbage dump. When we checked in, Mother marched up to the clerk at the reception desk. "I'd like a room with a view, please," she said. From that moment on, "a room with a view" became our watchword for all less-than-first-class accommodations.

Our first concert away from home, on April 20, was, ironically, in my former home, Cleveland. The trip there was
not exactly what I had expected. Rather than a seamless
sweep from one city to another, I found my forward motion
stopped again and again. I had to wait on my corner for a
taxi to take me to La Guardia Airport. I had to wait again
at the airline counter to check in. Then I waited at the boarding gate, and once we were airborne I even had to wait to
use the lavatory! When we landed I waited for my baggage,
for yet another taxi to my hotel, to check in at the desk, and
for the elevator. By the time I opened the door to my room,
the glamour of travel had thoroughly evaporated.

With this first concert away from home, the full force of
our togetherness struck me. The Guarneri Quartet not only
played, rehearsed, and conducted business together. We
found ourselves traveling and eating, even going to parties
together. I began to know the guys' habits, predilections,
quirks, and all their stories. Over a delicious meal in a private
home after the Cleveland concert, I heard Michael tell a joke
about a couple in an old-age home. It was a delightful joke
and he had delivered the punch line artfully, but I couldn't
laugh. I had already heard it three times that week.

Several members of the Cleveland Orchestra attended the
party and we greeted each other with bear hugs—an expression of affection for our vast shared experience over the
last years. But being in an orchestra has some of the feeling
of island culture, in that it is self-sufficient and insulated
from the rest of the musical world. It takes an effort to leave
its security, camaraderie, and regularity, but once that was
accomplished, I felt a gulf between us. I had made the great
journey away from that island, not to the mainland but to
another, much smaller island.

Next morning, I attended the last part of the orchestra's
rehearsal in Severance Hall and then knocked on Szell's door

to say hello. Szell took one look at me and almost yanked me into his room. "Arnold, I heard the Guarneri Quartet's broadcast of Mozart K 590 from the Frick Museum recently and I've been waiting to talk to you. Very well played, I must say, but one must think of the first movement in two, and also, why do you use such old-fashioned fingerings in the last movement? Modern listeners no longer want to hear the shifts from one position to another." I had to think: he hadn't seen my fingerings, he had *heard* them. Moments later, my visit (or was it a lesson?) with Szell was concluded. If Szell had been a member of our quartet, a healthy debate would have followed on the heels of his suggestions, but he wasn't a quartet player, he was Georg Szell, conductor and king of the Cleveland Orchestra. Stepping out of Severance Hall, I knew with even greater certainty that my island move had been the right one.

Along with my complaints about being always bound together, I soon realized that traveling as a foursome had decided benefits. You were never lonely. Our concert-pianist friends spoke with envy of our togetherness. Theirs were isolated lives on tour, alone everywhere they went except for that glittering moment onstage before an adoring public. We could dine, go shopping, even see a movie on a free night, with Guarneri company. A quartet was a traveling social club, if you wanted one.

It was good to have the luxury of ever-available companionship, wasn't it? Or was it bad, day in day out, year after year, to have the same four people bound together like Siamese quadruplets? This depended entirely on one's mood. The four of us liked each other and got along well; that was never in question. But how much togetherness could one take? John seemed to have the least tolerance for socializing. He rarely went to post-concert dinner parties and often ate alone. He could be the warmest of people, but Michael, David, and I recognized early on that John's people battery gave out quickly. The rest of us enjoyed people more readily, especially after a day of traveling, practicing, and performing in a strange city. A musician on tour is an outsider always trying to look in on other people's lives through the little windows that only occasionally present themselves. The after-concert party was such a window. There, we could rub shoulders with music lovers, be entertained, and return the favor by telling the jokes and stories we had picked up on our travels. But for all of us there came that moment when the mind and the body said, *No more.* We all had an almost physical need for private time, a time for the "I" rather than the "we."

Traveling with the quartet presented us with another unexpected consideration—the constant dividing of money. On that first trip away from home, the four of us crowded into an airport taxi en route to the Howard Johnson Motel, where we were staying. "That will be thirteen dollars," the driver informed us as we pulled up to the door. Who was to pay? While I wondered about this, the guys disappeared. All right, I said to myself, I'll pay. Let's see. Thirteen bucks, a two-dollar tip, that makes fifteen dollars. Divide by two. That's seven-fifty. Divide by two again. That makes, hmm, three dollars and seventy-five cents apiece.

I entered the lobby and joined the others at the registration desk.

"Three dollars and seventy-five cents each, gentlemen," I announced.

"Do you have change for a ten?" John asked. I didn't. "Then I'll have to owe it to you."

"David, you owe me four dollars for dinner last night. Pay Arnold three seventy-five and you owe me a quarter," said Michael. David pulled out a ten-dollar bill.

"Then I owe you seven-fifty, Arnold. Do you have

change?" I looked in my pocket and came up with two dollars and twenty-five cents.

"Okay. I owe you twenty-five cents."

This convoluted exchange over an insignificant taxi fare! The procedure became an unavoidable fixture of quartet life over thirty-three years, as we applied higher and higher mathematics to compute what we owed each other for auto rentals, air fares, meals, tips, gifts, and telephone calls.

In those early years I was eager to settle our debts with one another justly. It was not as if we couldn't afford it. It was more the principle of the thing. Perhaps I was concerned that we be judged well when and if we ever arrived in quartet heaven. Nancy Dalley and Janet Soyer joined us on our first trip to Europe that summer. The tour took us to Geneva, Basel, Amsterdam, Cologne, and Spoleto. There were many taxis to take along the way, but six people obviously couldn't fit into one cab. We had to split up. I would find myself in a taxi with, say, David and his wife, Janet. How much should we pay individually? Should I pay only one-quarter of one fare, my share if no wives had come along? That seemed a little extreme. Should David consider Janet and himself a unit, in which case we would split the fare in two, or were we three separate people, paying one-third of the fare each? What was right? You could make yourself a little crazy thinking about these things, which at heart were all pure nonsense. Who really cared about a few cents one way or another?

Other situations arose, however, where time, money, and even personal responsibility were at stake. Once, John's alarm clock didn't go off and he missed his plane for an afternoon concert in the South. John took the next flight out and would have made the concert on time but the plane was delayed. The concert started and finished late, and we missed the last plane back to New York City, necessitating an overnight stay in a hotel. Who should pay? The alarm-clock episode could have happened to any one of us and John had acted responsibly by allowing for a backup flight that should have gotten him to the concert on time. On the other hand, we were out a good sum of money. There was no easy answer.

In many situations, there was no right or wrong, merely a gray area. As time passed, it ceased to be important whether I split the taxi fare in two or three. Why clutter the mind with such drivel? Michael once suggested that we take a Talmudic scholar on the road with us for such eventualities. He could decide about taxi fares and even about some tempos in the Alban Berg Quartet, Opus 3, which we had yet to agree on. The three Jews in the quartet, Michael, David, and I, gleefully approached John, who is Christian, with this idea. He thought about it for a moment and then the slenderest of smiles crossed his face. "Sometimes I feel so lonely in this group," he said.

⌁

THROUGH THE MANY REHEARSALS and concerts of that first year, I began to notice a change in our playing. It was more a feeling at first. By the time the quartet arrived in Europe in the summer of 1965 for our first concerts there, we had begun to relax with each other during the most problematic ensemble passages. A natural by-product of ensemble difficulty is a certain tightness and stiffness. It is so hard to play together that a young quartet, instinctively, will avoid any freedom or individuality that rocks the boat. Their first performances tend to be well played, synchronized, and bland. In those problem areas we were no different from other quartets, but once our ensemble playing was in order, we each began to feel more freedom onstage. The passages John and I had together in the slow movement of the A minor Mendelssohn, for example, had initially sounded cautious in our effort to play them in perfect ensemble. As we got to know each other's playing styles, we became more confident, even daring. Problem passages could now surge forward and then hesitate at the end if we so desired, and still we'd be together. If Michael decided to play a viola solo rhapsodically in the Hindemith, he was more confident that we would follow him. Three months earlier, our inexperience might have forced him into a more sedate version. And it was a point of pride for the three of us to mesh with David after a long leap he made from one note to another in the slow movement of Mozart's F major Quartet, K 590, a leap he blithely chose to play differently at every performance. To be honest, we weren't always exactly with David, and this presented him as well as us with a problem. He could curb his artistic impulse and retreat to a more static and predictable rhythm that would be easy to follow, but he never did. There was a danger inherent in the lockstep, marching-band character of ensemble playing that threatened our music-making, and we strove mightily to rise above it.

The last stop on our first European tour was Gian Carlo Menotti's Festival of Two Worlds in Spoleto, Italy. In the daily noon concerts that took place in an old theater off the main square, we were expected to perform as a string quartet, but also in combination with a roster of exciting young players that included the cellist Jacqueline Du Pré and the pianist Richard Goode. We had become a little turned in on ourselves in the intense efforts to forge a new quartet. Playing with other people who had different musical ideas came as a small shock. Quartet life reminded me of the terrariums my elementary-school teachers kept in their classrooms. In large glass bottles partly filled with gravel and water, they had fish, snails, plants, sand, and shells, with a cork stopper in the opening. For the entire school year we children witnessed an independent and completely self-sufficient life system at work. A quartet was like that. It could, in perfect four-part harmony, shut out the rest of the musical world if it wanted to. But with other musicians added to the mix, the cork was out of the bottle.

An unassuming nineteen-year-old with long blond hair, wearing a simple print dress and looking more like a milk-maid than like a cellist, showed up for our first rehearsal of the Schubert Two Cello Quintet. There was something en-dearing about her loping stride and her slightly wacky sense of humor. But when Jacqueline Du Pré sat down to play the quintet with us, these impressions vanished. She swayed with an almost animal-like joy and intensity, and the music poured out of her. The beauty of her playing swept across the musical assumptions we had acquired in these months of working together. As perfect a thing as a string quartet was, it was vital for us individually and as a group to step back into the other, real world from time to time.

Spoleto came to a close in the middle of summer. The Guarneri String Quartet had actually completed a year to-gether, and we were still speaking to one another. It had been a hard year, smoothing out enough of the rough edges of our four personalities to mesh properly but not so many as to make the surfaces smooth, bland, and uninteresting. It had been difficult to have my young and still somewhat fragile ego assaulted endlessly, and to remember that often enough I had been the assaulter as well as the victim. But somehow I think we all understood that this was a necessary feature of string-quartet work. We had come together with a goal in mind, the performance of string quartets, and reaching it depended on our being able to break through our heavily fortified attitudes in order to understand and relate to each other.

The Guarneri Quartet was evolving into a disciplined, supple, expressive group. That was certainly cause for celebration. Besides, I was surprised to realize that with every discussion, disagreement, and adaptation, I felt a growing personal strength and self-confidence.

Now was undoubtedly the time to take inventory, but there was no doubt in any of our minds about the quartet's going on. Even *The New York Times* concurred. "Guarneri Quartet Displays Tone of Satin" had been the headline of its review of our New School debut. Besides, Judson, O'Neill, Beall, and Steinway had booked us thirty-five concert appearances for the next season. Never mind that Ruth O'Neill had the unsettling habit of calling me Michael when she came backstage after concerts to congratulate us. As long as she didn't confuse the Guarneri String Quartet with the Budapest or the Juilliard, I didn't mind. There was more exciting news. In early June, we had made our first recordings with Max Wilcox for RCA Records and they were soon to be released.

To paraphrase Winston Churchill: this wasn't the end, and it certainly wasn't the beginning, but this was probably the end of the beginning.

Diary. September 27, 1996. Tonight's concert is in Wels, a small but beautiful Austrian city. It is always a question whether the quartet will be fêted or ignored in a new city, but in this case the presenter lays out the red carpet for us. We are picked up at the airport and whisked away to a restaurant whose national identity and age are everywhere to be seen—ancient plastered walls, hand-carved beams, paintings of bucolic landscapes and hunting scenes on the walls. A memorable beer in outsized glasses is served. The level of good cheer rises slowly but inexorably as chopped cabbage in a vinaigrette sauce, dumpling soup, and various smoked and marinated meats arrive. John, who has made one of his rare social appearances, orders an ice-cream and whipped-cream heart-clogger. I am encouraged to eat a "moor in a shirt." This masterpiece of political incorrectness turns out to be a round brownie covered in chocolate sauce and surrounded by puffs of whipped cream—tasteless name, tasty dessert.

For some unfathomable reason, the conversation turns to burial plots. From across the table, we hear Michael divulge that he plans to be buried in a Vermont cemetery next to several musician friends we all know. John tells Michael that he must cancel these plans immediately. There is no doubt in his mind. The Guarneri String Quartet must be buried together! Peals of laughter crisscross the table.

Later, I think about the idea. Do I really want to be with these guys for eternity? I imagine our bereaved widows laying wreaths on our graves and hearing, to their astonishment, voices from inside. "You were too loud for me in the Haydn." Two graves down comes the answer: "Better than being out of tune. You were always out of tune in the Schubert." From a third grave: "Stop arguing! Did you hear the joke about the couple in the old-age home?" From the three other graves: "Not that joke again, please!"

7

The Metal Ear

WHEN MAX WILCOX told us that the Guarneri String Quartet would make its first records in a place called Webster Hall, the name conjured up images of burnished wood paneling, stuffed leather armchairs, and even academia rather than a recording studio. There was nothing Ivy League, however, about its location at 125 East Eleventh Street on the Lower East Side of Manhattan, a once thriving Jewish neighborhood whose last visible remnants were a few delis, kosher restaurants, and public baths.

Walking up the front steps and into Webster Hall on that June day in 1965, I was surprised to find myself in an ample ballroom out of another era. In fact, my mother recalled attending union dances there in the 1920s. Its hardwood floor had been left clear, with chairs lining the perimeter, presumably for dance couples spent from their exertions in the fox-trots, polkas, rumbas, and tangos that had been Webster Hall's principal industry over the last half century. Now it had been leased by RCA Records, which installed a soundproof recording booth and listening room along one wall. Max Wilcox obviously relished guiding the four of us around.

Webster Hall's most spectacular feature by far was a garish chandelier, adorned with two concentric rings of electric lights, which hung in the center of the ceiling. As we gawked at this monstrosity, Max unobtrusively drifted over to a nearby wall and flipped on a light switch. White, yellow, blue, green, and red lightbulbs lit up. We cackled with glee. Max flicked the other switch. The two circles of light began to move briskly in opposite directions. A collective gasp was all Max heard from us. This was to be the beginning of a long-standing tradition. No recording session at Webster Hall (and there would be many) was complete without the ritual of turning on the electric chandelier.

It was time for the business at hand. Our plan was to make two initial recordings—the last two Mozart quartets, K 589 and 590, for one, and in a contrasting vein, Mendelssohn A minor, Opus 13, and Dvořák A flat major, Opus 105. Richard Gardner, our recording engineer, busied himself with the equipment while Max ushered us onto the ballroom floor, where the four chairs, four stands, and a bevy of hovering microphones awaited us, looking forlorn and curiously out of place. As we approached, I imagined an elaborate, very stately cotillion about to begin, with engineer Gardner, producer Wilcox, assorted chairs, stands, microphones, and members of the Guarneri String Quartet all bowing, curtsying, and swaying. It was, after all, a dance hall. Max suggested we start playing for ourselves while he and Gardner made their preparations.

Webster Hall's acoustics were superb—just enough resonance to put a bloom on the sound but not so much as to make it muddy and indistinct. This was a quality that would be heard by the listener in the stereo comfort of a living room as well as by us in the hall. Dry acoustics are a musician's curse, sapping the luster of his sound and nibbling at his confidence.

We continued to play while Max fussed with the microphones. Then he stood in front of us as if to gather in the sound of our playing like a human recording machine. He moved quickly back to the recording booth to compare what he had just heard with the sound now issuing forth from the loudspeakers there. Shuttling back and forth from live musicians to machines, Max kept moving the microphones and adjusting their height in search of that elusive match in his inner ear between the two sounds. This process took no inconsiderable amount of time, but finally Max deemed us ready for a trial recording to test the quality of sound and instrumental balance. The tape recorders rolled, and we dutifully churned out three minutes of Mozart. Then John, David, Michael, and I marched expectantly to an alcove alongside the ballroom to listen to playbacks.

What we heard was disheartening. The balances were off, the tempos not altogether convincing, and aspects of my own playing a not altogether pleasant surprise. Was this what we and I really sounded like? It was the same feeling of discomfort and mild shock I had experienced recently in the men's section of a department store while trying on a new jacket. Standing in front of a three-way mirror, I had caught a glimpse of my profile as others presumably saw it. Was my nose really shaped like that, did my chin do that funny thing? And, in this case, was my vibrato really so unrelenting? As if on a prearranged signal, we began to complain to Max all at once: a whole catalogue of grievances about balances and the quality of our individual and collective sounds.

Max was unruffled by this assault from an unhappy four-headed monster. He seemed almost to expect it. When the complaints ceased, he emerged from the recording booth and began repositioning our dance partners, moving microphones fractions of an inch one way and another. With a continuous, repeated triangulation of playing, listening, and readjustment, we began to approach a recorded sound that was realistic. But it never was exactly right. The microphones seemed to hear differently than we did. On the playback, David's Domenico Montagnana cello sounded realistic enough in the high register but the bass end boomed excessively. The recording was both good and bad news for Michael. The mikes could be positioned to rectify the chronic problem of the viola facing away from the audience in the traditional American quartet seating, but Michael, still a fledgling violist, was playing on a brand-new instrument made by a relatively obscure maker, one Harvey Fairbanks from Binghamton, New York. As good as this instrument was, it pitted a young wine against old and noble growths, three Italian and French instruments whose combined age was more than five hundred years. The acoustics of a great hall might forgive and equalize the differences among instruments, but the microphone highlighted the newness of the viola's sound. John and I, who presumed we were well matched in concert, seemed curiously unbalanced on tape. John's violin, made by the French master Nicolas Lupot, produced a big, strapping sound in the playbacks, while my Italian violin, the work of Santo Serafino, one of the last of the Cremonese makers, had a softer, sweeter, more complex quality. Not only did the microphone hear differently; it seemed to take a shine (in its steely way) to certain instruments and turn its tempered nose up at others.

Listening to the last and best playback of the morning, I thought we might now, after two hours of adjustment, begin the real recording, but a taciturn Dick Gardner made an observation that had escaped all of us: there was a small but audible hum in the test recordings.

Dick led us back onto the dance floor to listen. It was impossible to hear a hum or even a howl with all the talking going on.

"Quiet, please," Dick pleaded.

The conversation faded away and we were left in a thick silence.

"I don't hear anything," David commented skeptically.

"Oh, I do," Max said with the assurance of his calling.

"What do you hear?" I asked, unconvinced that this was anything but our imagination.

"It's the sound of Michael's wallet," John volunteered.

"Shh!" Dick hissed. Then after a moment, "I think the sound is coming from one of the ceiling lamps."

Dick needed some time to exorcise the errant noise from the room. The quartet stood around glumly. It seemed that the recording session would never begin.

Max broke the mood by inviting us to his favorite deli on Second Avenue, a street that was once known to locals as Yiddish Broadway. Over matzoh-ball soup and juicy pastrami on Jewish rye, we discussed the recording process. Were we hearing our playing for the first time, warts and all, or did the metal ear of the microphone simply hear differently from a human one? Max confirmed that microphones not only gather sound differently than the human ear, but due to their various designs, they hear differently from one another. We complained about a certain shrillness in the recorded sound. Max suggested we try the old RCA 44BX ribbon mikes, a mainstay in recording since the days of the 78 r.p.m. record and now usually replaced by condenser microphones, the Neumann U47 in our case, which picked up more of the highs and lows in the sound spectrum.

Old photographs of radio actors reading soap-opera scripts showed them facing one another with the older ribbon microphones poised between them, their distinctive hexagonal shape picking up sound from front and back but not the sides. With these oldsters, we would be sacrificing a certain hard-edged realism for a more rounded, appealing sound— something akin to the soft camera lens that hides nature's crueler signs of aging with a beneficent candle-like glow. We were sold on them.

In the coming years, Max and the recording producers who followed him continually brought in new microphones to try. One was brighter, another more mellow. Some favored the violins, while others would bring out the deeper resonance of the viola and cello. The producers also tried different recording approaches. Individual microphones were assigned to each of us, so that lapses in the balance of voices could be readjusted in the studio, months or years after the fact. The downside was that you tended to look at trees in the forest, not the forest itself, hearing the individual voices rather than a homogeneous quartet sound. The very opposite in recording philosophy was to have one microphone perfectly positioned for optimum balance and the hope of a golden sound, but then the balance of instruments would be, unfortunately, sealed in aural stone. If someone grumbled about not being heard, there was no court of appeal. RCA tried recording in quadraphonic sound for a while. The listener who had bought a second speaker when stereophonic sound was introduced was now asked to buy two more, so that he could be surrounded by sound, immersed in an aural bath, when listening to the Guarneri Quartet, Arthur Rubinstein, or Elvis Presley. Presley's name, incidentally, was always mentioned with great respect in the halls of RCA's Red Seal classical division. It was said that the profits from his record sales single-handedly kept the division afloat.

Elvis Presley and classical music were odd bed partners, to say the least. His records were as ubiquitous as peanut butter, but I daresay that most rock-and-rollers were unknown to classical musicians. Mention the name Jerry Lee Lewis or the Coasters, famous rockers from the 1960s, to one of our ilk and you would get, most often, a blank stare. And Jerry Lee Lewis may well not have known who Jascha Heifetz, Arturo Toscanini, or the Budapest String Quartet was, settling the score. The primal harmonies and primitive rhythmic drive of rock-and-roll were considered by the cultured to be a plague that had settled on the earth, would run its course, and finally ebb away. The fact that the Guarneri Quartet played in a hall and the Beatles (whose music I enjoyed) in a football stadium, or that they sold a hundred times more records than we, didn't bother us particularly. Classical music had never succeeded in capturing more than a sliver of the music lover's pie. Why should we be an exception? If Elvis was willing to foot our bills, it was fine with us.

⤆

THE RESTORATIVE POWERS of a delicate matzoh ball in chicken soup are impressive. After lunch, we returned to Webster Hall refreshed and ready to work. Dick Gardner was waiting for us, looking pleased. He had located the hum's source and removed it. The culprit was an errant lightbulb in an exit sign. It was time to record. Max and Dick retreated to their soundproof recording booth and we assumed our quartet positions. "Mozart Quartet, K 589, first movement, take one" came over the intercom, and the quartet prepared to play.

Even before the first note sounded, something was wrong or, at the very least, missing. The ballroom was empty, devoid of any audience. As performing musicians, we exist not just to play but to play for *someone*, to interest, then involve, and finally, move the live, receptive listener sitting expectantly before us. The pianist Arthur Rubinstein always picked a specific member of the audience to play to (preferably a beautiful woman), to woo her from his piano, creating a bond and, ultimately, a deep relationship. Playing before the microphones hanging there so mutely on movable stands eliminated a whole series of transactions between performer and audience. Gone were the familiar sounds of the concert hall that drift across the footlights: the rustle of programs, the infuriating latecomer rushing breathlessly to his seat, the occasional cough, the intense silence of concentration, and, finally, the applause. With that "Take one," the quartet began to play, not for an audience, but for a collection of impassive metal objects that were seemingly unimpressed and unaffected by us.

The microphone inevitably divides musicians into two groups: those who feel uncomfortable before its metal ear, and those, fewer in number, who embrace its cool presence, even revel in it. Glenn Gould went to the extreme of entirely forsaking the concert stage for his beloved recording studio. He complained about the concert experience, "the non-take-two-ness of it all." Of those who are comfortable playing before the microphone, a few old-fashioned types still regard the experience as a performance, but most others depend on frequent stops to stitch together a final product.

My old friend Lincoln Mayorga, a partner in Sheffield Lab, a recording company that caters to customers who have top-quality high-fidelity equipment, tells a revealing story about their return to the then outdated process of direct-to-disc recording in the 1970s. In the days before digital recording, every transfer of music from one recorded medium to another caused a deterioration of the original sound, not unlike a photograph that loses its sharpness with continued reproduction. By eliminating the tape machine entirely, Sheffield hoped to improve the sound quality of the recordings, but it meant playing twenty-two minutes of music, the length of one side of a long-playing record, without interruption, for, with no tape machine, there could be no splicing. The older musicians who had begun their careers recording with the 78 r.p.m. format, four to five minutes of uninterrupted music on a single side of a record, seemed to function well in the twenty-two-minute time frame. But the younger musicians, used to splicing together whole sections from small pieces, even single notes, tended to be uncomfortable.

Just as film differs from theater in that its success or failure may lie in the editing room, a recording may consist of dozens, even hundreds of bits and pieces combined to make a convincing and spotless performance. The splicing of sections of tape together, made even easier in the digital age, means that after the performance has been completed, the final practicing, so to speak, and the last artistic input take place.

As we played the Mozart quartet's first movement, it was uncertain to what extent we would learn to love the microphone, but "take one" came to an end and we moved into the sound booth to listen to it: whether we or the microphones were responsible for our grievances was now irrelevant. In the next two takes we realigned voices and readjusted details of our phrasing so that we liked what the mikes heard. The middle of the afternoon was already upon us by the time all the elements needed for recording came together. The spadework had been done and we still had enough stamina and concentration for a take four, and possibly takes five and six before we gave out completely. Years later, another of our record producers, Peter Dellheim, would announce over the intercom at this juncture, "Take four, gentlemen. It is now time to *gird* your loins."

Max preferred a complete take as a basis for the final record. If someone squeaked or the garbage trucks chose to empty cans during a moment of musical reverie (which happened with perverse regularity), then those spots could be replaced by grafted splices on the main trunk of the complete take. But using the head, torso, and legs from three different takes of any given movement was not recommended. Music recorded like that could wind up like the composite sketch of a wanted criminal—disjointed and lacking the authenticity of a coherent structure.

A record producer of my acquaintance, faced with the task of recording an aging violin virtuoso, found a section of the music so poorly played that he had to piece it together almost note by note from many different takes. Tape runs at fifteen inches a second on a professional machine. A sixteenth-note might be two inches of tape, a long note could be sixty or seventy. The producer carefully laid the thirty or forty pieces of tape he ultimately decided on side by side on his couch. On each he placed a scrap of paper indicating its pitch and its place in the sequence. It had taken him the better part of a day to get this irregular collection of plastic strips together, and there was no way that he could have known or protected himself from what was about to happen. His dog walked into the room, sniffed the tapes out of curiosity, and sneezed violently. A day's work was now scattered all over the floor. Perhaps the dog knew better than his master how the finished work would sound.

Movement by movement, we waded through our recording sessions at Webster Hall. As time went on, the Mozart seemed to bear less and less resemblance to a live performance. For better or worse, our performances were meant to be organic wholes. But in the recording studio during a long day the stopping and starting broke up the natural flow of the music into a series of mistakes, glitches, and outside noises. When Max announced over the intercom, "Two bars after letter B, take twenty-seven," it was hard to focus on the musical task at hand. We might initially play take twenty-seven cleanly, but the frame of reference could easily slip away, inviting another "perfect" stillborn record to invade the marketplace.

When our records were finally released, I was pleased. I thought that we sounded surprisingly good, and we had even managed to retain some of the energy one expects in the concert hall. There was our name in large letters on the record jacket with a suitable accompanying photograph. On the other side were liner notes and then, almost as an afterthought, Max Wilcox and Richard Gardner's names in unobtrusive small letters at the bottom. Max had used our best takes while eliminating our slips, the sounds of airplanes approaching La Guardia, and noise produced by the New York City Sanitation Department. With the ever-increasing power of technology in the recording process, I wondered why Max Wilcox's name wasn't featured prominently on the front cover and ours writ small below the liner notes.

～

WHEN THE SUBJECT of recording technology arises, I invariably think of Pablo Casals. Casals approached music reverentially, almost religiously. All else seemed to recede in importance when he communed with his muse, and his recordings were no exception. But even for a cellist of Casals' stature, an occasional blemish appeared in the recorded performance. The producer would inform him (in the gentlest way possible) that there was, say, a note out of tune. Casals would readily acknowledge it. "Yes. That is the way I played it." The producer would then ask him to repeat the passage where the errant spot had been heard. "But why?" Casals asked. "That is the way I played it." Indeed, the only way

Casals might be induced to repeat a movement, which he considered a performance before the microphone, was for the producer to trick him, saying there had been a technical malfunction.

Let no one think that because Casals had principles he was not of this world. When his earliest recordings made on 78s were rereleased on long-playing records, he was livid to learn that his royalties had been cut in half. But Casals' convictions—from his well-known stand against General Franco to something as insignificant as his stage manner—were unassailable and incorruptible. When in 1904 he had arrived in the United States as the foremost of living European cellists, his programs had featured Bach. (At his debut, a Bach unaccompanied suite was his encore.) In despair over half-empty houses, his manager begged him at least to adopt a more pleasant stage manner. "If you would just *smile*," pleaded the manager. "If you would just try to be a little pleasant when you come onstage, I'm sure American audiences would like you so much better." Casals' answer was to change his manager. Years later, with people fighting for a ticket to his concerts, Casals remarked acidly, "And I'm *still* not smiling!"

The four of us in the Guarneri Quartet joined the Marlboro Festival Orchestra for several remarkable recordings conducted by Casals between 1960 and 1973, including Bach's six Brandenburg Concertos and four Orchestral Suites, and several symphonies of Mozart, Beethoven, and Mendelssohn. The orchestra comprised some of America's finest orchestra, chamber, and solo musicians. Many would ordinarily have avoided the musical confinement of a large ensemble, but they all played happily for Casals, a man who regarded an orchestra as no different from a chamber group or a soloist, and therefore answerable to the basic principles of his music-making: variety, form, freedom. The result was an energy and suppleness that is rarely heard in an orchestra usually weighed down by the demands of good ensemble.

Thomas Frost, the producer of many of these recordings, recalled that Casals' approach remained the same as it always had been. He was above the recording process, focusing on the things that were important to him—creating an interpretation, a mood, a feeling. During the recording sessions, Frost felt instinctively that it would be inappropriate to talk to Casals about inaccuracies or technical difficulties. Retakes were usually initiated by Frost or Alexander Schneider, who made the orchestral preparations and served as concertmaster during the recordings.

Frost went to see Casals a few days before the recording of Mendelssohn's "Italian" Symphony and found him studying the score. Casals had founded an orchestra at an early age in Barcelona and therefore knew the standard repertoire inside and out, yet here he was studying the work with the delight and enthusiasm of a young man at the beginning of his career. The hallmark of a Casals interpretation was the freshness he brought to it, a special labor of love. Occupied with the pieces he loved most, Casals approached them with joy. Frost remembered, almost reverentially, "Those were special times."

Remarkable as Casals was into his nineties as both cellist and conductor, the inevitable signs of age were beginning to show. His step to and from the cello and the podium was halting, and he paused longer between movements to gather his energy, but these last recordings show no concession to age in the music-making itself. If anything, Casals harnessed the aging process to his advantage. Although many of the tempos he chose in later life were much more leisurely and reflective, these changes seemed only to heighten his interpretations, now stripped of everything but the music's most essential elements.

~·

IN 1966, THE Guarneri Quartet decided to record Tchai-kowsky's sextet, "Souvenir of Florence," with Boris Kroyt and Mischa Schneider from the Budapest Quartet. Boris and Mischa were both friends, colleagues, and mentors, and already in their late sixties. We had the feeling they wouldn't be playing forever. As it turned out, the Budapest disbanded soon after, and the Tchaikowsky was one of the last professional recordings the two men made together.

What better musicians than Boris and Mischa, both born into the Russian language, culture, and music, to guide us through this Russian landscape with an Italian name? Tchai-kowsky's "Souvenir of Florence" bears little resemblance to the city. If it is about Florence at all, the sextet is about the city's Russian Quarter. Boris and Mischa both knew the work, but when rehearsals and recording sessions commenced, they were again intoxicated by Tchaikowsky's genius and the sounds that reminded them of their homeland, which they'd left more than half a century before.

"Ach, Boris. Leesten to this. Only Tchaikowsky could have written such a loffly melody," Mischa would exclaim, looking upward as if for some higher confirmation.

"Ya, vanderful," Boris agreed. We all did. Slavic melodies roam through the "Souvenir" enticingly, lengthy sequences hypnotize, and alluring rhythms beg to be danced.

And that is exactly what happened. The six of us were huddled together listening to the melancholy and lilting opening of the third movement float out of the speakers. Abruptly, the mood is shed for a joyous dance that sparkles with deft scales and castanet-like rhythms. Boris Kroyt, ordinarily a reasonable, measured kind of man, could not contain himself. He bolted onto Webster Hall's dance floor and began to pirouette and leap around the room. His shock of gray hair bobbed up and down as if it were a dance partner. Around and around the ballroom floor he flew as the rest of us, jaws dropping, looked on amazed from our front-row seats. Boris danced as if his life depended on it. Only the reappearance after the scherzo of the movement's opening Slavic melody doused his exuberance. He returned to the booth and resumed his accustomed manner. In the years to come, I never heard him talk about his balletic outburst, but the quartet dined out on the story.

~

IN THE LATE 1960S, RCA asked us to record the complete cycle of sixteen Beethoven string quartets, an invitation that we had to consider very carefully. One by one, we had been learning and performing the Beethovens, and had performed our very first cycle of them all only recently. Both the performance and recording of the cycle were rites of passage for any serious quartet—were we ready for such a weighty project? Shouldn't we have a few silver hairs among the gold before recording this cornerstone of the repertoire? We shared our trepidation with Max Wilcox. "You'll do it well now and you'll do it differently the second time around" was his laconic reply.

Despite our relative inexperience as a quartet, the appeal of recording the cycle and Max's encouragement proved irresistible. We agreed to a project that would take us almost three years to complete, slipping recording sessions into openings in our concert schedule when time allowed. Against conventional wisdom, we did not record the works chronologically. Starting with the middle, and continuing with the late, we finished the cycle with the early quartets. Even in our relative innocence, we had the good sense to realize that the early Opus 18 quartets were dangerously difficult. Under a halo of Haydnesque classicism, their transparency and radiance had to be served to perfection. Better to forestall them as long as possible while we logged additional concert experience. The later quartets, with their wider dynamic range and broader gestures, were in certain respects easier. The bonds of restraint could be eased in this music. The Great Fugue even begged for a kind of craziness, turning four string players into wild boars crashing through the fugal forest. Our recorded cycle was released in 1970, in time to celebrate Beethoven's two hundredth anniversary.

Mastering these works in order to record the entire cycle became, inadvertently, a useful experience. Not that I recommend a young quartet make records as a substitute for other kinds of rehearsal and performance, but the microphone, with its mechanical innards placed outside the human body, claims a certain objective vantage point that can be helpful. A microphone doesn't have a set of human ears or, for that matter, a heart and soul, but it has no preconceptions, either.

On the concert stage, I find myself separating into two entities—the performer who is swept away emotionally by the music, and a second, cooler, more detached observer who sends in directives to the command center: more ritard here, a little more volume there, be careful with the passage coming up which you tend to flub, and so on. The microphone assumes that second function, I realized when we listened to the playbacks: they were served up clinically by a disinterested party.

As the quartet sat down to record the slow movement of Opus 132, we were still having difficulty deciding on its tempo. In addition to the traditional tempo indication in Italian, in this case "Molto adagio" (very slow), for the opening chorale, Beethoven took the unusual step of adding a highly personal description in both Italian and his own

German: "Solemn Song of Thanksgiving to the Deity, in the Lydian Mode." A movement with this billing demands a special feeling and, therefore, an appropriately slow tempo. But the "Song of Thanksgiving" is an epic twenty minutes long—three sets of chorale variations separated by two contrasting sections also with their own specific directives: "Feeling new strength." Our problem was, without lapsing into a world of static boredom, to find a dirge-like tempo that emphasized the deeply felt thanks Beethoven was offering for his recent recovery from illness. The line that separated these two states was difficult to find; that is, until we heard the first playback. With the complete tonal picture before us, it took only a minute for us to form a strong opinion. The complaints began arriving from one member of the group after another.

"Too slow."

"Boring."

"Where is the sense of motion?"

"This is a song of thanksgiving, not a funeral service."

Our comments were remarkably similar. For the first time, all our rehearsals and performances included, the quasi-glacial tempo which had slipped in and out of our grasp became crystal-clear.

⌀·

WHEN MAX WILCOX pronounced, "You'll do it well now and you'll do it differently the second time around," we had all laughed at the preposterous notion that the Guarneris would still be in existence as a quartet to make a second Beethoven cycle recording. But that is exactly what happened when, more than twenty years later, Philips Records asked us to do the cycle again. In the acoustical splendor of the auditorium of the American Academy of Arts and Letters, on Manhattan's Broadway and 155th Street, producer

Hein Decker and engineer John Newton helped the quartet grapple all over again with this sixteen-headed monster.

Did the Guarneri Quartet play the cycle differently the second time around, and if so, how? The answers to these questions are yes and I'm not sure. In more than three decades of playing the quartets regularly, individually, and also in some thirty complete cycles that we have offered around the world, change has been inevitable. Every performance has added a layer of experience and understanding. The quartets have become old friends whom we know and love deeply through our many encounters. At the same time, we are aging physically. Did our fingers move as quickly, did our brains function as clearly when we recorded the cycle for a second time? And what happens when age meets experience?

It is futile to ask a musician to assess objectively the extent and quality of personal change in his own playing. But against my better judgment, I pulled our two versions of the cycle from my bookshelf and blew the dust off them. Listening to my own records is not a favorite pastime. Where should I start in this ill-conceived effort? Sheepishly, I could only think of comparing their respective timings. Like some television sportscaster trotting out stats, I let my eyes wander across the movement lengths printed on the CD covers. A superficial numerical sign might lead to something more worthwhile.

I picked a sample movement from each period of Beethoven's work: the slow movement of Opus 18, no. 1; the last movement of Opus 59, no. 3; the cavatina from Opus 130. The timing of these movements was concrete data I could hold on to in a sea of subjectivity, but did it reveal anything of value? The adagio affetuoso from Opus 18, no. 1, said to be inspired by the tomb scene from Shakespeare's *Romeo and Juliet*, was 9:39 in the first version and 10:21 in the second. The Guarneri had taken forty-two seconds longer the second time around. I listened to the earlier adagio for the first time since its release. Our rendition was well played and musicianly, but it seemed too innocent, too rushed to capture the full tragedy of Romeo's and Juliet's death. The second version was much more satisfying. The extra time afforded us an expansiveness, an ample space to dwell on the details of phrasing and the drama of the writing. I was pleased. The quartet in middle age was acquiring a certain wisdom.

But my verdict on Opus 59, no. 3, was somewhat different. The fugue, marked "Allegro molto," was played so fast in the earlier version that I almost dropped my cup of coffee. There was little time for details in a performance that took only 5:25. Nevertheless, I liked its raw energy. The later recording, at 5:43, was only eighteen seconds slower, but what a difference those seconds made! The tempo was fast enough to be effective, but the earlier headlong brilliance was replaced by a certain sturdiness of character that seemed less electrifying. If I had to choose, it would be the first one.

Would the cavatina determine whether youth or age triumphed? The two performances brought me no closer to a decision. The cavatina, marked "Adagio molto espressivo," was touching in a straightforward, heartfelt way in the first recording, at 7:14. To my surprise, our impending old age prompted a second performance in 7:01, thirteen seconds faster, but this cavatina had more detail and shaping in the phrasings. I found both versions affecting and was at a loss to choose one over the other.

My experiment had to end there with inconclusive results. I have neither the time nor the patience to listen to both cycles in their entirety. Besides, everything I had heard was a product of something more than age and experience. Each note had been recorded at a specific point in time, a creation of that one single moment framed by our physical well-being, preparation, and disposition. What if we had recorded twenty-four hours later? Perhaps the sun no longer would have been shining, the atmospheric pressure might have been lower, and the four of us in a different mood. The cavatina might have been faster, slower, but certainly unlike any other rendition before or after. There are certain elements of a performance that the recording studio cannot stifle.

∾

DURING THE YEAR that we recorded the Beethoven cycle for the first time, Max Wilcox began to scheme. In addition to the Guarneri Quartet, he regularly recorded the pianist Arthur Rubinstein, and Max thought it would be an excellent idea to bring us together.

Rubinstein visited the RCA studios regularly to record and listen to the final edit of new recordings. He was pleased with the final version of his latest solo disc, Beethoven's C minor Concerto with Erich Leinsdorf and the Boston Symphony Orchestra, which Max was now playing for him. He leaned back, lit up a very, very good cigar, and began telling stories. Next to playing the piano, this was undoubtedly his favorite pastime. Between the end of one tale and the beginning of another, Max gently asked whether Rubinstein might like to hear the newest recording of a gifted young quartet in the RCA stables. With cigar smoke curling around his leonine head, Rubinstein listened thoughtfully to a record of our playing. Perhaps in his next life, Max will be a professional matchmaker, for Rubinstein liked us and proposed that he, a man already in his eighties, and the youthful Guarneri Quartet join forces for the Brahms Piano Quintet.

Such a collaboration was something that none of us would have dared to imagine. We were young and at the beginning of a career, while Rubinstein was in the twilight of his, one of the most renowned pianists in the world. With such a disparity in age, culture, and experience, it was hard to predict what the chemistry would be like.

As a teenager growing up in Los Angeles, some fifteen years earlier, I had had a brief preview of Rubinstein's personality. My violin teacher, Peter Meremblum, had founded and led a very well-known young people's orchestra in which I played. The Southern California Junior Symphony had acquired enough quality and reputation to be featured with Jascha Heifetz in the 1939 film *They Shall Have Music.* Meremblum seemed to know everybody in music and was able to lure some of these great artists to his Saturday-morning rehearsals.

Arthur Rubinstein appeared at one of these. Everything about him was striking: his shock of curly hair, his prominent nose, his husky voice, his grace, his poise, his humor. But when Rubinstein sat down and began to play the Tchaikowsky Piano Concerto, even we youngsters could tell that he was struggling with passages that came out blurred and somewhat uneven. Suddenly, Rubinstein stopped, rose from the piano, and addressed us. "I want to apologize for my playing. Last night I smoked too many cigars," he said with a conspiratorial wink, "had too much to drink, and stayed up far too late. What I really need now is not the Tchaikowsky concerto but two aspirins and a good snooze." There was complete silence in the orchestra as we tried to digest what Rubinstein had just said. More than a great pianist stood before us: a person of his stature who could admit his shortcomings and even apologize to kids, some of them with acne sprouting on their faces, was indeed a great man. With his confession, a cloud seemed to lift off Rubinstein. He resumed his place at the piano and played the Tchaikowsky concerto with an electricity and verve the memory of which all of us will carry to our graves. It was beyond my imagination to think that I might be playing chamber music with Rubinstein little more than a decade later.

At our first rehearsal for the planned recording, Rubinstein himself ushered us into his New York City apartment in the Drake Hotel. It was the same Rubinstein who had appeared before our children's orchestra, only now his hair was almost white. For an eighty-two-year-old man, he exuded a seemingly unquenchable vitality. Rubinstein kept up a stream of convivial conversation as we entered a well-appointed room with a grand piano featured prominently at one end. It was quite impossible to forget the stature of the man with whom we were about to rehearse. There was such a theatricality of gesture and voice, even in his self-mocking stories. On the other hand, there was none of that discomfort one feels in the presence of a powerful personality who has fought, manipulated, and connived to get to the top. A big ego was obviously at work, but Rubinstein's interests extended outward beyond himself and music into art, literature, politics, the world, and with a charm and intelligence that were all but irresistible.

Despite his display of sociability, Rubinstein soon seated himself at the piano, eager to rehearse. Out came chairs, stands, and instruments, and we began to read through the first movement of the Brahms quintet. Three truths were immediately evident: Rubinstein was not very well prepared, he seemed somewhat cavalier about whether we played exactly together, and his playing was exquisitely beautiful. There was a leisurely sweep and suppleness to his phrasing, never forced or excessive but organic and natural. You could almost hear his sound and musicality as you watched the movements of his body. His torso remained at rest, but all movement from his shoulders to the tips of his fingers was directed to having his hands sink firmly but lithely onto the keys, almost in slow motion. With a minimum of real effort, an enormous and alluring sound bathed one's senses.

Rubinstein seemed blithely unconcerned with wrong notes and the occasional uneven passage. At the end of the movement, he smiled at us, but we could see that his thoughts were directed inward. We had just played Brahms with a man whose first ten years of life had overlapped Johannes Brahms' last, and who as a youngster enjoyed a special relationship with Brahms' great friend the violinist Joseph Joachim. Rubinstein had carried on a lifelong love affair with the music of Brahms. He had played the Rhapsody in B minor in his Paris debut as a seventeen-year-old, and he remembered vividly into old age the impression made on him by the piano quartets in A major and C minor that he heard for the first time only months after Brahms died. The Brahms quintet was no stranger to him—his last performance of the work had been with the Budapest Quartet at the Library of Congress in 1961.

Rubinstein had a faraway look in his eyes when he said, "It has been a half of a century since I have played chamber music regularly. Between the two world wars, we used to gather in the summers at the estates of wealthy European music lovers. There were no summer music festivals then. We played for the sheer pleasure of it and for the company of other musicians. I played chamber music with Casals, with the great English violist Lionel Tertis, with Kreisler, and with Eugène Ysaÿe. Ysaÿe! What a magical violinist he was. All the others sounded like children next to him—even Kreisler." Ultimately, his thoughts returned to the Brahms at hand.

We read through the other three movements. The music intoxicated Rubinstein. He would often stop and exult over a harmonic progression, a special moment. That, in turn, might remind him of a story, in which case the rehearsal simply stopped. Starting the tale seated at the piano, he would become animated and stand up to act out the various plot twists and even assume the voices and facial expressions of its characters, who were often some of the leading musicians of the turn of the century. Rubinstein demonstrated the punch line of a long tale about a famous pianist with a drinking problem by making his way onstage, walking shakily to the piano, bowing with exaggerated dignity to the audience (in this case, the four of us), and then turning around and retching violently into the piano. We were an adoring audience, happy to be in the presence of this extraordinary raconteur who for those brief and delicious moments ushered us into a world that had long since vanished.

Several days later, Rubinstein and the quartet arrived at Webster Hall for our first session. Rubinstein ignored the recording equipment and microphones. After greeting everyone, he proceeded to a private corner of the studio with his briefcase. Out came a comb and a long-handled mirror, which he used as he shaped his mane of white hair, camouflaging the thinning areas. (Did I detect powder on Rubinstein's face?) Only then did the playing begin. When we were not rehearsing or recording, he often remained seated at the piano and would go on playing. He practiced the Brahms, or played solo pieces, or even improvised—looking off into the distance, his jaw dropping a little. Rippling arpeggios reminiscent of Sergei Rachmaninoff's music would fill the room.

Rubinstein, who was generally sparing in his praise of other pianists, worshipped Rachmaninoff. Between takes, he told us of a dinner with Rachmaninoff at his home in Southern California sometime around 1940. Rubinstein's latest recording of the Grieg Piano Concerto had just been released and he was especially pleased with it. Knowing that it was

Rachmaninoff's favorite piano concerto, he couldn't resist playing the recording during dessert and coffee. Rachmaninoff sat impassively as they listened, while Rubinstein squirmed. He was hoping for a favorable response from the man who was generally regarded as the greatest pianist of his time. When the Grieg finally came to an end, Rachmaninoff remained seated at the dinner table for what seemed like an eternity. Eventually, he roused himself from his introspection. "Arthur," he said. Rubinstein leaned forward expectantly. "Yes, Sergei." Rachmaninoff thought a moment more. "Arthur, piano out of tune." It was vintage Rubinstein: a story with him as the butt of the joke.

Our early sessions were all recorded, but they had a rehearsal-like aspect to them. Rubinstein had been less than prepared at the first rehearsal in his apartment, undoubtedly because of his busy concert schedule, but he was a quick study. Enormous hands, a seemingly effortless technique, and a powerful musical conviction swept him forward. One of the quartet's concerns in playing with a man of Rubinstein's stature and age was that he might be set in his ways and unable or unwilling to accept new ideas from us; that he would play and we would follow. Uneasily, I approached him with a suggestion about a different way to make the transition from the exposition to the development section of the first movement. One had to speak loudly, for old age had made Rubinstein slightly hard of hearing. But he treated my suggestion evenhandedly and considered it on its musical merits. Though it was impossible to forget that we were playing with the great Rubinstein, not one of the boys, we were soon quite comfortable with a man who was both reasonable and accessible.

An enormous bonus came with Rubinstein's music-making. We were able to witness up close an artist who seemed to enjoy himself and every aspect of life immensely—

music, people, art, food, wine, the world. He once said that even a toothache gave him pleasure! Really, Mr. Rubinstein. On the presumption that even the most joyous people have an opposing, balancing dark side, I would secretly observe him for signs of it as we listened to the playbacks of sections in which Rubinstein had not played his best. But I could find none. He took it all in attentively; his attitude was relaxed, unworried, confident. But this was no Pollyanna at work. Rubinstein could be critical of everything—from people to politics. For example, when speaking of Heifetz, for whom he had a strong personal dislike, he promised, "When I write the story of my life, I will expose that man for what he is." And of a European string quartet's performance which had displeased him, he said, "You may call them the Loewenguth String Quartet, but I call them the Loewen*bad*."

Among the musicians we had known who were cautious, remote, insecure, and neurotic, Rubinstein stood out as a person completely comfortable with himself, an eighty-two-year-old experiencing the autumn of his life with the freshness of a child. And it showed when he played. There was a grandeur and expansiveness in Rubinstein's phrasing. He grasped both the scope and the details in the music, and took the time necessary to reveal them. In the trio of the Brahms quintet's third movement, for example, the opening pattern of six sustained, singing, melodic notes is broken up by three faster eighth notes. Pianists play these three notes in tempo or even rush them impulsively. Rubinstein, seated at the piano, with his head tilted upward and his jaw slack, held them back as if unwilling to relinquish their enjoyment. In the dozens of times we have played the Brahms since then, the glowing aura of these moments hovers over us.

When the Brahms sessions ended, Rubinstein, the quartet, and Max Wilcox went to Lüchow's Restaurant on Fourteenth Street to celebrate the completion of our record. Lüchow's had been a fixture of New York life since the beginning of the century, hosting such luminaries as Victor Herbert, Lillian Russell, and Diamond Jim Brady. It was December, and we were seated near an oversized, shimmering Christmas tree that filled the center of Lüchow's cavernous main room. As glasses were raised, Rubinstein turned to Michael and said, "Let's do the Schumann now." Michael's eyes widened. "You mean rehearse, don't you, Mr. Rubinstein?" Rubinstein looked at him impishly. "We will not rehearse. We will record," he said. Again, the recorded playthroughs gradually evolved into the finished record. In all, we recorded ten works with Rubinstein: the Brahms, Schumann, and Dvořák Piano Quintets, the three Brahms, two Mozart, Fauré C minor, and Dvořák E flat Piano Quartets.

The Mozart, Fauré, and Dvořák quartets were all done in RCA's new recording studio. It was sad to have left Webster Hall. What would life be like without the dance-hall atmosphere, the matzoh-ball soup, and the garbage trucks? But RCA's studio 1-A was specifically designed for recording. The acoustics were lively and, furthermore, adjustable. With the flick of a switch, the entire ceiling, which looked like undulating waves, could be raised or lowered. This might be construed as competition for Webster Hall's revolving chandelier. Even the recording equipment had a high-tech glitter. The massive new control panel with its maze of dials, knobs, and lights looked as if it had been designed for intergalactic space travel. But despite their elaborate plans for a dream studio, RCA made one near-fatal blunder. The garage elevators were so near the studio that come 4:30, when people began heading home, we had to compete with distant thumps and knocks. It was Webster Hall in new clothes. Here in the new recording studio my wife, Dorothea, a professional photographer, began to take photos of us and our guest artists for records and CD covers. Rubinstein, who was her first assignment, proved to be a difficult subject. The very qualities we loved in him—warmth, ebullience, and flair—guaranteed that his body and face were never at rest. In the scant available light in the studio, a photo of Rubinstein in motion would have had little clarity or detail. Only when he listened to playbacks was it possible for Dorothea to photograph him during a moment of rare reflection. When the shutter clicked, Rubinstein realized she had caught him. "You're a good photographer," he said later on, a treasured compliment coming from a man whose oldest daughter was a well-known photographer herself.

Normally, recordings are a natural outgrowth of performance, but in this case the process was reversed. Concert opportunities presented themselves in London, Paris, and New York City. This allowed us to see Rubinstein in the setting of his home, the walls lined with books and Impressionist paintings. That is where we rehearsed before the Paris concert. The day, starting at 10 a.m., was filled with a stream of rehearsals, stories, cigars, and food. In the morning, we rehearsed the piano quintets. Then Rubinstein's wife, Nela, served lunch, which featured a magnificent Polish dish with sausage. The afternoon and evening were reserved for piano quartets. With only one violin in these works, John and I took turns playing. Sitting comfortably in a stylish armchair when it was my turn to listen, I felt that I had wandered onto the set of a period play about turn-of-the-century upper-class Parisian life, a play in which the bigger-than-life actor himself, Rubinstein, was the star. The fact that my friends were playing with him lent a further air of unreality to the situation. I would leave by nightfall, exhausted. My last image of Rubinstein is of him seated majestically at the piano playing the Fauré C minor Piano Quartet with John,

David, and Michael. A boyish grin covers his face, and yet another cigar smolders patiently at his side, the only remaining audience that evening for a man whose vitality knew no bounds.

For our London concert in Royal Festival Hall, a Who's Who of music, it seemed, turned out to hear Rubinstein play the Schumann Piano Quintet with a quartet each of whose members could easily have been his grandchild. As we walked onstage and bowed, I could see that Rubinstein was pale. The man who had conquered the musical world was nervous playing chamber music. We were still tuning and adjusting our music stands when a look of alarm crossed Michael's face. Inexplicably, he lifted his viola and bow and lunged. Too late! Rubinstein, in near panic, had started the quintet without us. We had arranged that I would lead the five of us in the opening, but we entered one by one like so many slices of Swiss cheese. It was a credit to Rubinstein that after such an inauspicious beginning he was able to recover his poise and play so beautifully.

Our paths crossed again some ten years later, again at RCA. The Guarneri Quartet was making another record and Rubinstein, now well into his nineties, was there to hear one of his very last recordings. Max Wilcox led us into the listening room, where Rubinstein stood, immaculately dressed in a dark blue three-piece suit, an antique gold watch fob emerging from his vest. Aged and frail but still a fashion plate, he greeted us. "You know," he said almost apologetically, "I never imagined reaching this advanced age." A sheepish smile flickered across his face. "Frankly, I feel silly being this old."

I always hoped that, by osmosis, some of Rubinstein might rub off on me. It would be foolish, of course, to think that one person's artistry could be grafted onto another human being. I would settle for something more modest, a small portion of his outlook on life. When you are armed with such an attitude, all things are possible.

·~·

WE RECORDED with other artists. Pinchas Zukerman played second violist for our recording of the two Brahms String Quintets. Having planned to perform and record the G major, we decided spontaneously at the sessions' end to begin recording the F major the next morning. Pinky agreed, but only if we brought a second viola part to the session. He had never performed the work and had no music. When we protested that we should have at least a few rehearsals for him to learn the piece, he waved us off coolly. "Just bring my part." But the separate part for the second viola gives no clue about the others. Either you study the complete score or you gradually collect the necessary information about the other voices during rehearsals. At the next day's session, Pinky sight-read flawlessly, artfully; he fit into the ensemble as if we had been playing the quintet for years. I cannot explain such a gift.

By contrast, the cellist Leonard Rose could never get enough rehearsals out of us for our recording of the Schubert Two Cello Quintet. The more we rehearsed, the deeper the furrow on his brow. It was remarkable that such a great cellist would worry so much about a work that we all knew intimately. When the prerecording performance in New York's Alice Tully Hall finished, I heard him muttering behind me as we walked offstage, "We had no right to play it that well." It has been our experience that the learning curve rises dramatically with the first few rehearsals, falters for the next one or two, and then plummets, the victim of too much devotion. The Schubert recording by some miracle went well despite all the rehearsals.

෨

PERHAPS THERE IS a way to bring the concert hall into the recording studio. That was our thinking when we recorded all six Mozart two-viola quintets "live" at the Grace Rainey Rogers Auditorium of New York City's Metropolitan Museum in 1984–85. The violists Kim Kashkashian, Ida Kavafian, and Steven Tenenbom each joined us for a pair of the quintets that were the common theme of six concerts interspersed throughout the season. Microphones were set up to record both performances *and* rehearsals, just in case anything untoward occurred; coughing fits from the audience, slips of the fingers, any musical indiscretions. In a live performance, all those things do inevitably happen. Mistakes happen, but so do excitement and inspiration. We all know it, but few are willing to trade in their blemishes for something so unquantifiable. Our producer undoubtedly borrowed freely from takes of the recorded rehearsal, all of us being victimized by the pressure to have clean, sanitized recordings even when they are advertised as "live." Whether it be our recording "Live from the Metropolitan" or "Horowitz Live from Carnegie Hall," buyer beware.

෨

AFTER MAKING MORE than fifty records and CDs for three different companies—from Haydn to Henze, from the somewhat obscure Arriaga Quartets for Philips Records to the celebrated "Death and the Maiden" and A minor Quartets of Schubert on the Arabesque label—our feelings about the process are still mixed. We have not embraced with love in our hearts a process that the pianist Artur Schnabel called "preservation by destruction." Recording and performing are two distantly related species that we try to bring together as if we were genetic engineers. Unlike Glenn Gould, our hearts really lie with the non-take-two-ness of the concert stage.

Several years ago, the quartet was making a recording in London for the BBC. The session dragged on and we were tired. We couldn't manage a definitive take of the last movement of the Smetana quartet, the last piece on the program. Either the ensemble was ragged, a wrong note slipped into the mix, or the performance suffered from the shellshock of too many repetitions. Then Jacqueline Du Pré entered the studio. A real friendship had flourished among us since Spoleto days, and we were to have dinner with Jackie after the session. "I'm early. Do you mind if I listen?" she asked, draping herself over one of the few chairs in the studio. Of course we didn't mind. The very British voice of Eleanor Warren, our record producer, came over the intercom. "Guarneri String Quartet, Smetena's 'From My Life,' last movement, take fourteen." The quartet came to life, reinvigorated by an addition to the still life of inert microphones poised before us—a listener with ears, a heart, and a deep musical sensibility. The music flowed from us to the studio's solitary listener. With the three quiet pizzicato notes, the three heartbeats that end the work, Jackie embraced and congratulated us all. Eleanor Warren added her bravos and announced the obvious: the session was over. A recording at the last moment had turned into a performance, far better than any take.

If there is a god of recorded sound, he guards his domain jealously. There seems to be no perfect recording device, and no way of completely capturing the magic of the concert hall. Like the first person who had his photograph taken, or the very first witness to the flight of a heavier-than-air flying machine, I sometimes feel uncomfortable about recordings. If God wanted us to reproduce sound, wouldn't he have given us a miniaturized solid-state recording organ embedded somewhere between heart and gall bladder?

Still, there is some satisfaction in knowing that the more than fifty records and CDs the Guarneri Quartet has made are in the hands of music lovers—to be savored, compared, criticized, and finally considered (apart from their merit) as artifacts of a specific time in musical history. If the quartet never plays another note, our performances can go on forevermore. But forever comes in many sizes. The two complete Beethoven cycles we recorded, for example, are both still being sold, but our set of the six Bartók quartets, records we are particularly proud of, was pulled from the stores after only a matter of months, the victim of poor timing. Elvis Presley had just passed away and RCA must have felt that he took precedence over all else. Most of our records have suffered a similar fate. Each new wave of recording technology and each bevy of new recording artists pushes the older ones aside.

The glut of recorded music may be bad for record companies, but it puts the CD buyer in the catbird seat. If he decides to buy, say, a Beethoven string quartet, there is an embarrassment of riches before him. From this era, in addition to our CDs, he can pick from the Alban Berg, the Cleveland, the Emerson, the Vermeer, the Juilliard, the Tokyo Quartet. Going back a generation or two, there are the two Budapest recordings, the Végh, the Busch, and, reaching far back into the 1920s, the Capet String Quartet.

And what if the Guarneri Quartet's Beethoven cycle or even our newest CD of two Schubert quartets has the good fortune to be bought? It will arrive in its new home and be played once or twice before it joins its pals, the music lover's other records and CDs, in semi-retirement on a shelf somewhere. Even if our "Death and the Maiden" is lucky enough to become one of the collector's favorites, it may be heard only eight or ten times during its lifetime. If the concert performance is a spark in time, then the recording is only a brief flame.

Still, what's wrong with a little flame now and then?

Diary. October 8, 1996. Open rehearsal at the University of Maryland. We rehearse Bartók's First String Quartet for the first time in many years. The changes of tempo, unison passages, and complex rhythmic patterns that must fit together like a puzzle are more difficult than I remember. Lost in the work process, we run past our allotted time.

Every time the quartet has rehearsed the Bartók, the same disagreement ensues. One by one, Arnold, John, Michael, and finally David contribute our fugal entries that begin the work, a movement that Bartók called "my funeral dirge." The tempo is slow but comfortable. Michael speaks first. "We are nowhere near slow enough for Bartók's metronome markings." True. We start again, considerably slower, even painfully slower. At the snail's pace that Bartók indicated, it has become very uncomfortable to sustain the line and maintain a good sound. David loses patience and explodes. "This is ridiculous! It is too . . . slow . . . ! Let's not be slaves to a number on a piece of paper." He is so wound up that he is not aware that we all agree. For the third time, the movement commences, once again at a faster tempo. "It certainly is more comfortable to play," says Michael, his voice rising over our sounds. David, still suffering from the effects of the "correct" tempo, adds, "The point is, it sounds better."

[8]

Growing Pains

FROM THE START, we had little idea of how long it would take to establish the Guarneri as an ongoing professional group, or indeed whether it would happen at all. Very few quartets based in the United States during the 1960s survived primarily from concerts—the Budapest and Juilliard come to mind—since most quartet members bridged the bothersome need to make a living with other work that supplemented their quartet income: solo, other chamber music, teaching, freelance and steady orchestra jobs. David made $6,500 in a good year from concerts with the New Music Quartet in the 1950s, including recordings and a healthy supplement of children's concerts. It was nothing to write home about.

Yet it was far better than preceding generations of quartet players had enjoyed. During the Great Depression, a joke circulated about a man who gets into a taxi and finds a string quartet playing inside. "How come you have a quartet playing in the back seat?" he asks the driver, who laments, "I couldn't afford a radio." Orlando Cole, cellist of the Curtis Quartet, which formed in the early 1930s, told me that no group of that era could survive on concerts alone. You looked for a sponsor. The first great American string quartet, the Kneisel, was founded and sponsored by the Boston banker Henry Lee Higginson before the First World War. The Curtis Quartet had Mary Louise Curtis Bok as its benefactor. Elizabeth Sprague Coolidge helped the Budapest Quartet occasionally and ultimately financed the Coolidge String Quartet. And E. J. de Coppet, an American businessman, created and financed the Flonzaley String Quartet, the reigning quartet of the 1920s, naming it after his summer estate in Switzerland. De Coppet ran such a tight ship that he forbade the quartet's members to marry for the first ten years, requiring them each to sign a contract to that effect. "When the ten years were up, I had to marry my mistress. What else could I do, mon ami? I ran out of excuses," the cellist Ivan d'Archambeau confided to a young David Soyer.

It is difficult to exaggerate the importance of the Kneisel and Flonzaley quartets, which retired in 1917 and 1927, respectively, in spreading the gospel of chamber music to a public that in general displayed striking ignorance of it. At the end of one concert, an admirer asked whether the Kneisel Quartet would someday play an all-Wagner program, unaware that Herr Wagner had never written anything for string quartet. And at a Flonzaley concert a woman approached the second violinist and begged to look at his instrument. "Why," she exclaimed with amazement, "it looks exactly like a first violin." Both quartets started by playing to empty halls, but like earnest missionaries, they persisted long and effectively enough to see full houses for their concerts. The two quartets and their sponsors must have been gratified.

No such sponsor came our way. Besides our meager teaching position and a few personal contacts, the Guarneri Quartet depended entirely on our new concert management. But Judson, O'Neill, Beall, and Steinway—which sounded more like a Wall Street law firm dealing in mergers and acquisitions than like a music agency—was getting us concerts. That was the good news. The bad news was that the fees in the 1965–66 season were, to put it delicately, modest: Cleveland, Western Reserve—$900; Philadelphia Art Alliance—$500; Metropolitan Museum—$800; Ridgewood, New Jersey—$700. Even by 1960s standards, these were pittances. By the time you subtracted travel, meals, lodging, a manager's fee of 20 percent, and an occasional ice-cream cone, there was very little left. We grumbled about the paltry sums, but the feeling was that a quartet was lucky if it got any concerts at all, and we tried to put a positive spin on the money issue: since the fees were so low, there was only one direction in which they could go, up.

As the Guarneri Quartet began to accustom itself that fall to a life of performing and touring, our management was already booking concerts for the next season. Word began to spread about our group. Within several years, to our surprise and delight, we would be playing upward of 120 concerts a year and be on the road for at least four months. By the middle of one season, next year's concert schedule was already 90 percent in place. At any given time, we knew what we would be doing and where we would be doing it a year in advance. It was almost like having a regular job.

As if our future wasn't overorganized enough, Judson and partners were now demanding next year's programs from us, passing on the requests of the presenters, who had to organize, oversee, and advertise their concert series well in advance. The quartet had to read through old and new repertoire and come up with the four different programs that we planned to offer each presenter. In this way, we could somewhat control the quartet's destiny by creating programs we considered balanced and varied while allowing local concert committees the freedom to pick their favorites from our list.

By November, that year's programs were well in hand and only in need of regular maintenance as we played them again and again. Between then and January, when both our American and our European managers would be clamoring for new programs, we read through material and decided our musical fates for the next year.

On a frosty late-autumn day, we gathered at John's New Jersey home to audition music. His wife, Nancy, greeted us at the door. John had met her at Curtis, where she was studying flute with William Kincaid, first flutist of the Philadelphia Orchestra, so we had all been students together. The strands of their lives were interwoven with mine even as the two of them fell in love: John and Nancy would sometimes drop by my boardinghouse room in the early days of their courtship and bat their eyelashes at one another while I served them a hot drink, a stale doughnut or two, and tried to act as if my presence was needed. The task of selecting from the main body of quartet literature was relatively easy. It had essentially been done for us by more than two hundred years of string players choosing their favorite quartets frequently enough to qualify them as "standards." It was only a question of which ones to pick: a Haydn, a Beethoven, a Schumann, a Stravinsky, or a Bartók. On that particular morning we looked at quartets that were on the fringe of the repertoire, but as always, it was not just a question of separating the good from the bad. As when you are shopping for clothes, the music also had to look good on us. We would be looking for quartets that fit our particular style of playing.

Everyone brought his favorite pieces to the reading session. David offered the three Arriaga quartets, which he knew from his days in the New Music Quartet. Juan Crisóstomo de Arriaga, glibly called the Spanish Mozart because of his exceptional gift and because he lived only a little later than Mozart, had the misfortune to die just short of his twentieth birthday. The craft and originality of these quartets proved irresistible to all of us. Any one of the three would be an ideal program beginner.

I brought the Fritz Kreisler quartet, which I had studied and performed in Meadowmount some years before. For anyone who knows and loves the dozens of encore pieces Kreisler composed that re-create the grace, charm, and ambience of nineteenth-century Vienna, the four movements of this quartet are instantly recognizable. It was not the serious music that is usually associated with the quartet repertoire, but perhaps for that very reason, and the fact that the Kreisler brought a smile to the lip and a tear to the eye rather than a clenched fist and a sob, I was hopelessly under its spell. And because David, Michael, and John knew Kreisler's music intimately, I figured this would be a shoo-in.

The Kreisler quartet was shot down. After one movement, there was a frosty silence; after the second, John shook his head; and at the end of three movements, Dave complained that it wasn't even good Kreisler. The piece was in flames and I in shock. I appealed to Michael, who knew and loved Kreisler's music and as a boy had met Kreisler. Why, Michael even had a picture of himself and Fritz proudly displayed on his piano. But Michael looked soberly at me, not wanting to hurt my feelings, and gently explained why he thought it was not the best Kreisler.

Michael submitted the Kodály Second String Quartet. All

of us were familiar with Kodály's music. Aside from the well-known Háry János Suite for orchestra, there were several works for strings that we admired. We had actually met Kodály, a very old man, with his very young wife, in Marlboro. (Only later did I learn of his poignant marriage proposal: he asked her if she would be his widow.) We took an instant shine to the folk-like melodies and imaginative rhythms of this quartet. Both the Arriaga and the Kodály were especially appealing because they were relatively unknown to audiences.

John passed out some music to each of us. It was the Sibelius String Quartet. The Sibelius? Not again! Why was John doing this after the last read-through? Nobody cared for it then, nobody would care for it now. He was just being stubborn. Still, he was exercising his right as a member of the quartet. Even if he brought it in for the next fifty years, however, we wouldn't play it. It was just not a strong work. And rereading the Sibelius only reinforced my opinion.

David spoke first. "I've changed my mind. This music has a very special, haunting quality." My world was crumbling before me: it was incomprehensible that David could like a composition with so little originality, so little spine. Was he playing games just to stir up trouble? Time was running out for next year's program decisions. After the Kreisler debacle, this turn of events put me in a daze, but Michael became the lawyer for the prosecution, attacking the Sibelius vigorously. John and I sat quietly by while our proxies, David and Michael, argued the pros and cons of Mr. Sibelius' string quartet. After the dust had settled and the votes were tallied, we were deadlocked. The Sibelius was shelved for this year, but I recognized the look in John's eyes. We would be hearing from him again. And from me, as well! How could I abandon my friend Fritz? Next year, I would bring the Kreisler quartet once more.

Again and again, in our heated discussion, it was a solace to have an ally. When Michael joined my side to fend off our misguided colleagues who were advocating the Sibelius, I thought, This is a man I can work with; he and I, with a similar musical outlook, will push through the good point of view in times of disagreement. It will be like a political alliance, but instead of Republican and Democrat, first violinist and violist will work together. But the same Michael had voted down my beloved Kreisler quartet only half an hour ago! Some ally! And one hour into the future, John might be my bosom buddy as we locked horns with those *lower* voices. The truth was that you couldn't count on anybody. Better get used to alliances that shifted as easily as the wind.

Eventually, the four programs we constructed out of the new, the old, the celebrated, and the unknown were sent off to our managers. At least that issue was solved. Now we could attend to the *real* work of learning those twelve quartets for next season. What we hadn't reckoned with was births and deaths. Unfortunately, every composer has them. Concert promoters, ever eager for a ticket-selling angle, find the first, the three hundredth, and every birth and death day in between, irresistible. The concert may then be trumpeted as commemorating a composer's arrival in or departure from this world. The Guarneri Quartet was obligated to celebrate, for example, Beethoven's and Schubert's two hundredth birthday in 1970 and 1997, respectively, and the two hundredth anniversary of Mozart's death in 1991, with massive doses of their music all year long. It seemed to us that Ludwig, Franz, and Wolfgang were hardly endangered species. Why did we have to play even more of the most played music in the world? Wasn't this too much of a good thing? "What they need is an all-Schrattenholz festival," David liked to offer in trade for any given year's poster composer. Schrattenholz was a forgotten composer whom he invoked to poke fun at the promoters. Since there are dozens of esteemed composers, a year didn't go by without extra repertoire to learn.

Next year's planned twelve works were swelling with these special projects, and there was more to come. Judson, O'Neill, Beall, and Steinway called. "You can't play the Schubert A minor in Cleveland. The Juilliard is doing it. They want to know if you'll play the 'Dead Maid' instead." (That is what Harry Beall's assistant in charge of programs, Lynn Penney, insisted on calling Schubert's "Death and the Maiden.") The office called again. "Would you be willing to play the Dvořák Piano Quintet with Mitchell Andrews in Marquette, Michigan?" In quick succession, we had added two more works to the list.

Our quartet had its hands full, but practice didn't necessarily start at quartet rehearsals. Once in a while I could get away without personal practice before we gathered for the usual 10 a.m. session, but like brushing your teeth in the morning, scales or exercises for general maintenance of technique were a must. I was never privy to Michael's, John's, and David's early-morning instrumental calisthenics (good lord, some things must remain private), but I witnessed their different approaches firsthand when we warmed up before a concert. Michael and I usually tackled that evening's program first off, but our paths then diverged. I doodled with this and that, while Michael began working the calendar. Why is he practicing Webern's Five Pieces? I wondered. We're not playing them this season. But we were—two months from now. Dirk Nabering had requested the Webern for his concert series in Freiburg, Germany. He had decided to have a work by Anton Webern and Ferruccio Busoni on each program (no doubt, celebrating their birth, death, marriage, baptism, or other significant occasion). Michael was practicing now to avoid unpleasant surprises later. John practiced scales and arpeggios diligently and then went on to the solo violin repertoire. It could be anything: Maurice Ravel's Tzigane, Max Bruch's Scottish Fantasy, a Bach sonata, or the Sibelius concerto, all done somewhat undertempo so that John could examine each more carefully under his personal microscope. David practiced quartet parts and then seemed to wander off to a Bach solo cello suite with regularity. Who could blame him? The cello suites resonate and take wing.

Exercises out of the way, there were those feisty quartet parts to deal with that often rivaled the virtuoso repertoire in difficulty. Everything from Mozart's delicate filigree to Bartók's complex rhythms begged diligent study before rehearsal. Besides, it was bad form and a time-waster to fish for notes while the others sat around looking bored and tapping their feet impatiently. After rehearsal, further soul-searching might warrant some afternoon practice on problem areas as well.

The massive amount of work required to learn all these programs rapidly engendered a certain rehearsal style. We were, from the beginning, blunt with each other, quickly becoming like four brothers who have spent a lifetime together—affectionate, fun-loving, occasionally cantankerous, and certainly long past the need for etiquette. I began to notice that no compliments were passed around, a distinct departure from the behavior of other groups in which I had played, where you might hear, at appropriate moments when something went particularly well, a "Gee, I just loved your playing." The Guarneri Quartet was a compliment-free zone: if there was nothing to complain about, we moved on to the next order of business.

It felt a little strange at first. What could possibly be the harm in John's complimenting me once in a while? But then

I might be obliged to say to him, "Nice job," the next time we performed Alban Berg's Quartet, Opus 3, whose beginning erupts with a second-violin solo. And Michael and David (who also have feelings, you know) might be slighted if they were not verbally rewarded. Without a single explicit word ever uttered on the subject, the avoidance of compliments became a habit among us. When John turned an elegant phrase next to me, the word "beautiful" formed on my lips but remained stillborn. And with time I came to like the absence of compliments. It reduced competitiveness and emphasized the group rather than the individual. Still, a question lingers. What do my colleagues think of my playing? Do they think I play brilliantly or simply well enough? Have I ever moved them with my rendition of the *Beklemmt* section in Beethoven's Opus 130 cavatina? Because of the Guarneri's rehearsal style, I just don't know. And at this late stage, if John told me how much he loved my playing, I'd feel uncomfortable. I'd have to ask myself what he really meant by this bit of sweet talk. Perhaps on the very last day of the Guarneri Quartet's career, after the final note has faded away and the applause has ceased forever, we can hand out report cards to each other. There will be grades for promptness, comportment, work habits, technique, tone, musicality—and how I played the *Beklemmt* section of the cavatina.

In all these years of playing together, I can recall only one compliment being given within the quartet. We were rehearsing for a concert in our series at the Metropolitan Museum. John suggested a new fingering for a particularly alluring melody I was playing. "Frankly, John," I said ruefully, "as good as your fingering is, I don't think I can do it well." Then I completely forgot about it until the passage was directly upon me at the concert. We generally sell out the museum series, and that particular night there were stage seats almost hugging our chairs. Impulsively, and without having practiced it, I used John's new, improved fingering. The fingering worked, the melody soared to new heights, and John, himself in the act of playing, said in a voice loud enough for certainly everyone onstage to hear, "Good!" I almost dropped my violin.

There was little time to dwell on compliments or general rehearsal style, so preoccupied were we with the ongoing pressure to learn major segments of the standard repertoire. It was splendid music, but, when you thought about it, all by dead composers. At Harpur College, we met our first live one, the composer-in-residence William Klenz. Bill had been a cello student at Curtis and had gone on to study composition with Paul Hindemith at Yale. We agreed to perform a string quartet he had written, and Bill attended the last rehearsals before the Harpur performance.

I had thought that by the time a composer's ideas developed into an actual composition they were, like the Ten Commandments, set in stone. But Bill was surprisingly flexible and accommodating. To be sure, he had specific ideas about his quartet, but he was also a performing musician and, therefore, practical. If a passage that we played at a faster tempo than his printed marking worked better for us, he encouraged us to do it that way; if a crescendo was unsuccessful, he altered it.

In time, the Guarneri worked with many distinguished composers as we learned and played their works: among them, two of Leon Kirchner's three quartets, Vincent Persichetti's Piano Quintet, Ned Rorem's Third Quartet, and Mario Davidovsky's Concerto for Quartet and Orchestra (the last two works written for us).

Leon Kirchner was himself a marvelous pianist with a rhapsodic, quirky flair as a performer. We had heard him and played with him often, which gave us a leg up on the inter-

176 • INDIVISIBLE BY FOUR

pretation of his music, but his particular style was nearly impossible to emulate. Even if we had been able to come up with a close approximation, it would have been instantly recognized as performance plagiarism by those who knew Kirchner. All musicians who have heard music directly at its source have faced this quandary. Should Ferdinand Ries and Karl Czerny, students of Beethoven, have tried to sound like the great one when playing his music, or like themselves? And what about composers such as Sergei Rachmaninoff and Béla Bartók who have made powerful recordings of their own music? What should a performer do after being swept away by such a performance? A clue might be found in the recordings themselves. It is surprising just how far Rachmaninoff and Bartók wander from the printed score in bringing their own compositions to life. Even the revered score itself is at times negotiable. Schubert wrote down some of his most popular songs, "Erlkönig" and "Die Forelle" among them, over and over again, each time altered in small details. "Die Forelle" exists in five versions. It is the kind of compositional freedom that one expects from jazz musicians. When Bill Challis, Paul Whiteman's arranger, and Bix Beiderbecke, the great jazz performer and composer, sequestered themselves so that they could get Beiderbecke's famous "In a Mist" on paper, Challis was driven nearly to distraction. Beiderbecke was more than willing to accommodate his friend, but "In a Mist" came out differently each time he played it on the piano. And when Kirchner demonstrated a passage for us, it also came out shaded somewhat differently each time, as did his Sonata Concertante for Violin and Piano, which I had the pleasure of playing with him more than once.

When all was said and done, we had no choice but to find our own way with Kirchner's quartet, and he was experienced enough to be able to coax us along. Kirchner explained, gestured, supplicated, played the piano if one was handy, and sang (a stylized moan) if one was not. Ultimately, he seemed happy enough to leave his quartets in our safe-keeping, to let us play them in our distinct manner, even though a very different performance would have taken place if he himself had been playing the parts.

When his composition goes out into the world, like a child who has grown up and left its parents, a composer relinquishes control of it. He must accept that every performance will be different, some far afield from his original premise. In a sense, the composer who plays his own music reverts to the same status as all other performers. True, he has an inside track on the score, but the technical and musical difficulties are now as much his as anyone else's, and somehow he must find a way to breathe life into a work whose umbilical cord has been severed from him.

Working with living, breathing composers was important because it reminded us that the dead ones were also once alive. Mozart, who was both an excellent keyboardist and a gifted violinist, must have used his improvisational genius not only in composing but also when, as a freelance musician, he had to deal with divas, bad flutists (an instrument he disliked), and even good instrumentalists who played his music differently than he envisioned. He was known to rewrite arias on the spot to fit the singer's vocal range and temperament, and he replaced the entire second movement of his Fifth Violin Concerto because the soloist complained about the original. Musicians who worked with Mozart, think what they might about his compositional skills— good, excellent, or genius level—still regarded him as a working colleague. When he died, and slowly receded from the memories of his contemporaries, finally joining the pantheon of composers whom we honor at the highest level in our concert halls, something was lost. The reverence and awe

we have for Mozart resemble suspiciously the fear and trepidation with which we handle museum objects. "What is
the correct way to play Mozart?" I have been asked more
than once by students, as if they were talking about an insect
sealed in amber. It was the way history had been taught in
school, and why George Washington seemed such a wooden
figure—as wooden as his wooden false teeth, which I learned
about only years after graduation.

The awe factor often intruded on our effort to bring Mozart's works to life. His K 168, a slender work by a
seventeen-year-old, has charm, cohesion, and brilliance. It
was on our stands and opened to the slow second movement,
whose two sections bear repeat signs. The repeats themselves
were troubling us: the fragile beauty of this slow movement
seemed to sink under the weight of the repetitions. Since
there is an unwritten tradition among performing musicians
that it is all right to eliminate the second repeats, we had
few qualms about doing just that. The movement then
sounded better, but it was still top-heavy. Doing away with
the first repeat, which had come from the pen of the mighty
Mozart, was a bigger hurdle. Would I be able to sleep at
night if we defied his markings? Concert after concert, we
dutifully repeated the first section, always looking for new
ways to solve the problem of its monotony. Finally, one evening, we gathered up our courage and risked going to hell.
We launched the movement without any repeats at all. For
the first time, it felt balanced and effective.

Leon Kirchner's endless variety in the act of playing gave
me a strong sense not only of his music's life force but also
of the constant reinvention that all music must undergo with
each performance. When those of us who know Kirchner,
his unique style, and his era, are gone, it will be ever more
tempting to place him comfortably in our music books under

the heading "Composers, Twentieth Century, American," and to lose sight of his music's energy and its beating heart.

·❦·

OUR CONCERT MANAGEMENT suddenly shrank to half its size and half its age when Arthur Judson and Ruth O'Neill announced their retirement. From now on, Harry Beall and Fritz Steinway would represent us. As the younger, more vibrant partners, they were the ones we had usually dealt with, anyway. Indeed, after the initial excitement of our first concerts, a major concern was that Beall and Steinway might be doing their job too well. In the first few seasons, they were able to book us for marathon four-week tours. I began to feel like a visitor in my own apartment when I got home.

One such adventure in early fall took us almost exclusively to warm climates, with the exception of two concerts in Alaska. Why should I schlepp an overcoat through the Arizona desert and the orange groves of Southern California just for two silly concerts in Alaska? How cold could Alaska be? When we arrived in Fairbanks, it was fifty below zero. But aside from surviving to tell that tale, I felt the tour had been too long—we'd been too long away from family, friends, and clean clothes.

How long should a tour be, and how many concerts in a row was too many? If Beall and Steinway were clever enough to do their job well, why shouldn't we be Flying Dutchmen forever on the road? The answer was athletic as well as artistic.

To the outsider, the playing of string instruments looks like sissy work. It couldn't possibly take much effort to play one of those little things that you hold under your chin or between the legs, and go shrum shrum. The instruments aren't very heavy, and the bows! Why, they weigh next to nothing. It must be like fencing with a feather. But coming off the stage after a concert, drenched in sweat, we four look more like athletes after a bruising game than like musicians. And the sports injuries you read about in the newspapers are often similar to the ailments professional musicians develop—repetitive-motion syndrome, tendinitis, and simple overuse of certain muscles. I have been meaning for years to count the number of notes contained in the last movements of the Mendelssohn E flat and Beethoven Opus 59, no. 3, Quartets. There must be thousands of notes, and they are all played at full throttle. If you harnessed a quartet to the electrical system of a hall during the closing moments of the Beethoven, when fingers are flying and bows whizzing up and down at a manic pace, the lights would brighten sufficiently to read the program notes. It is exhausting work to practice, play a concert, travel with instruments and luggage, and then pick up your tired body day after day to repeat the process. Well-meaning as Fritz, Harry, and our European managers were, they sat behind their desks and moved us from city to city like pieces on a Monopoly board going from Marvin Gardens to Park Place. We might never know the trouble they went through to get us an engagement in Des Moines, but they would have only an inkling of how we got there from New Orleans and still managed to play a good concert.

In one of our frequent business meetings with Fritz and Harry, it was settled that we would go for no more than two weeks on a major tour anywhere in the world, and play no more than four or five concerts in a week, without prior consultation. This was fine with them. Fritz and Harry were warm and concerned guys, and besides, our good health was their continued good business.

꙾

THE GUARNERI QUARTET, would-be missionaries for the cause of chamber music, eagerly went out into the world to play concerts. We thought of ourselves, naturally, as four individual people who, arms linked, had formed a musical group. But many people found it easier to lump us together as a unit, with no individual parts. "The Guarneri String Quartet plays an all-Mozart program tonight at the Shmichik Center for the Performing Arts" went the radio or newspaper advertisements, with no mention of our names. There might be practical or financial considerations: it cost money to mention individual players. But sometimes we were introduced at parties as the Guarneri Quartet, as if we were one monolithic formation that would eat, talk, and laugh in unison. Even the concert program itself occasionally omitted our names—which could be downright discouraging.

From our infancy on, parents, teachers, and the community had encouraged each one of us to think of himself as special, even unique, and now our identities were being taken away because we had joined a string quartet. Well-meaning people after a concert would sometimes present the quartet with a single gift, such as a bouquet of flowers or a bottle of wine. That entitled each of us to four daisies, one rose, and several swigs from the bottle we might pass around later that evening. Once, as a token of their appreciation for the many times we had played for them, a concert society awarded us a leather-bound diary with a lock. Did they imagine that, kneeling in unison, we said our prayers together every night, and before getting into the same bed and turning out the light, we wrote in the diary together, "Today *we* met a mysterious stranger"?

We used every means available to deal with this identity crisis. Beall and Steinway stipulated that our names appear in the program, and a short bio of each of us was included with publicity material sent out. Once, at an airport, the young lady assigned to pick us up approached David. "Are you the Guarneri String Quartet?" she asked timidly. David assumed his most magisterial pose and answered, "I am." We would have to speak to him about that.

As the quartet became known in musical circles, other issues started to grate. No matter how well we played and how celebrated we became, our fees would never match those of a commensurate soloist. Quartets at the top of the heap made about the same per concert as one well-established pianist or violinist, so our individual fees were one quarter of an average soloist's. And when a soloist joined us for a piano quintet, the fee was rarely split five ways. The quartet and the pianist got their agreed-on fees, negotiated separately. The violinist Lewis Kaplan, founder of the Aeolian Chamber Players, once invited me to his apartment for dinner with our former teacher, Ivan Galamian. Lewis is a well-known chamber musician whose apartment was, coincidentally, in the same building as those of two other violinists, Itzhak Perlman and Pinchas Zukerman. Galamian arrived and immediately saw that the apartment was the same as Itzhak's or Pinky's, but smaller. Why was it smaller, Galamian wanted to know. Lewis explained that the original apartment had been broken up into two smaller ones. Galamian's face lit up with comprehension. "I see. Pinky and Itzhak have soloist's apartments. You have the chamber-music one."

Then there was the name-recognition factor. We were known as members of the Guarneri Quartet, but were less well known as individual personalities. "Daddy, how famous are you?" my six-year-old daughter wanted to know. After considering my nuanced response for a moment, she said, "I think I'll name my car Arnold." It was difficult to give my daughter more than a vague estimate of my standing, because it always lagged behind that of the group name. Even the members of a quartet like the Beatles suffered that fate. Many of the fans couldn't remember the individual names, or got them confused. (It was John Lennon who played the sitar, wasn't it?) Pinchas Zukerman and I were once having pizza together when a man approached us excitedly. "I know you two. You're, you're—" "I'm Arnold Steinhardt and he's Michael Tree," Pinky said, with the authority of someone who knows who he and his friends really are. "Yes. That's right. That's who you are," the gentleman agreed, and left contented. I had the secret pleasure of knowing that even a great soloist's name gets lost in the mix sometimes.

These were some of the aggravations of being one tree in a grove rather than a single oak standing free. But none of us could claim surprise. Having trained to be soloists and to varying degrees performed as such, we had, intentionally and with some knowledge of the consequences, renounced the spotlight for lower-profile stage presences.

Although the absence of individual recognition often rankled, none of us complained unduly. There was so much to treasure in our life as a foursome. We were playing the great quartet literature for audiences who knew and loved Beethoven, Brahms, and Bartók. There were almost too many masterpieces, each one a universe to explore, for us ever to get bored, and we were constantly challenged by the process of learning music and working together. The slowly evolving nature of the group from a generic well-running four-cylinder engine into a quartet with a recognizable musical profile was also satisfying. When you heard our unrepentantly individual voices dissolve into a homogeneous sound, our emotive and exuberant style shed like a skin for something more angelic or otherworldly, like it or not it had become immediately recognizable as that of the Guarneri String Quartet. There was very little conflict about the life we might have had as soloists. Rather, conversations about musicians and their travails often ended with our thinking how lucky we were.

The quartet also profited from the luck of perfect timing. When we formed in 1964, chamber music was a dusty little corner of the American musical world. The Budapest Quartet was about to retire and chamber-music activity was nominal. In this environment, the Juilliard Quartet was a true pioneer, having been formed directly after the Second World War, and carrying the two banners of the string quartet itself and the cause of new music. But like a surfer who has caught a perfect wave, the Guarneri Quartet's arrival coincided with an enormous swelling of chamber-music interest. Old concert societies expanded, new ones sprouted up throughout the country, and suddenly a music student's wish list included playing chamber music and being in a string quartet. In America, outstanding quartets began to form on our heels, among them the Cleveland, Tokyo, Vermeer, Emerson, Colorado, Orion, American, and Shanghai, and they all were making a living primarily from playing quartets. The Guarneri Quartet was now working in a rich and varied environment, and chamber-music enthusiasts were in heaven.

It was rare to find a free night with another group in hearing distance, and for that reason the occasions when we could listen to other quartets stand out in our memory: the Amadeus in Berlin, the Cleveland in Los Angeles, the Juilliard at Tanglewood, the Vermeer in New York City. Aside from the admiration we had for their artistry, I always had another reaction listening to other string quartets: so it can be done *that* way too!

What caused this burgeoning interest? The following is nothing but an unscientific guess. The American standard of living was rising, and with more money and time for the so-called good things of life, concert halls began to fill. The 1960s were also a time when the country began questioning whether bigger was necessarily better. People were exploring the other end of the scale: small business, small town or rural life were becoming more attractive; the idea that all politics is local was gathering steam; and the era of self-exploration had arrived. If you could leave a steady job to meditate at the feet of a guru in India, why not trade an orchestra position for the more intimate, personal expression of a chamber-music group? A golden age of quartet playing was upon us.

⌒

BEALL AND STEINWAY called again, but not about another single concert. Wooster, Ohio, had asked for a Beethoven cycle. Hearts must have missed a beat all around our group. There can be no greater event in a quartet's life than performing all sixteen of Beethoven's string quartets. Individually, they are works to ponder and enjoy for a lifetime. As a collection, they both span a major portion of Beethoven's adult life and trace his evolution from brilliant classicist to daring modernist. And the cycle is more than a complete collection of Beethoven's quartets in several concerts: the individual works cast light on each other, highlighting the connecting threads of Beethoven's creative mind. The totality of them, like a collection of epic sagas, acquires a weight in performance that overwhelms both player and listener. The Guarneri had already played most of the quartets during the past three years, and if we accepted, the invitation would spur us on to learn the rest. It was a gargantuan task, but an inevitable one that we thought we must accept.

A concert or series of the works of one composer may be a novelty, but it presents the danger of a certain sameness. Beethoven seems to be the exception. In his symphonies, piano sonatas, and certainly in his string quartets, each work feels and smells different. For each of three discernible periods in his life, Beethoven seems to have consciously reset his compositional compass. The works of his middle period are longer and more complex than, say, his early Opus 18, with its concise classicism. And the late quartets are, for the most part, even more extended, both in actual time and in concept, often breaking the conventional four-movement mold and entering into remarkable new spheres of feeling.

Like a scientist in his laboratory with the periodic table in front of him, Beethoven gives the impression of using a different earth element as the building block for each new quartet. In his case, it is pointless to blame promoters for "cycleitis" as a cynical means of selling concert tickets: both audiences and performers are mesmerized by the creativity and variety they encounter in a Beethoven string-quartet cycle.

Beethoven himself took the string quartet very much to heart, as evidenced by the vast number he composed and his frequent return to the form throughout his life. His first effort, a series of six quartets, Opus 18, was tantamount to a coming-out party, for the quartet genre itself was already held in very high regard at the time. The quartet form was still on his mind when he wrote Opus 135, his last completed work, only months before his death. Beethoven even went to the trouble of totally revising the first quartet, originally sent to his old and good friend Karl Amenda a year earlier. On July 1, 1805, he wrote Amenda: "Be sure not to hand on to anybody your quartet, in which I have made some drastic alterations. For only now have I learned to write quartets; and this you will notice, I fancy, when you receive them." His sketchbooks reveal no fewer than nine different versions of the opening of the quartet that would be his first published one, Opus 18, no. 1.

How do you program a Beethoven cycle—chronologically, for those with a sense of historical evolution, or drawing from each period of Beethoven's life, for greater variety at each concert? We opted for variety. And in how many concerts should sixteen quartets be presented? Being young and foolish, we gave in to Wooster's cries of poverty and agreed to play the cycle in only five concerts. (Cheapest, of course, would be to play all sixteen in one concert.) It takes no mathematical genius to figure that one of the five concerts was a marathon, with four quartets, and that each and every other concert would be monumental in length as well as content. The excessive length of these concerts, all played in a fairly short period of time, almost brought us to our knees.

The Beethoven cycle had been an epic journey, as advertised, but it was easy to conclude that we should play all future cycles in six concerts. If we were ever asked again, there would still be the problem of the cycle's order, which had almost endless permutations. In a bind, we could simply shuffle the quartets like cards in a deck and pick the programs blind.

Our next invitation to play the cycle came from Buffalo, New York, and with it, an improbable solution to the question of its order. Frederick Slee, a lawyer by profession and a passionate amateur string player, had set up an endowment to have the complete Beethoven cycle played in Buffalo each and every year by a first-class professional string quartet. To my knowledge, it is the only such ongoing cycle in the entire world. There was a condition attached to the invitation to play, however. The cycle had to be (wisely) in six concerts, and Mr. Slee also stipulated the exact order of the quartets. For all his generosity and initiative, an amateur's high-handedness in dictating the sequence makes the professional musician bridle. Who does this part-time musician think he is? But Slee knew his quartets. Starting with Opus 127, the first of the late quartets, and finishing six concerts later with Beethoven's very last, Opus 135, the cycle unfolds beautifully in the Slee configuration. Mischa Schneider confessed to grave misgivings about the order until the Budapest played their first Slee cycle, but then liked it so much that all future Budapest cycles were done that way.

In a sense, this was our true debut playing the cycle. The quartets were in a coherent order, the number of concerts was comfortable, and besides, we held the last rehearsals in Mischa Schneider's house. It was here, only a few years earlier, that Mischa had invited me to my first all-Beethoven quartet concert, and it was Mischa who had continued to be our most valued mentor, telling us when he "loffed" our playing and also when he did not: "too fast. You played like meshuganas."

By the time we arrived in Buffalo for the cycle, we had done our major work, but there were perilous spots, an obstacle course of technical problems, that needed special attention. The scherzo of Opus 131 in C sharp minor was one of the wickedest. The movement, which employs ponticello (playing near the bridge, to create a whistling sound), rushes along at a headlong pace. Its difficulties are compounded by sudden ritards. When a freight train is roaring (in this case, whistling) down the tracks, four people will have different ideas about how to stop it quickly.

This was our problem as we rehearsed in Mischa's living room. The running notes we were playing in lockstep at a presto clip had to slow down dramatically in only eight notes, and we had to play them perfectly together. Over and over we tried, with only limited success. Everybody's read on the ritard was different. The notes often sounded as if a basket of tennis balls had been tipped over, the balls all hitting the floor at random intervals. Then the doorbell rang. It was Sonya Kroyt, wife of the Budapest Quartet's violist, Boris Kroyt. We rose to greet her, but she held up a hand. "I hev cold. I'm nut keesing enyeboddee," the Russian-born lady said. Greetings were exchanged at a respectable distance and we returned to the problem of the eight notes. Again the passage went poorly. There was silence.

Credit for the suggestion then offered, an idea of considerable genius, was later claimed by more than one member of the quartet. "Why don't we use Sonya's last spoken words to help us through this passage? As we play the last eight notes, just say to yourself, "I'm nut keesing en-ye-bod—dee!" Smirks, groans, and chortling filled Mischa's living room. Another silence. The proponent of the idea came forward again. "If no one has any better suggestion, at least try this one." The lowered heads and general body language betrayed muted embarrassment, but no escape route out of our dilemma appeared. We began the passage once again, adding Sonya Kroyt's vocal part.

For mysterious reasons, "I'm nut keesing enyeboddee" rolls off the teeth, tongue, and lips easily. Say it out loud once or twice and it is stored firmly in the memory. Then say it to yourself and it passes down the brain's corridors with equal comfort. "I'm nut keesing en-ye-bod—dee" was to those eight notes as a compass to a plane's flight. The passage went perfectly.

The night of our first Beethoven concert arrived. Waiting in the wings to launch the cycle with Opus 127, I thought of the letter Beethoven had required the Schuppanzigh Quartet to sign before their premiere performance of the quartet:

To the Schuppanzigh Quartet
My Dear Fellows   Vienna, March 1825
Herewith each of you receives his part and is bound to understand on his word of honor to perform in the best possible manner, to distinguish himself and to emulate his fellow performers in excellence.

Everyone who takes part in this said matter must
sign this sheet.

Beethoven

Schindler, *Secretarius*

Schuppanzigh
Weiss
Lincke
much abused cello of the great Master
Holz
the last, but only in signing this paper.

If Beethoven himself had appeared before us at that moment,
we would surely have added our names to the sheet. A sense
of import hung in the air as we strode onstage. The E flat
major chords of Opus 127, like blocks of granite being
moved into place for some monumental structure, announce
the beginning of the work, the concert, and the entire cycle.
"Ladies and gentlemen," Beethoven seems to be saying, a
master of ceremonies at heaven's portals, "let the saga begin."

What impulse prompted Mr. Slee to establish the annual
Beethoven cycle? Many of us have our passions, our pet projects, but few act upon them with this kind of fervor. Slee
played string quartets in his home every Sunday, come rain
or shine. Perhaps because he and his wife, Alice, had no
children, a powerful impulse to give birth to something else
through his endowment took root. The collection of Beethoven's sixteen quartets has an especially powerful hold on
us as a musical event, and the public never seems to tire of
it. Some ten years ago, four complete cycles were performed
in New York City during a single season, and the Guarneri
Quartet has played the cycle over and over again: in New
York, London, Geneva, Athens, Mexico City, Buenos Aires,

and even in Beethoven's birthplace, Bonn. As richly endowed as these cities are, it is only the people of Buffalo who have had the good fortune to be given the gift of a Beethoven cycle in perpetuity.

Frederick Slee's cycle inadvertently presented me with a gift as well—one of inestimable value. At a party the Schneiders gave us after one of those Beethoven concerts, I met my future wife, Dorothea von Haeften. She spoke in halting English, and I was incapable of saying more than a few words in her native German. It seems that my German class at Curtis with Frau Schumway had been a complete failure. Still, we sat in a corner of the living room and talked—about our lives, my music, her photography. The language barrier and even the subject matter seemed of little significance. Aside from the glow of a powerful attraction, I felt a sense of profound familiarity, as if Dorothea and I had known each other always. Not too many Beethoven cycles later, we were married.

Our Beethoven cycle took place at the University of Buffalo, where we had appeared in white tie and tails, our standard concert attire. Tails had been our stage uniform of choice for at least two reasons: they bestowed formality on our concerts, a feeling that a special event was taking place, and they were very comfortable to play in. Their free cut under the arms gives a string player more freedom to execute the swashbuckling motions often called for in virtuoso passages. But the 1960s were a time of increasing informality. Students were giving up ties and tweed jackets for jeans. We began to feel funny dressed in tails while across the footlights kids were wearing bib overalls. We worried that formal dress might be creating a barrier between classical music, a rare and fragile flower in the best of times, and the young people who were our future audience. Buffalo was not an isolated

192 • INDIVISIBLE BY FOUR

incident. Colleges and universities, acting like latter-day Medicis, accounted for half of our American engagements. We decided to bridge the fashion gap by changing to dark suits, white shirts, and ties.

The Guarneri proceeded uneventfully through the season in our new rags until we arrived in more formal Europe for our next concert tour. As we were warming up before our Frankfurt concert, the organizer announced that concert time was fast approaching and we had better change into tails. "Tails? We don't play in tails anymore. We play in suits," someone informed him. Herr Organizer marched off in a huff, and we walked onstage and played.

That very morning, seated on a train that traced the willful meandering of the Rhine through Germany, I was trying to read a German newspaper, a daily ritual to improve my language skill in a country we often visited. I came across the words *"schmal spurig."* Consulting my German–English dictionary, I learned that this meant, literally, narrow-gauge, as in railroad tracks. Used in the article I was struggling to read, *schmal spurig* described a state of narrow-mindedness.

The Frankfurt concert came to an end, and the organizer charged backstage to berate us about our attire. He spoke in German, but even with our shaky grasp of the language, his message was clear. "How dare you play for us in street clothes? My subscribers are from the highest levels of society, and they expect musicians to be dressed properly, in tails," he shouted, turning an apoplectic red. We looked at each other in incredulity. A difference of opinion about dress was understandable, but this overreaction was pointless and, yes, disrespectful. One eruption provoked another. I lost my temper with this officious busybody. Turning crimson with anger myself, and frustrated at not being able to express myself well in German, I sputtered, "You are, you are . . . *schmal spurig!*" The man flinched as if I had hit him. *"Schmal spurig?"* he cried in disbelief, and fled the room. John, David, and Michael looked at each other quizzically, and then at me.

"What did you say to push his buttons like that?" John asked suspiciously.

"It sounded like Shmuel is sure big," Michael volunteered.

"Schmal spurig," I repeated, still overwrought.

"What the hell does that mean?" David wanted to know.

When I explained, the quartet was impressed by the aptness of the words and intoxicated with the expression itself. For the next several days, as we traveled through Germany, the four of us could think of little else. When I ate a boiled egg two days in a row, Michael accused me of being *schmal spurig*. When John remained opposed to a ritard in a Bartók quartet, we condemned him as *schmal spurig*. It has remained an effective weapon for all of us. After all, how would you like to be called narrow-gauged?

In the matter of dress, whom should you try to please—the uninitiated with a show of informality, or the already converted who expect full dress with their full concert? Perhaps it didn't matter one whit, but the Guarneri Quartet eventually decided on a compromise, tuxedos, thereby running the risk of satisfying no one.

◦

IF YOU NOURISH an organism, it will flourish. In our young string quartet, we were hoping for quality, not numbers, notwithstanding the now apocryphal story of the quartet fan who came backstage and enthused, "I love your little orchestra and I hope it just grows and grows." For us, the regimen of daily rehearsals was both basic food for learning new music and the soil in which our own group personality began to evolve. When a work is put under intense and prolonged scrutiny—on the operating table, so to speak—how could it and we not change?

The process of growth continued in performance, although its path was less clear and harder to chart there. When we performed a work twenty times during a season, the piece itself seemed to change. But, of course, it was the other way around: with each performance of a Beethoven quartet, the contour and details of its terrain came more and more into focus for us.

Even to attempt an exact replay of an interpretation night after night goes against the nature of change in all things. Something as unthought-out as writing one's name, one's own signature on letters, checks, or automobile license forms, unwittingly changes over the years. Without my paying any particular attention, mine has evolved significantly from childish scrawl to earnest schoolboy penmanship, from early-adult propriety to midlife quirkiness.

This process is well illustrated in Haydn's "Seven Last Words of Christ," which the Guarneris play at Easter time in New York City every year. In the interim, we do not perform or study the piece, but somehow it manages to change from year to year. What interior process is at work? Even more mysteriously, our ideas often change together. Last year, for example, the quartet agreed that an ascending passage in the sixth movement, "It Is Fulfilled," should be dramatized by emphasizing each change of note. There was little discussion, since we all agreed. This year, nobody liked the idea. Someone suggested that we play the figure simply and let it speak for itself. Again, there was little discussion—it seemed so natural this way. I suspect that, as with wine in a cask, a fermentation process is going on of which we have little control or even conscious awareness. The Haydn resides in each of us over the year and simmers, mixing ideas, age, and experience. How will we play the rising group of notes when we come together next year? Stay tuned.

In the course of the two dozen times we played Beethoven's Opus 59, no. 3, several seasons ago, change was, therefore, inevitable. Some was of the unwelcome kind. Ragged ensemble and intonation tended to creep in with repetition. We called regular rehearsals to keep the quartet engine running smoothly. It was not very different from bringing your car in for a tune-up. Sometimes our changing ideas would warrant a special rehearsal—mostly small ideas: more ritard here, less crescendo there. But bigger issues would arise. "I hated the tempo of the slow movement—so sentimental!" someone groused. "Sentimental stems from the word *sentiment*," another retorted. "Tell me what's wrong with sentiment in this movement?" There followed a half tongue-in-cheek squabble in order to eliminate the "al" from sentimental.

Then there was the change brought on by individual work on repertoire. While on tour, we spent a sizable amount of time in our hotel rooms practicing. On the way to my hotel room after lunch, I often heard the guys working. I would hear scales, sometimes unaccompanied Bach, but, most often, the music of that evening's concert. I had my own work to do—for example, several cadenza-like passages in the first movement of 59, no. 3, that gave me trouble. Two of them finish with seemingly endless chains of eighth notes. What bowings, what fingerings were best? I experimented endlessly. Finally, John commented on my phrasing—or lack of—at a rehearsal. The passages were beginning to sound like études, he claimed. Once I passed David's room while he was working on a feisty cello passage from that same movement. I stood by his door, unable to resist eavesdropping. He ran the passage several times up to tempo, with only partial success. Silence. He resumed practice, only slower this time, and now something else was different: David had changed the fingering in the middle of the run of quick notes that go up to the cello's stratosphere. The new fingering worked well enough when he played it slowly for him to have another go at it at full tempo. The new fingering was a vast improvement and I tiptoed away from David's room with satisfaction, wondering if John, too, had ever listened outside a hotel door. The quartet was evolving.

∽·

BEFORE CONCERTS, WE often had "dry" rehearsals. Instruments remained at rest and we aired our comments and grievances, without playing. In the midst of a yearly European tour, we played in Eindhoven, Holland. The program was to finish with Opus 59, no. 3, the inevitable position for a work that ends with a fugue of driving energy and speed. During intermission, Michael came to my backstage room. "I just want to warn you. I'm going to try a slower tempo for the last movement." Michael made the tour of dressing rooms, informing John and David of his plan. I was hardly surprised. The tempo of the last movement was one large question mark. Beethoven's metronome indication was laughably fast and at the twilight zone of impossibility. Purists insisted that any musician worth his salt must adhere to the master's instructions (a whole note was marked for 84 on the metronome), but here the plot thickened. Opus 59, no. 3, had been written before Maelzel had invented his metronome, and Beethoven had added the tempo markings years later, when he was totally deaf. Still, being young and rambunctious, we tried our hardest to approach his speed of light, racing through the movement as if menaced by the metronome's flailing rod. The question of what constituted a good tempo was still very much alive as we prepared to continue the Eindhoven concert, but I gave little thought to Michael's backstage announcement. After all, he played the first fugal entry by himself. One by one, John, David, and I added our voices, but Michael controlled the tempo. Whatever he did, we would do.

The last notes of the third movement, upper and lower voices in contrary motion, settled into a final dominant seventh chord—four voices poised tranquilly at the water's edge before diving one after the other into the whirlpool. The embers of the chord faded away and Michael began the fugue. His plan had been to ratchet down our usual tempo one or two notches, a change from wildly fast to simply fast, but Michael had somehow miscalculated. In his effort to slow the fugal theme, he overshot the mark, and it emerged sounding like a fast practice tempo. The rest of us exchanged looks of disbelief as we waited our turns to enter. No whirlpool here! This was a hot tub that each of us entered at leisure, with a glass of Chardonnay in hand. But it was hard to play so slowly. After willing your fingers for a lifetime to be fleet, they tended to stumble over each other in slow motion.

Such is the brilliance of the fugue, however, that even played somnolently it makes an impression. The Dutch public clapped enthusiastically. Striding into the wings, we fell upon Michael. "What kind of a tempo was that?!" we demanded in that brief moment out of public view, and then we reemerged onto the stage, smiling insincerely, for a bow. We returned to the wings. Off came the smiles. "I told you I would try a new tempo," said Michael, covered in sweat and consternation as he faced his accusers. Out for another bow and back to the wings. Smile, then glower. The clapping continued. "We really should play an encore," David said above the din. "And the encore will be"—John uttered these words with glee—"the same movement, but *faster*, Michael!" "Yes, *faster!*" David and I added in chorus. We heard

Michael, already halfway onto the stage. "All right, all right. I'll start it faster." There was an edge to Michael's voice that should have warned us. We had hardly seated ourselves when he bolted out of the starting gate—it was the fastest tempo I had ever heard. Again David, John, and I looked at each other in disbelief, but one by one, we were sucked into the maelstrom. The Guarneri Quartet achieved the speed of light.

Meanwhile, in another part of the universe, Beethoven is listening. "They have finally played my tempo," he exults, a beatific smile on his face. Or perhaps not. There might just as easily be a furrow on his brow. "You know, that tempo doesn't work. I really ought to change the metronome mark."

◌

ONE CONCERT FOLLOWED the last with pleasing regularity. Chamber-music series that had liked our performances often rebooked us, and Beall and Steinway were able to serve up a full season of concerts again and again. Our career for the foreseeable future was set, and with each successful concert David, John, Michael, and I were slowly being wed to each other. This is what we had dreamed of and planned. But now hard reality set in. We could never get away from one another—not for very long, at any rate. There was no way to play quartets without the full measure of our four personalities interweaving and interacting. The silly jokes, the bad moods, the musical squabbling bore down on us with increasing intensity as our career solidified. Sometimes it was stifling. We enjoyed each other's company, but it was not healthy to be so interconnected: we spent more time with each other than with our wives, our children, even our friends. Were we in quartet heaven or was this a cleverly disguised prison?

In our frequent business meetings to discuss fees, bookings, and programs, there was never an item entitled "ways to alleviate the effects of constant togetherness," but individually we began to create zones of privacy. I have, in a box of miscellaneous photos, a picture of the quartet sitting together by a canal in Amsterdam. Before our first concert in that city, we had taken a tourist's boat ride together, and a street photographer had snapped us as we disembarked. Five years later, this outing could not have happened. Out of self-preservation, we had built little cocoons around ourselves. We didn't avoid one another, and occasionally we did things in two's and three's, but more and more we ate at separate tables in the hotel dining room, each often armed with reading material whereby we would gain entry into a world that excluded the others—I might have a book of E. B. White's essays, David the latest Philip Roth novel or just as easily some action-adventure thriller. Michael might bring Jane Austen or Shakespeare along, often annotating and underlining significant passages, and John was never without a book of challenging crossword puzzles. If I went for a walk, it was alone. I had been with David on the plane that morning, rehearsed with him that afternoon, would play a concert and even attend a party with him that evening; why should I invite him to the mall to look at socks and shirts?

We did not necessarily fly together anymore. John lived in New Jersey and another airport was practical for him, but each of us, in the course of developing different friends and interests in the cities we visited, found ourselves with individual travel needs. We often arrived for a concert on four different planes. The organizer waiting to pick one of us up at an airport would ask, obviously troubled, where our colleagues were—a crack outfit was supposed to travel together. "Where is Mr. Dalley?" was most often asked. John went about his business quietly, independently, and without fuss.

Why should he inform anyone of his arrival when he was perfectly capable of taking care of himself? We usually didn't know ourselves where Mr. Dalley was, but we never worried. John could be counted on to show up at the right time and place. But we did wonder. Where's John? was a question we asked ourselves a thousand times—in airports, hotels, backstage at the concert hall, and even afterward, when fans would request autographs. "Thank you," a young man said as I added my signature to the two already on the program. "Where is Mr. Dalley?"

I looked up from my violin case, but John was already gone, disappeared without a trace. It is illegal to forge someone else's signature, but I became adept at signing his name—never quite so stylishly as John himself did, but well enough to satisfy hundreds of fans over the years.

A Miami taxi driver finally got it right. On the way to the airport, he asked David, Michael, and me if we were part of an orchestra. "No, we're a string quartet." He looked us up and down in the rearview mirror. "Where's your fourth guy?" "He's not with us." The driver thought about this for a moment. "So, you're a quartet with only three people in it." Exactly. That was our traveling persona in a nutshell. I would reckon that the three of us travel without John 90 percent of the time. In between concerts, we should by rights be called the Guarneri Trio plus one.

Each of us cultivated pet interests on tour, all of which separated us further. Michael often called ahead to arrange for tennis wherever he could. Arriving at the Gainesville, Florida, airport, we were met by a couple from the local concert organization, who shook our hands and said, "We have a tennis pro lined up for you, Mr. Tree." Michael, who regularly travels with his racket, got excited. "A pro! You shouldn't have," he protested. "I'm only a club player. A duffer." This courtly little dance continued for a while: you must be a crack player; oh no, I'm really just a bumbler, etc. Finally, David could contain himself no longer. "Do you mind if I check into my hotel now, or should we just stand around listening to your tennis plans?" David, whose cousins were the well-known American painters Raphael and Moses Soyer, has always had a serious interest in art. He would seek out the museums, homing in on the exhibits that most interested him. I myself loved to nose around antique and junk shops. For no special reason, I once bought an old lock— not very valuable, but something about it pleased me. "What is that thing?" Dorothea asked suspiciously when I brought it home and put it on the mantelpiece. "Just an old lock." "And just what exactly are you planning to do with it?" The way she picked it up and wiped it clean gave every sign that the lock was a carrier of the plague. "Oh, I don't know. Nothing much, I guess." It was an honest answer, but the next time I wandered into an antique store while on tour, I asked the proprietor whether he had any old locks. Soon I had seven of various sizes and shapes. "Come see my lock collection," I beckoned to two friends who were visiting me. They looked the locks over. "Nice, but this is no collection. You need eleven items of one kind to make a collection." Eleven? This was news to me but, oh joy, the quest to create a collection was going to add new relevance and meaning to my traveling life. And John? I regret that I cannot report on any of his activities on tour. They are unknown to me.

In the early years, the quartet played through the summer. A young group takes whatever bookings it can get to make a living and a career. But once we had established ourselves, a twelve-month playing season seemed overwhelming. A little vacation was in order—perhaps two or three weeks during the summer to clear the head. It felt so good that we extended it the next year by another week. Year after year, the antidote for a hundred-concert season was a slightly longer convalescent period. The "right" amount of time turned out to be the traditional summer vacation for students and teachers, from the middle of June through Labor Day. For nine months our heads were filled with the sounds of string quartets and the opinions of four musicians echoing in their self-imposed cloister. For three months we shed our robes and did anything *but* play quartets—hit a tennis ball, sail, garden, hike in the mountains, even fiddle with other musicians. It was what the doctor ordered, a summer unhitched from one another.

I must confess something. During our vacation, I don't think about the guys. They have so saturated my system that there is no more space left for them in my psyche. The quartet rarely finds its way into my dreams. I suspect that dreams are about things that have not been given enough attention or that are unresolved during waking hours. No such problem with this group!

I remember dreaming about my quartet buddies during the summer only once, some two or three weeks before a new season was to start. It was a typical musician's anxiety dream, in which the first concert of the new season is just about to begin. David, John, and Michael are ready to perform, but I can't find my violin. The appointed time has long passed and the audience is restless. The others decide to go onstage and wait for me there. I find my violin, but now the music is nowhere to be seen. To my distress, the audience begins to boo. I find my music, but now my concert clothes have disappeared. I am close to panic, especially since an ominous, ever-swelling groan is emanating from the audience. John, Michael, and David return from the stage, anxious to find out why I have not joined them. Aha! Just then I spot my suit behind the door, but now I can't get my leg into the pants. I try again and again but it won't go past a certain point. I awake. My leg was being pinched by the bedcovers. (Why does my wife tuck in the sheets so tightly at the end of the bed?) Sun was streaming through the windows and I still had two weeks of vacation left.

But there was a reason for that dream. Somewhere in the recesses of my brain, thoughts of the coming season were beginning to ferment. Never mind the mundane stress of showing up for a concert on time, dressed, with violin and music in hand. It was almost time to get to work. I was rested and looking forward to the music and to my colleagues—their latest jokes, the endless discussions, the disagreements, and the entire process that would lead us to this year's interpretation of the great literature. I missed playing string quartets.

Diary. October 11, 1996. Chicago. Concert with the Orion and Guarneri String Quartets. It is of high interest to see another quartet in action. Hermetically sealed in our own capsule, we can easily lapse into the opinion that our way of music-making is the only way. The Orion is an outstanding group, but they definitely play with a different point of view. This is apparent when the two groups come together to rehearse to play in Chicago tonight. Michael Tree joins the Orion as second violist in Mozart's G minor String Quintet, then violist Steve Tenenbom and cellist Timothy Eddy join us in Brahms' G major Sextet, and finally we all come together in the only obvious conclusion to the program, the Mendelssohn octet.

The playing differences of the two groups are striking. The Orions are refined and thoughtful, the Guarneris are swashbuckling and boisterous. The attempt to bring two quartets together, like mating two species with different chromosomes, can be a disaster, but in this case, it is successful and highly enjoyable. We seem to respond to each other's differences by meeting comfortably in the middle—they opening up their dynamic range and sense of rhythmic freedom, we reining ours in a bit.

Besides, they have a sense of humor, we have a sense of humor. The mixture makes for entertaining rehearsals. Violinist Daniel Phillips does his interpretation of a bad violist playing the Bartók Concerto. Timothy exhibits his now famous imitation of Pablo Casals. John shows off his "bad violinist trying a new violin" routine, and violinist Todd Phillips plays the last movement of the octet with the motions of the right and left hands going at different speeds to produce chaos, a difficult joke to perform after a lifetime of coordinating them. We all laugh until it hurts.

[9]

In Perfect Four-Part Harmony

"YOU IN SOME kind of musical group?" the cab driver asked as David, Michael, and I made our way to La Guardia Airport.

"Yes, we're part of a string quartet."

"A string quartet, you mean *only* strings?" The driver turned in his seat to scrutinize us more closely.

"That's right. Two violins, a viola, and a cello."

"It couldn't be any good with just strings," he said darkly, his eyes fixed on us in the rearview mirror. "You need a rhythm section. Four strings are nothing by themselves."

We tried to digest this information.

"Drums are good with strings, you know, and I happen to be a drummer."

"Really?" We made eye contact with each other in the back seat while feigning interest.

"I'm not just any drummer, I'm a member of the musicians' union. Hoboken local. Why don't we get together?" He turned around again and smiled enticingly. "You're under no obligation."

The taxi arrived at La Guardia. We paid the fare, tipped the drummer generously, and declined his invitation. In retrospect, I regretted not accepting, if only to see the look on John's face as a yellow New York City taxi pulled up to his suburban house and the driver deposited a drum set on his front porch.

In my humble opinion, the taxi driver was wrong. The string quartet sounds full, satisfying, and complete all by itself. A voice inside me ridicules the idea. "Of course Steinhardt likes it. That's what he does for a living." True. But I also find Bach chorales, barbershop quartets, and the Beatles satisfying—wildly diverging types of music with nothing remotely in common except four-part harmony.

Is there something significant about groups of four? Perhaps, but again, look who's asking. All these years in a string quartet tend to create a certain outlook. Immersed in fourness, I am like the plumber who sees pipe fittings rather than a house, or the cardiologist who while gazing at a beautiful woman also considers whether her heart valves are opening and closing properly. I am aware of fours everywhere. Are there not four seasons in the year, four suits of cards, four legs on a table? But on inspection these examples suffer a bit. I have heard that the Laplanders divide their year not into four but into eight seasons, based on the reindeer's life cycle, and why couldn't a deck of cards have five, six, seven, or even nine suits? Come to think of it, there are three-legged tables.

The case for the number "four" in music is also murky. Classical compositions are most often in four movements, but they are usually published singly and occasionally in groups of two or three, less often in groups of four. (If any numbers are significant in this respect, they are six, as in Bach suites or Beethoven's Opus 18 string quartets, and twenty-four, as in Paganini caprices and Chopin preludes.)

In musical harmony, however, the number four has great value. A single note unadorned may please, but it is a naked and lonesome thing. Add the interval of a third to it and a major or minor tonality is announced. Combining this with the fifth degree of the scale forms a triad, the basic building block of tonal harmony, and a chord with a certain fullness. And by adding a fourth note to the triad, the octave above the chord's root, you have put a roof on the house. The four notes together have a satisfying completeness to them. They foster an almost physical sense of well-being. What's more, the four-voiced chord is ready to travel. It can go on any number of journeys with its four passengers on board. In the right hands, it can move adroitly from one harmony to another and modulate to other keys, each independent voice moving gracefully while fitting into the texture. The four-note chord contains what is essential, even of interest, but nothing superfluous or ornamental. Albert Einstein, himself a passionate string-quartet player, once observed, "Everything should be made as simple as possible, but not simpler." He could have been talking about four-part writing.

~

LIKE MUSIC STUDENTS in conservatories all over the world, I was required to take a course in harmony at the Curtis Institute of Music. Constant Vauclain, always dressed immaculately if somewhat warmly in a wool suit, taught the class. He led us solemnly through great numbers of exercises almost entirely in four-part harmony. "In four-part harmony" was the phrase that assignments had in common. "Class, please demonstrate the use of the plagal cadence in four-part harmony," or a deceptive cadence, or a raised fifth at the dominant. We were required to acquaint ourselves with a great variety of chords and their harmonic functions, and also to develop skill in manipulating four voices so that they progressed from one chord of four notes to the next in a pleasing and natural way. Vauclain stressed the importance of independence and beauty in each vocal line, the essence of counterpoint. (This had not always been so. In the sixteenth century, the top and bottom voices were often held together by unobtrusive harmony, a filling that was sometimes called *ripieno*, a cooking term that means "stuffing.") When a triad is to be played or sung in four parts, one of its intervals inevitably must be doubled, and rules governed the way this doubling was done; the triads had to be interconnected fluidly. An example from an old harmony book in my library: any tone of the triad may be doubled, but the root is best suited for this, the fifth less so, and the third least of all, because this latter, forming a major or minor third with the root, is most sharply prominent in characterizing its triad as major or minor.

Our great Maker created a harmonic universe in which the four-note chord sounds complete, and whether by design or accident, humans have the vocal range to establish four basic classes of voice to service it: soprano, alto, tenor, and bass. Mr. Vauclain's students were drawing on a rich European choral tradition in place for hundreds of years. Hand in hand, the voice and four-part music writing have journeyed from early Church hymns to Christmas carols and beyond. A footnote in an 1893 book entitled *A Manual of Harmony* by S. Jadassohn states, "Our reason for choosing a four-part mixed vocal chorus as the imaginary executant of these as well as of all following exercises is immediately apparent. All our exercises are preparatory studies to counterpoint, which requires the independent leading of each part, and its innermost essence is *vocal*. In *all* contrapuntal compositions, even if not intended for singing, every part must be *melodious, and its leading governed accordingly.*"

Four-part harmony, the choral tradition, and Western European music in general have not been here forever, although some of us carry on as if they had. Stravinsky wrote, "The superannuated system of classical tonality, which has served as the basis for musical construction of compelling interest, has had the authority of law among musicians for only a short period of time—a period much shorter than is usually imagined, extending only from the middle of the seventeenth century to the middle of the nineteenth." Ancient Greek and early Church music consisted largely of a melody without harmony or counterpoint. I wonder whether its gradual evolution into the satisfying, full sound of four-voice parts, which came into being only about the middle of the fifteenth century, is an arbitrary man-made product or a result of inevitable physical laws of sound. Certainly the two notes of the octave have a physical connection. They are the easiest for untrained voices to sing, blending so well that they almost sound like one note. They are mathematically related, the higher note being double the frequency of the lower. Pythagoras is said to have discovered this in the sixth century B.C. when he "stopped" a stretched string at its midpoint and found that plucking either half sounded an octave higher than the entire string vibrating unstopped. Pythagoras found that when you divide a string in three and pluck two-thirds of it, a fifth is sounded; that dividing in four produced a fourth. Next to the octave, the intervals of the fourth and fifth appear to be the easiest to sing together. In medieval times, these three intervals, the octave, fourth, and fifth, were the only ones considered concordant, or "perfect." But it is in the harmonic series that the entire triad appears in an unquestionably natural form. When a string is plucked or a column of air vibrates, the single note we think we hear is actually overlaid with many other notes, called overtones or harmonics. Although these can be produced and measured in a laboratory, every string player knows about them from their continuous appearance in the repertoire. If, for example, you lightly stop the G, the lowest string on the violin, at its middle, the octave above is sounded with a primal, almost flute-like timbre. Gliding up the string lightly with the left hand while bowing with the right, reveals the overtone series of pitches, shimmering one by one, like so many pipes or whistles: the octave G above middle C (as mentioned), D (the fifth above that), G (two octaves above the principal G), and E above that. The series continues into the stratosphere as you stretch the left hand to the end of the fingerboard, and the pitches become so high that humans stop hearing and dogs start barking, but *voilà* the three notes of a major triad have already appeared, plus two additional octaves thrown in for good luck. Before we congratulate ourselves on this discovery, the disquieting absence of a minor chord in the overtone series should be considered. According to Robert Schumann, the major chord is active and masculine; minor, passive and feminine. Does the absence of minor mean that masculine is natural and feminine not? It is my fervent hope that the universe has no sexual bias on this subject. Two possibilities present themselves: either a G major triad and the laws of physics are inextricably linked, or these musings are the self-centered conceit of a Westerner who believes that the sun rises and sets only on his own music.

I was not happy doing my harmony exercises. Mr. Vauclain's rules of do's and don'ts in voice leading seemed tedious and never-ending, even though I dimly sensed their importance. It was easy to recognize as four-voiced the moving chorales of Bach's *St. Matthew Passion*, the vocal quartet in Beethoven's Ninth Symphony, the French horn quartet in Carl Maria von Weber's overture to *Der Freischütz*, and the solemn brass choir of Brahms' First Symphony, but it took longer to realize that the symphonic music of the eighteenth and nineteenth centuries is overflowing with choirs of strings, winds, and brass instruments playing in four-part harmony, individually or together. Like spores traveling through the air, four-part writing seems to appear everywhere—in symphonies, in chamber music, and even in the popular vocal quartets of our 1950s student days.

We loved listening to the Mills Brothers singing "Up a Lazy River by the Old Mill Stream" so sweetly, the Modernaires, and the Hi-Lo's, who pushed the harmonic conventions far for their day. A favorite passed around by Curtis students was a record of the Hollywood Saxophone Quartet, which dazzled us with its brilliant playing and daring harmonic progressions. You would think that four saxophones were too similar in sound to hold the listener's interest for any length of time, but each instrument laid stake to a specific register, and the common quality of sound was cohesive and unifying. In retrospect, I realize this is suspiciously like the rationale for a string quartet. And another type of music served by four-part harmony, rock-and-roll, was just around the corner. Soon, older citizens would be biting their knuckles in horror over the antics of the Coasters or the Beatles. Civilization may have been going to hell, but it was doing it in four-part harmony.

~

WHEN WE WERE WELL into our career, examples of four-part writing were still coming from surprising directions. Several years ago, the Guarneri Quartet was checking into an upstate New York hotel. We were just signing the hotel register when the elevator doors opened behind us and a glorious if unexpected major chord filled the lobby. Four men in full voice stepped into the lobby and sang their hearts out. We stood there, keys in hand, unable to tear ourselves away from this barbershop quartet which so deftly wove melody and harmony together. As their song came to an end, other quartets seemed to come out of the woodwork in all directions. A barbershop convention was in progress and all the participants exhibited a cockeyed, almost delirious enthusiasm for their calling. Perhaps it was a mistake that I let slip to one of them that I played in a string quartet. Our relationship changed instantly: I was swept into the elevator by festively garbed gentlemen and invited to their rooms. When the elevator doors opened on a floor completely taken over by the convention, we stepped into a strange and awesome cacophony. The doors of all rooms were open and in many of them a barbershop quartet was singing. My self-appointed host took me around. At each door, introductions were made, hands shaken, and, without hesitation, each group burst back into song. They swayed as one with the beat, almost swooning with each passing purple harmony. My host turned to me and yelled above the dissonance caused by groups singing simultaneously in different keys, "We are brothers in harmony!" At that moment, it was hard to remember what a Beethoven quartet sounded like, but I grinned and nodded, almost ready to commit some primal act of blood exchange as proof of kinship. A manic, hot energy that might have been harnessed either to cure disease or to create mayhem pervaded the floor. I worried about what the headlines in the morning paper might be: Barbershop Quartets Terrorize Upstate New York Town. National Guard Mobilized to Quell Acts of Violence, Vandalism, and Lasciviousness. Excessive Harmonizing Blamed. Curfew on Singing Sweet Adeline After 10 p.m. Enacted.

The act of singing, especially in four parts, must tap into some deep-seated need. Mendelssohn even considered the person's location while vocalizing important. He composed a book of four-part songs intended to be sung in the open air. "The most natural music of all," he wrote a friend, "is that which comes from the heart when four people are strolling together through a wood or out in a boat."

That evening, as the Guarneri Quartet warmed up backstage before our concert, I couldn't get the barbershop experience out of my mind. I had swooned along with those groups that had so expertly served up songs from a bygone era. Someone had harmonized these standards with craft and imagination. Mr. Vauclain would have approved. "Good voice leadings, no parallel fifths, a nice feel to it," I could hear him mutter half to himself as was his habit when he pored over our assignments.

⌁

THERE WAS an enormous gulf between "Sweet Adeline" and the Mozart quartet we were about to play. But if it had been Mozart and not me checking into the Rochester Holiday Inn, what would he have thought about the barbershop quartet in the lobby? Considering his curiosity about other music and how seriously he took his own four-part writing, I suspect Mozart would have enjoyed it immensely.

In a letter to his father, Mozart related the difficulties he was having in fashioning six string quartets good enough to be worthy of his teacher and mentor Joseph Haydn. This should dispel the notion that his masterpieces, prepackaged like frozen dinners, came effortlessly out of the oven whole and perfect. On February 12, 1785, Mozart, his father, Leopold, and Anton and Bartholomäus Tinti played three of the "Haydn" quartets in Mozart's apartment for Haydn himself. What musician wouldn't have listened breathlessly at the keyhole? To have commandeered one of the Tintis' places to play with the two Mozarts and to hear Haydn say afterward to Leopold that he regarded his son Mozart as the greatest composer of his age—that would have been something!

The first edition of those six "Haydn" string quartets by Mozart contains a well-known dedication that reads in part:

> To My Dear Friend Haydn,
> A Father who has decided to send his sons into the great world thought it his duty to entrust them to the protection and guidance of a man who was very celebrated at the time and who, moreover, happened to be his best friend. In like manner, I send my six sons to you, most celebrated and dear friend. They are, indeed, the fruit of a long and laborious toil . . .

Mozart was paying homage to a great artist of his time and, coincidentally, the father of the string quartet.

Although the string quartet evolved from other instrumental configurations, it was inevitable that sooner or later the vocal quartet, which had gradually made its way into Reformation churches in the singing of hymns, would also influence instrumental writing. What instrument has not tried to emulate the voice, and what teacher, at one time or another, has not coaxed the student to "sing" on his chosen instrument? The violin, viola, and cello, without valves, or keys, or the frets of their cousin the guitar, can glide from one note to another almost as the human voice does. And the strings of our instruments are set into motion when stroked by the bow's horsehair, not unlike the way in which a column of air activates the vocal cords. Perhaps this is why string instruments mime the human voice so well. Haydn, who at the age of eight became a choirboy at the Cathedral of St. Stephen in Vienna, must have made the connection. The man who had difficulty writing one of anything (108 symphonies, 47 piano sonatas, 26 operas) composed 83 quartets for two violins, viola, and cello, a form that Marx once called "the refined, intellectual conversation of a small and intimate circle."

Haydn's inspired writing primed the pump for an outpouring of string quartets that continues to this day. If one considers only quartets written by the most celebrated composers of the eighteenth and nineteenth centuries, the numbers are impressive: 83 Haydn, 27 Mozart, 16 Beethoven, 15 Schubert, 3 Schumann, 8 Mendelssohn, 3 Brahms, and 12 Dvořák quartets—more than 150 quartets without looking in unusual corners of the repertoire or even scratching the surface of the twentieth century.

Ultimately, a body of such illustrious compositions was amassed that writing a string quartet became a composer's rite of passage. How could you be a composer without writing a string quartet? It was like calling yourself a man before shooting a tiger. Composers who wrote only one quartet must have felt that way, yet the list is long. Debussy wrote one, the only work he deemed worthy of an opus number. Ravel also wrote only one. So did Jean Sibelius, Edvard Grieg, César Franck, Niccolò Paganini, Edward Elgar, Anton Bruckner, William Walton, Amy Beach, Samuel Barber, and Gabriel Fauré, practically on his deathbed. With rehearsals for the Naples production of his opera *Aida* postponed, and stranded in a hotel room for several weeks, Verdi produced a quartet, the only piece without vocal writing he ever composed. Even Benjamin Franklin, taking a well-deserved break from American history, wrote one. The names of those who wrote more than one string quartet would fill pages. From nineteenth-century Russia alone, Peter Ilich Tchaikovsky, Nikolai Rimsky-Korsakov, Sergei Taneyev come to mind. Both Puccini and Liszt thought a quartet was best suited for the dead—Puccini's "Chrysanthemums" and Liszt's "At the Grave of Richard Wagner" were intended for funeral services.

It is easier to list composers who are quartet-less, for their number is small. Wagner, a worshipper of Beethoven's quartets, never produced a string quartet, except for one written when he was sixteen, which was subsequently lost. Considering his description of the last movement of Beethoven's C sharp minor Quartet (in Ashton Ellis's lively translation), one wonders why he avoided the string quartet so completely:

> Tis the dance of the whole world itself: wild joy, the wail of pain, love's transport, utmost bliss, grief, frenzy, riot, suffering, the lightning flickers, thunders growl: and above it the stupendous fiddler who bears and bounds it all, who leads it haughtily from whirlwind into whirlpool, to the brink of the abyss—he smiles at himself, for to him this sorcery was the merest play—and night beckons him. His day is done.

Mahler never wrote a quartet, but here is a curious footnote. He thought so highly of Schubert's "Death and the Maiden" quartet that he transcribed it for string orchestra. Hector Berlioz, Modest Mussorgsky, Aleksandr Scriabin, and Leonard Bernstein never wrote quartets. Why? It may have been Beethoven's overpowering presence that paralyzed them. "The deaf one," as Debussy purportedly called him, had set such an awesome example that by their own admission both Saint-Saëns and Fauré were cowed into waiting until the very end of their lives before daring to write a string quartet.

In 1908, Arnold Schoenberg produced the first works in which the tonal system is suspended—"the emancipation of dissonance," he phrased it. The finale of his second string quartet, the endgame in a series of changes in the logic and constructive power of harmony, presented the distinct possibility that it would become a requiem for four-part harmony and therefore for the string quartet itself. But Schoenberg, the great destroyer, nevertheless continued to write quartets in the new key-less twelve-tone language he had just created. The phoenix had risen from its ashes.

This century has produced an almost endless supply of quartets by the likes of Sergei Prokofiev, Igor Stravinsky, Dmitri Shostakovich, Béla Bartók, Zoltán Kodály, Ernst von Dohnányi, Alfred Schnittke, Leoš Janáček, Alban Berg, Anton Webern, Charles Ives, Roger Sessions, Elliott Carter, John Cage, Benjamin Britten, Alberto Ginastera, Heitor Villa-Lobos, Krzysztof Penderecki, György Ligeti, György Kurtág, Ned Rorem, Lukas Foss, and Leon Kirchner.

By contrast, the quartet's next-door neighbors, the string trio and the string quintet, are easy to enumerate, since there are few of them. The celebrated trios can be itemized on the fingers of two hands, the quintets by adding a few toes. What, then, was the defining characteristic that brought the string quartet into such prominence? Einstein put his finger on it: simple, but not any simpler. Four lean and economical voices that completely free the creative spirit to look inward. No hundred-piece orchestra, no myriad of instrumental colors to juggle or be seduced by. Nothing left but the naked ideas the composer has created and must confront.

Perhaps this explains the many visionary and personal examples in the repertoire: Haydn's religious epic "The Seven Last Words of Christ"; the shocking Great Fugue of Beethoven; Smetana's deeply autobiographical "From My Life"; Shostakovich's Eighth Quartet, dedicated to the victims of fascism and war, which quotes a song known to all Russians—"Exhausted by the hardship of prison"; the Barber String Quartet, whose devotional adagio has become one of the best-known classical compositions in the world; the radical Bartók quartets; and Berg's Lyric Suite, with a recently discovered soprano part revealing the existence of a clandestine and torrid love affair.

Three composers in particular, Haydn, Beethoven, and Bartók, not only wrote quartets that spanned their entire creative lives but used the quartet's small, enclosed, private space to move their compositional language forward, to confess their musical secrets, to dare. To this day, almost two centuries after the deaths of Haydn and Beethoven and fifty years since Bartók's passing, even the uninitiated sense something fresh, even revolutionary in their quartets. When I was eighteen, a friend pulled me into the listening booth of a record store to hear the Juilliard Quartet's brilliant recording of Bartók's Fifth String Quartet. For us, this had all the excitement of hearing a controversial if not treasonous speech given by a great orator. The sets of repeated notes which open the first movement like an ominous and urgent signal of warning finally burst into a babble of angry and contentious voices. I did not understand this music on my first hearing, but I sensed its significance and visceral excitement.

The stringed instruments have an advantage over all other instruments, including the human voice, that may explain in part their attractiveness for quartets. Since each instrument has four strings and up to four notes can be played at a time, a string quartet can leave the world of four-part harmony entirely. Ask a listener to close his eyes while listening to the return of the opening statement in Debussy's String Quartet and he will swear that the sheer volume and wealth of voices is the work of an entire string orchestra.

As the twenty-first century approaches, the quartet remains fresh and functional. The Guarneri is sent many unsolicited works every year by composers eager to cut their eyeteeth on this daunting form. Sometimes there are unexpected turns. Darius Milhaud composed his fifteenth and sixteenth quartets to be played separately *or* together. Leon Kirchner's Third Quartet is for four strings and prepared electronic tape. Morton Feldman's Second String Quartet is more than five hours in duration, and recently, the Arditti Quartet, specialists in twentieth-century music, played a new Karlheinz Stockhausen work in which each player is installed in a different airborne helicopter connected musically only by earphones. Over dinner one night, the members of the Arditti related the adventure to the bemused members of the Guarneri.

In an age in which computers, the information revolution, and digital recording and manipulation are influencing the way young composers regard the string quartet, we string players stubbornly continue to play instruments made and repaired by hand with methods little changed in the last three hundred years. Entering an instrument shop on the eve of the new millenium, you will find the chisels, gauges, knives, finger planes, saws, and calipers, the glue made of cow's or rabbit's skins, the air redolent with newly cut and planed wood, the freshly applied varnish tweaking the nostrils that were the basic trappings of Stradivari's workshop. It is hard to imagine what the future offspring of this unlikely union will sound like—an instrument maker's experience, intuition, craft, and artistry coupled to the newest glittering technology—but musicians are bracing for a seismic creative shift.

Exploring the nature of the string quartet must inevitably lead to a question about the musicians who choose to play quartets. Are there identifiable markings by which we can distinguish them from other musicians? "Those who can, do; those who can't, teach" goes the mean-spirited cliché about teachers and performers. There is a similar perception that those who can are soloists; those who can't, become chamber musicians. The image endures of four doddering, elderly men playing string quartets (perhaps instead of shuffleboard). But nothing in the solo literature is more difficult than the many first-violin cadenzas scattered through the Beethoven quartets, the second violin's finger and bow twisters in the Great Fugue, the Smetana Quartet's heroic opening viola statement, or the knotty cello cadenzas in Hindemith's Third Quartet. In reality, the best string-quartet players are outstanding instrumentalists whose interests simply head in a different direction from that of the soloist.

Musicians who by temperament are drawn to the world of instrumental showmanship have few quartets to sink their teeth into. Although virtuoso elements are plentiful in the quartet form, by and large it has not attracted the attention of the virtuoso composers. Paganini, Wieniawski, Vieuxtemps, Ernst, Hubay, Ysaÿe, Popper, and Kreisler, great soloists who also composed, either wrote no quartets or wrote nothing worthy of entering the canon of frequently played quartets.

The four-part form has also eliminated those egos who prefer to stand alone on the stage rather than share the spotlight. For the soloist who wants complete control, playing in a quartet is a form of hell. The soloist's artistic impulses are continually monitored, amended, or vetoed—impersonal expression dictated by a committee. But artistic control is elusive in any setting. In a broad sense, most music that a soloist encounters involves ensemble playing of some kind. A string player rarely performs in a vacuum. Unlike a piano soloist, for example, he almost never plays an entire program completely alone. A recital program most likely contains two or three sonatas with piano, in which case the irritating rules of chamber music apply, since the pianist will undoubtedly have a set of ideas requiring some compromise on the solo-ist's part. And the concerto experience, supposedly a soloist's crowning personal expression, requires dealing with a con-ductor, an orchestra, and all its individual members, each of whom may have other opinions or limitations that put the soloist in an interpretative straitjacket. The concept of the completely independent soloist looks less clear-cut, more theoretical, by the minute.

Also, soloists do play chamber music. They even form permanent chamber-music groups, occasionally. There have been celebrated piano trios: the Rubenstein–Heifetz–Piati-gorsky and Istomin–Stern–Rose trios come to mind. But despite the very real ensemble difficulties in the piano trio form, the independent writing allows the three members to operate as much like soloists as chamber musicians. Soloists play all kinds of chamber music—duos, string and piano trios, piano quartets, string and piano quintets, sextets—everything except string quartets. They play quartets for fun in someone's living room, but they are, curiously, absent from the soloist's public chamber-music ventures, off-limits, *verboten,* not to be considered. The most dazzling violin vir-tuoso of the nineteenth century, Niccolò Paganini, often enjoyed playing the quartets of Haydn, Mozart, and Beetho-ven with friends, but never in public. For a soloist, the string quartet is the Bermuda Triangle of music. It has an ominous reputation for being too difficult, too time-consuming, and capable of unleashing the darkest forces of human nature.

A psychiatrist, call him Dr. Smith, is making his morning rounds in the insane asylum. He is informed that a new patient has just been admitted, one who will especially in-terest the doctor because of his profession. He is a violinist, and Dr. Smith is himself an avid music lover. The patient is sitting peacefully under an oak tree as the doctor ap-proaches.

DR. SMITH: I understand you are a violinist.

PATIENT: Yes. Actually, a concert violinist.

DR. SMITH: Really. Where have you played?

PATIENT: Just about everywhere. I made my debut with Karajan and the Berlin Philharmonic. Since then, I've played with most of the world's major orchestras.

DR. SMITH: My goodness! Do you perform as a recitalist?

PATIENT: Of course. I recently played the entire cycle of Beethoven violin and piano sonatas throughout Europe with the great pianist Alfred Brendel, and I have toured four continents as a recitalist.

DR. SMITH: Good grief. This is extraordinary! And what about chamber music?

PATIENT: Oh yes! I have played a variety of chamber music with some of the world's most distinguished artists—there's not enough time to go into details, but let me just say that they have been wonderful experiences.

The doctor is overwhelmed by the sheer scope of this man's musical career. He is also perplexed. The patient seems so successful, so fulfilled, so well adjusted. Why is he here?

DR. SMITH: Tell me, have you ever played string quartets?

PATIENT: Aaaaieeeeeeee!

Attendants rush in, the patient is placed in a straitjacket and removed, kicking and screaming.

Musicians who gleefully tell this story come from both sides of the asylum walls. String-quartet players know it, of course, from the inside, but I have also heard the story told by concert pianists, oboists, and conductors. The nasty little secrets of the string quartet are out of the closet.

Even among those who do want to work in the rarefied, high-risk environment of the string quartet, few have the qualifications. The ideal string-quartet player has a very particular profile—is capable of being a soloist but prefers not to be, is willing and able to give up center stage for a communal effort, and has an artistic sensibility commensurate with the quartet repertoire. Each of these requirements winnows out a section of the string pool, and those who remain are a meager minority indeed. To begin with, mastering a string instrument is a user-unfriendly enterprise. Practicing for hours daily from a tender age to ingrain the awkward hand and arm positions guarantees no success. It is a minor miracle when a string player arrives at the very top level. Furthermore, working well with fellow musicians under stressful, sometimes stifling conditions is not taught in music school. And what would they teach? Sensitivity Training 101, Learning to Love Your Tormentor, Living with Criticism, Zen and the Art of String-Quartet Maintenance? Only by playing in a string quartet do musicians get an inkling whether they are among the chosen few who might survive.

Unlike an orchestra, string quartets have no union rules limiting the length and number of rehearsals. If five rehearsals are planned but ten are ultimately needed for a work to evolve into its finished state, then the gym workout, the dinner for two, the ball game, and even (God forbid) attending a string-quartet concert, may have to be forgone. Playing quartets is a nine-to-whatever job.

Last, a quartet of substance challenges the string player's mettle. The string quartet by its very nature selects those musicians who have the temperament and ability to probe as a team into the music's essence. Each player must be willing to take whatever time is necessary to examine and discuss the big ideas of an epic Schubert quartet, as well as the intimate world of little gestures that lives alongside, not unlike the cosmologist who looks out at the far reaches of the universe and at the same time into the microworld of particle physics. And "the deep difficulty of excellence," as

Spinoza put it, only gets deeper with time. Each added day of experience and understanding pushes the goals of performance further along. The quartet player's work is the stuff of high emotion laced with a powerful intellectual component.

Violists and cellists look lovingly at the string-quartet literature if for no other reason than because composers have written so few concertos for them. Even their wealthier friend the violinist, with almost limitless concertos on tap, has none by Schubert, Grieg, Fauré, Kodály, Smetana, Borodin, Debussy, or Ravel, all of whom wrote quartets. The first-rate repertoire for cello is small, and for viola an embarrassment. But the string-quartet legacy offers a world of interesting music as well as a ticket out of the orchestra and onto a more personal concert stage.

⁓

THE COMPOSER WRITES in four-part harmony and we performers play. What about the listener? What is the nature of this beast who is attracted to a concert experience that is aurally stark and visually minimal? The fellows and gals who come to hear the Guarneri Quartet, four men dressed in plain black tuxedos sitting on a stage devoid of anything but chairs, stands, and perhaps a floral arrangement or two, are not looking for visual excitement. Otherwise, they would be watching the elephants in the second act of *Aida*.

Not surprisingly, our audiences also dress without show. These are not people who have come to concerts to be seen. The men are most often in conservative suits or jackets. The women dress nicely, tastefully, but untheatrically. When I look out onto my audience as I bow, there are no wild colors, no heart-racing décolletage, no off-the-shoulder extravaganzas. It is a different crowd than you see at the opera. Oscar de la Renta would starve here. These people have come to hear their beloved music, and for them it is a spiritual event, as much like a religious service as a concert. Our audiences expect to be drawn into the deep emotions of a late Beethoven, the ethereal feeling of a Haydn, or the desperate melancholy of a Bartók quartet. It would be inappropriate to be flashy.

Marketing experts can undoubtedly pinpoint our public far more accurately than I can—their age group, income, level of education, etc.—but my eyes and ears tell me they are in general older, middle-class and up, and well-educated. Chamber music is most often the last stop in the evolution of musical taste, and therefore it is not surprising to see gray hair decorating our halls.

String-quartet audiences undoubtedly draw greatly from the professional classes. Sometimes I suspect they are all doctors—everything from podiatrists to psychiatrists, since there seems to be a mysterious and powerful underground railroad linking medicine and music. Perhaps music is an equally effective agent of healing, and doctors and musicians are part of a larger order serving the needs of mankind. Perhaps they recognize each other as brothers and sisters.

This can work to a musician's advantage. With an infection in my chest, throat, and ears that had dogged me for several weeks, I asked our organizer moments before a concert in Charlottesville, Virginia, whether there was a doctor in the audience. She laughed. Of course there was. In fact, many. There always are. At the end of the concert, a Dr. Corbitt arrived. He closed the door behind him and examined me. I offered to pay him for his time, but he declined, proposing instead to barter his services for three minutes of discussion. He wanted to talk about the piece that had just finished our program, Beethoven's Opus 135. Intrigued, I agreed. The doctor contended that Beethoven knew he was dying and that this work, his last, reflects the classic pattern of the terminally ill as outlined by Elisabeth Kübler-Ross in her book *On Death and Dying*: first movement, questioning; the middle of the second movement, rage; third movement, mourning; fourth movement—with the words "The difficult question: Must it be? It must be" written over the introduction—final acceptance. My flu symptoms fell away as I listened to the doctor's dramatic concept.

Doctors and music, what a relationship! There are doctors' orchestras, doctors' string quartets. Our family doctor upstate is a cellist. For many years, David and I had the same internist in New York City, a violist. Michael Tree's doctor is an amateur violinist. At his annual checkup, the doctor asked Michael about quartet repertoire and was horrified to learn that we start one program with a Mozart quartet. "Are you mad? It's too difficult, too stressful, and therefore bad for your health to begin a program with Mozart. Please! As your doctor, I strongly advise you to change the order."

A good minority of our audience are amateurs who regularly play string quartets at home. They come to our concerts not unlike weekend tennis hackers who go to professional tournaments, to pick up pointers as well as to enjoy the event. Music played in the home, *Haus Musik*, draws on an old European tradition. Many of the lawyers, doctors, dentists, mathematicians, scientists, teachers, professors, and other amateurs who play with almost clock-like regularity in living rooms all over America sport European accents. I bump into them quite often. An elderly woman standing next to me on a bus identified herself as an avocational violist, saying, "Excuse me, Mr. Steinhardt, I want you to know that I consider myself a Guarneri Quartet grrrroupie." Recently, at the corner of Manhattan's Broadway and 105th Street, a lady barely five feet tall approached me and said, without introduction or greeting, but with a distinct Austrian accent, "I hear even *you* have difficulty with

Opus 161." She was referring to Schubert's epic quartet in G major, his last. "Madam," I replied, trying to be at once whimsical and philosophical, "everything is difficult for me." She looked at me alarmed, my attempt at humor lost on her. "Well, *I* certainly have difficulty with it," she confessed. Further conversation revealed that this eighty-six-year-old woman still plays quartets weekly for her own enjoyment. Her age and accent placed her among the thousands of cultivated German-speaking refugees who were lucky enough to escape the Nazis and take up residence in America. Our audience would be greatly diminished without them, an entire generation of Central Europeans who consider chamber music as essential as a roof over their head.

Amateurs are sometimes deadly serious about the music and even about themselves. Years ago, a German shoe manufacturer invited the Guarneri Quartet to his home after a concert. The conversation turned to Mozart's "Dissonant" Quartet, which we had just played. "My group played the very same Mozart quartet last week," Herr Shoemaker informed us. He paused for effect. "*We* play the adagio slower."

A remarkable organization is at the amateur chamber-music player's service. In joining, you are required to give your name, instrument, and level of ability. Applicants must grade themselves, and all this information is then entered into the organization's handbook, distributed to its members throughout the country. A lawyer from Philadelphia with a client in Los Angeles no longer has to stay in his hotel room watching television when the day is done—not if he is a card-carrying member. He has looked up his Los Angeles counterparts at a similar playing level and arranged for an evening of string quartets. He simply takes along his instrument together with legal briefs and a change of underwear. It will probably be heavenly. But a wisp of a shadow hangs over the event—the system of self-evaluation. What happens if the lawyer, a poor violist, thinks he's God's gift to the instrument, while the dentist from Sherman Oaks, a cellist of considerable skill, suffers from an inferiority complex? Their egos as well as playing level may be mismatched, and mangled during the evening. Fortunately, the second violinist will be able to smooth things over. She's a shrink.

Professional string players have a curious, many-layered relationship with amateurs. The amateur's love of string quartets is the original, all-important core feeling that has touched all of us who would eventually play quartets professionally. A woman who by her own admission is a poor violist told me last spring that, for her, playing string quartets was a step toward heaven. I know that, but would I say this to another professional musician? Probably not. I'd be embarrassed to wear my heart on my sleeve. As an amateur, she felt no such constraints, and I enjoyed her outpouring, if only to connect with that spontaneous feeling of wonder that I had and still have for the great literature. The Russian composer Alexander Glazunov liked to say that amateurs would make the best musicians, adding after some thought, "If they only knew how to play."

Yet non-professional musicians are often an information resource for us. They are interested and curious enough to poke around in dusty, little-noticed corners of the repertoire in search of unknown string quartets that have hardly seen the light of the concert stage. Bertrand Jacobs, a New York psychiatrist, and his wife, Veronica, regularly come backstage, shake my hand, and say something like, "Congratulations. Nice concert. By the way, you should look at Frank Bridge's First String Quartet. It's really a lovely piece." (We subsequently performed the work.)

While professional string-quartet players with few exceptions are only making a modest-to-good living, some amateurs have hit the jackpot in other fields. These lucky people can then buy the finest old instruments for their beloved chamber-music hobby. A symbiotic relationship may follow. Those who can do justice to a Stradivari or a Guarneri enjoy hobnobbing with those who own one. Having a professional play his treasured instrument is a validation of the amateur's purchase. The difference in their playing skills drops away when amateur and pro share the experience of admiring the luster of a varnish, the shape of a scroll, the style with which a master cuts the F holes, and the golden sound of a fine instrument.

Some amateurs become highly knowledgeable about string instruments while pursuing their four-part addiction. Paolo Jori, a doctor by profession and a connoisseur of fine instruments, once invited us to his home after a concert in Naples, Italy. "Before we eat and drink, would you kindly show me your four instruments, so that I may guess what they are," he requested solemnly. The cello, viola, and two violins came out of their cases and were placed side by side on his sofa. Paolo stopped before each instrument and examined it intensely. Finally he stepped back. "The cello is a beautiful example of Andreas Guarneri. I do not know the viola's maker, but it is unquestionably Venetian and from the middle of the eighteenth century. John's violin is a classic Lupot made around 1800. And Arnold has a Guarneri del Gesù made in the late 1730s, but with questionable varnish and recarved F holes." Paolo looked challengingly in our direction as if daring us to contradict him. He was completely right, down to the last detail. (My violin had purportedly been painted black and hung on a wall for a hundred years before being revarnished and the F holes misguidedly altered.) Paolo only failed to come up with the viola's maker, the obscure Dominicus Busan, because he was known primarily for his double basses.

When a weak amateur with a great instrument meets up

with a professional string player, the relationship often becomes tenuous. I was once invited to the home of a surgeon to admire his three violins, one Stradivari and two Guarneri del Gesù, fine examples from the two most famous master violinmakers in the world. I played them one after another before his assembled guests. The quality and complexity of their voices could inspire poetry, and a tinge of envy slipped into my heart. "I'm not like most amateurs," their owner boasted to me. "These violins don't lie neglected in their cases. I make it a point to play one of them for at least five minutes each day." "I know how you feel," might have been my retort. "It bothers me if I don't perform a minimum of five minutes of brain surgery each day."

But some of the amateurs who are collectors of great instruments have a philanthropic streak. They lend their instruments to worthy young artists just setting off on careers but as yet unable to pay the dizzying prices that great string instruments garner. Some of these fine instruments are eventually willed by amateurs to music schools where their usefulness can be more long-lasting.

Several years ago William Steckler, a retired lawyer and enthusiastic amateur violinist, came to us with an unusual request. Bill wanted not free tickets to a concert or that we try his newly acquired fine old instrument, but to come on tour with the Guarneri Quartet. He thought it would be fun to experience the highs and lows of the traveling life and to revel in our concerts and camaraderie. Ordinarily, we would have refused. Who needs a fifth party getting in our hair while we're playing concerts? But Bill is an old friend and entertaining company. After all, it was Bill who, during the Second World War, found himself going into a stall in a men's room as the great violinist Jascha Heifetz entered the adjacent one. Bill was a soldier in the army and Heifetz was entertaining the troops. What does one do sitting on a toilet seat only inches away from the world's greatest violinist sitting on another? Bill started to whistle the opening of Bach's Double Violin Concerto, and four bars later, at the second violin entrance, a whistler in the next stall joined him in harmony. It is hard to say no to such a man as Bill. He accompanied us on our annual European tour. He ate muesli with us at breakfast, traveled up the Rhine by train with us, watching the castles go by from the dining car, attended the evening concerts, drank good German beer with us afterward, and repeated the process each and every day for two weeks.

I can put myself in Bill's place if I think, as a baseball fan, of being allowed, say, to live with the New York Yankees for a time—to watch them at batting practice, to sit in the dugout with the players, go on the road and hear great ballplayers analyze the last game, talk baseball, and simply be themselves. I understood. And besides, Bill was contributing something special to our journey—new jokes and stories, a different point of view, and as a fifth member of the group, unwittingly creating a whole new network of connections among us.

As a retired person, Bill Steckler would have plenty of company at a string-quartet concert, but missing from these musings about our audience is the most crucial element— young people. Our future performers do appear at concerts, some with an incipient curiosity about quartets and others already full-fledged chamber-music fanatics; and they often come backstage afterward. Perhaps young musicians feel that shaking our hot, moist hands directly after a performance, with the sweat still rolling down the backs of our necks into sopping-wet tuxedo shirts, will give them a clue about music-making that cannot be transmitted in the more circumspect atmosphere of the teaching studio. The future quartet players want to thank us but also secretly hope that between their "That was great" and our "Thank you," some hidden link is formed. Let them think so. It is gratifying to hear positive comments about a performance, especially from students—a prelude to more serious talk and study at a later date.

How do you draw the young to a string-quartet concert when it is so laden with forbidding connotations? We have heard all the charges. String quartets are snooty, stuffy, boring. Quartet concerts are only for the rich. You have to know a lot to enjoy the music. Go to a string-quartet concert? You must be kidding. By some miracle, the message that an evening of quartets might be stimulating sometimes gets through to people before arthritis and receding hairlines set in. Our young listeners have to reposition the more typical order of evolving taste: from popular to classical, from orchestral music and opera to the relatively unshowy world of chamber music far down the line.

Even the idea that quartet players themselves are otherworldly creatures involved in lofty aesthetic considerations isolates them, or so potential new listeners may think. Two starstruck young ladies once shook our hands after an afternoon concert in Providence, Rhode Island, many years ago. From the look in their eyes and their reverential tone of voice, it was evident that for them we were no mere mortals. They regarded us as high priests of art, clearly a notch above the rest of mankind. David and I exited the hall shortly thereafter, and walking down the street, we spied a beautiful old Jaguar roadster parked at the curb. It was too stylish not to comment on. The young women who had left the hall directly behind us overheard our conversation. "Did you hear that?" one of them said in a loud whisper. "They're talking about cars. Oh, how human."

Still, if you can simply expose someone to a string quartet, just once, the process of appreciation can at least begin. Madame Alba Buitoni, a grande dame of music and art in her native city of Perugia, Italy, once told me a story I can never forget. She had put on a record of the slow movement of a late Beethoven quartet. When it finished, she left her study unexpectedly, and surprised her maid, who had been listening outside the door. Tears were streaming down the young woman's face. Madame Buitoni said that her maid came from a small village where she had received no more than a grade-school education and certainly had never heard any classical music before. For this lucky woman, the process had begun.

⌒

A NAME FROM THE PAST leaped out from the Curtis Institute of Music's most recent monthly publication. The school had presented a concert of Constant Vauclain's music, and the composer had attended. My old harmony teacher was still alive! On an impulse, I obtained his telephone number and called him. Even though we had not spoken in forty-three years, his voice was unmistakable. He remembered this recalcitrant student and was delighted to speak with me. Not only was Vauclain still alive, but at eighty-nine he continues to compose daily and run three miles every other day. Eventually, I confessed to him how burdensome his four-part exercises had seemed, half a lifetime ago. It was ironic, I added, that after such a shaky beginning I found myself in a profession devoted exclusively to four-part writing. Vauclain laughed. "Four-part harmony was of the greatest importance to my teacher Rosario Scalero, and to me as well. Three voices are skimpy, four are complete, somehow. I have composed several string quartets, you know." I waited for what must follow—a few words that would finally reveal the essence of four-voiced harmony, but Vauclain went on to other things. Could it be that after Vauclain's lifetime of teaching and composing, the subject remained as elusive to him as to me?

As we talked, I shuttled back and forth in my mind between two distant polarities, the dutiful if unwilling schoolboy and the professional quartet player. Vauclain was certainly not responsible for my present status, but with hindsight, he seems like a musical Zen master who gently guided a beginning pupil in his first steps. On this journey, no one whispered in my ear, "Play string quartets!" The succession of seminal figures who followed in Vauclain's footsteps—Gingold, the Schneiders, Szell, and Szigeti—had themselves long ago succumbed to a form rich in meaning, small in physical size and public recognition. In sharing their enthusiasm, their passion for quartets, they had unwittingly beckoned me.

Although I was delighted to speak with Vauclain, the conversation was eerie. The eighty-nine-year-old at the other end of the line was too vibrant, too clearheaded, too enthusiastic for someone his age. Had he made a pact with the devil? Or, a different and much better scenario, was four-part harmony the long-sought-after fountain of youth? I asked Vauclain whether we could meet in the fall to continue the conversation about four-part writing. "Oh yes. There is so much to talk about. The relatively new discipline in music theory of psycho-acoustics may help to explain why four-part harmony is so meaningful." Some light might shine on the subject, after all!

While Vauclain and I were having this unlikely discussion, four-part writing was heading into outer space, literally. A twelve-inch gold-plated disk containing twenty-seven musical selections had been placed in the Voyager 2 spacecraft and by 1990 had already left the solar system. The contents of the record were selected for NASA by a committee chaired by Dr. Carl Sagan. Among the selections, which included a Pygmy girls' initiation song, "Melancholy Blues" performed by Louis Armstrong and his Hot Seven, and the Sacrificial Dance from Stravinsky's *Rite of Spring*, the committee had chosen the cavatina from Beethoven's String Quartet no. 13 in B flat, Opus 130, to end the ninety minutes of recorded music. As Sagan noted, "The spacecraft will be encountered and the record played only if there are advanced spacefaring civilizations in interstellar space."

When the distant future is the present and extraterrestrials find and decode this record, what will they think of the four-part chorale that begins the cavatina? And how will they react to the middle section marked *Beklemmt*, which we of the human race find so moving? *Beklemmt* translates loosely into "oppressed," or "anguished." Will the aliens find it so? It is a four-part question that will take some time to answer.

*Diary. November 8, 1996. The morning after our concert in Port-
land, Oregon. At the airport, David, who always buys a seat for
his cello, is asked by the boarding agent whether his instrument is
a giant violin. Moments later, as he enters the plane, the stewardess
asks, "Got your dancing partner there?" Over the years I have heard
dozens of remarks about David's bull fiddle, his guitar, his oboe,
his banjo, balalaika, bassoon, and even his cello.*

*Then there are the regulations. The cello has to be in the bulkhead
seat. The cello cannot be in the bulkhead seat. It can't be brought
on board without the pilot's approval. The cello has to be buckled
in. The cello must be strapped down. It has to go first class. It can't
be by the window. David, who is known to lose his temper, used to
flare up at these contradictory instructions, but over the years he has
developed an almost spiritual equanimity. In the bulkhead? Fine.
In the coat closet? Fine. In the cockpit? Fine, too.*

*"Giant violin. That's a first," I hear Michael say as he trails
David into the plane. Later, leaving the airport, David asks win-
somely whether there isn't a medal given out for schlepping his cello
around, or at least a tax deduction.*

*David cannot explain why his cello has more frequent-flier miles
on United Airlines than he does. Has his cello been dancing with
someone else on the sly?*

10

A Long Journey

CAN YOU TELL when something is going to go on for a long time? It is the sort of unanswerable question a child might ask his parents. Grownups know better. Nailing down the immediate future is hard enough. Better not to think too much about long-range plans; leave them in the hands of the gods. Still, I can't help wondering, after all these years together, not only how we managed to survive as a group far longer than anyone's expectations, but also whether there wasn't an early sign that we were to receive the gift of an unusually long life together. Perhaps one or two small clues embedded in the Guarneri Quartet's tenth birthday celebration on the stage of New York City's Tully Hall revealed to the acute observer that two decades later, the average life span of a woman in Roman times, we'd still be performing on the world's concert stages.

If we had paused for reflection, the signs were certainly

there. The quartet was playing well, we were healthy, and Harry Beall, now our lone American manager after Fritz Steinway's retirement in the early seventies, was still able to book us concerts year after year. What better sign than that could we ask for? As we blew out the candles of the birthday cake that proclaimed our years together in icing and chocolate, the four of us kept to ourselves any thoughts about what might be in store for the quartet. I don't recall a single conversation about five- or ten-year plans, or even about the future in a larger sense. There was no point. In five years, anything might happen. David could come to hate my playing, I might tire of Michael's jokes, or John could decide to become a full-time violin bow maker, a calling that had involved him more and more. We thought about the future only in concrete terms, and that was next year's concert schedule.

In the late fall, Harry handed out the skeleton of the coming season's touring itinerary, previewing concerts both close to home and as far away as Australia, where we would go for the first time. Holding the stapled pieces of paper in my hand gave me a glow. We could pay the rent and feed our families by doing something we continued to love! You weren't supposed to be able to do that in this world! Life's likelier script called for either making a lot of money in some dog-eat-dog business or, if you followed a more noble calling such as that of schoolteacher or social worker, settling for canned beans more nights than not. Being a professional musician was supposed to be a noble calling, but many musicians most decidedly did not enjoy their work. A recent study had listed orchestra players at the bottom of the job-satisfaction list.

Although money was certainly not our primary concern in a life of playing chamber music, by the ten-year mark the Guarneri Quartet was making a very respectable living.

With all the talk about a life of monastic deprivation, we four monks had apartments or houses in the New York area, cars that ran, and even vacation homes to escape to in the summer. Our fees rose gradually but steadily in the United States, and dramatically in Europe as the post–Second World War economy took off.

An unpleasant fringe benefit that came with foreign fees was the concert agencies' frequent custom of paying us in cash. At the end of each concert, a representative would appear with an envelope full of the local currency. One of us would sign for the fee to be split up later in the hotel. It felt good at first. There were no checks, no waiting, just cold cash on the spot. My brother-in-law suspects that the custom was a holdover from an older order in which, after the juggler, clown, or entertainer performed, the king threw him a coin or two. But as we went from city to city, the bulge in our jacket pockets got bigger and bigger, and with it, the concern about being robbed. I began to regard anyone standing next to me with suspicion. As we arrived each day at another hotel, I felt obliged to obtain a safe-deposit box from the desk clerk for my accumulated savings. This led to other complications. I once lost my safe-deposit key and professional safecrackers had to be brought in. On another occasion, Michael was paged in a taxi by the hotel we had just left. He had forgotten to take his money out of the safe. Yet another time, David did the same thing, but only missed the lump in his pocket after he was in another country. Eventually, he got his money back.

The quartet once tried to simplify life by asking to be paid for all our Australian concerts in one lump sum at the end of a tour. We had played in most of Australia's principal cities, so the amount paid us after our last concert was considerable. Dividing it would take some time. We spread the money out on a bed in one of our hotel rooms to count it more easily, and ordered sandwiches and drinks from room service. The waiter entered the room just as the four of us finished making four massive piles of money on different parts of the bed. His eyes bulged as he set the tray down unsteadily. Looking alternately at us and at the money, he began to back nervously out of the room. Michael was the quickest to react. "You haven't seen anything, right?"

"Right" came the waiter's answer in a strangled squeal as he fled the room.

With good fees coming in, we were beginning to think of ourselves as people with a certain amount of heft. At one of our regular business meetings with Harry Beall, David brought up the idea of the Guarneri Quartet incorporating as a business. He had heard that there was some kind of tax advantage in being a group rather than four individuals. Harry said he would look into it. A week later he set up a meeting with one of New York City's prominent entertainment lawyers. As we entered a Manhattan skyscraper on the appointed day, I began to have visions. Groups such as the Beatles and the Rolling Stones must be incorporated. Why not us? I envisioned soft cowhide attaché cases for our music, embossed in gold with the words *Guarneri String Quartet*, expense-account business luncheons with fellow musicians at swanky restaurants, and, letting myself run amok, Lear jets with champagne on board to take us to concert engagements, all of this paid by our corporation. Those endless Beethoven quartet cycles would be less wearing with our own pilot waiting in the wings for Opus 135 to finish so that he could whisk us home.

We shook hands with a man dressed in a nondescript suit and tie. I had expected something more flamboyant.

"Gentlemen, let me not waste your valuable time and mine any more than necessary," the lawyer said, after the most minimal greeting. "You're thinking of incorporating?"

We nodded.

"Does your quartet make over a million dollars a year?"

We shook our heads.

"Then there is no financial advantage in incorporating."

As the lawyer uttered these words, he was already standing, extending his hand to each of us. "It was a pleasure to meet you, and good luck," he said, ushering us out of his office. Our very important meeting, the gateway to a life of privilege and luxury, had lasted all of two minutes. The four of us rode down in the elevator in silence.

Even with a sizable tax advantage, a corporate arrangement would in fact have taken a toll on us that all the leather attaché cases in the world might not have made up for. It would have drawn us into the mire of even more togetherness, what with regular business meetings for filing papers and general planning. Being somewhat disorganized myself and afflicted with just a touch of sloth, I could easily see being a pest come tax time, looking fruitlessly for records I had lost or misplaced and intruding still further into my colleagues' lives. Let the Beatles have their tax havens. *We* didn't need them.

A friend of mine recently observed that one of the most important commodities in present-day capitalist society is privacy. She was speaking of land. Buy yourself a little house in the suburbs or several hundred acres in the wilderness, depending on your needs and resources, and you can effectively seal yourself off from unwanted people and the trappings of commercial civilization. Unless the added income resulting from incorporation was enormous, the four of us would each rather pay more money in individual taxes in return for a little more of that privacy. In many, many small ways we could each purchase the commodity of privacy when we needed it. You could take your own taxi to a rehearsal, or rent a car at the airport when the quartet was away from home, when and how you wanted it—without conferences, without coordination, and without company. After ten years together, it was clear to each of us that the less time we spent with one another outside the sprawling quartet landscape, the more we enjoyed each other in it. A certain amount of private time was like a battery charge to be expended at quartet sessions later on.

∾

THE FACT THAT we maintained our private lives as we came and went to quartet engagements led people to talk. When we arrived at a concert at different times, sometimes in four different planes, the gossip mill churned out stories that eventually made their way back to us. The Guarneri Quartet wasn't getting along, they weren't talking to each other, they were about to break up, Steinhardt couldn't take the strain and was moving to Hawaii. These tales seemed to have their origins in the idea that a musical group not only plays together but must also *play* together.

In the Marx Brothers' film *A Night at the Opera*, three aviators make their appearance, dressed exactly alike, sporting the same long beards. When Groucho Marx tiptoes through their stateroom at night, you see them even sleeping together—side by side, like sardines in a tin, with their beards neatly arranged over the covers. People seemed to need to believe that the four members of a string quartet, living in blissful harmony, do everything together, and when its members don't, theories of strife, intrigue, and conspiracy spring to life. The members of the Budapest Quartet, who liked each other well enough, had a philosophy similar to ours about privacy, but an article about them appeared in *Life* magazine and the notion that they didn't get along was sealed in print. The photographer Gjon Mili thought that the four of them seated in different parts of an empty train-station waiting room, each alone with his thoughts, would make a nice picture. It did, but to this day, a good forty-five years after that photograph appeared in *Life*, people still believe that the four great musicians of the Budapest did not talk to each other during their career. They did talk to each other—in Russian, as a matter of fact—and as an interesting footnote to the need for breathing room in a quartet, members of the Budapest always used the formal "you" to each other in conversation.

We had other issues besides privacy to contend with as the Guarneri Quartet headed into middle age, and they surfaced in the form of a question asked with increasing frequency in interviews with the press: Don't you become stale, playing the same repertoire over and over? You would think that after several years a predictable, monotonous routine would settle in. The Guarneri Quartet plays about a hundred concerts a year, and in a given year we might offer three or four different programs. Individual works may be played some twenty or thirty times in a season. And after several seasons, there are inevitable repetitions of compositions we especially enjoy. The great pianist Artur Schnabel was once asked why he devoted himself almost exclusively to the music of Mozart, Beethoven, and Schubert. "I only play music that is better than I am," he retorted. Our standard repertoire draws from many different parts of the world, but I would guess that a full 90 percent rests with nine composers whose mighty string-quartet output, by virtue not only of size but of depth and brilliance, is an irresistible magnet. These musical giants—Haydn, Mozart, Beethoven, Schubert, Schumann, Mendelssohn, Brahms, Dvořák, and Bartók—are composers with whom we can happily grow old, and whose compositions we might refer to, as Schnabel did to the music of three of them, as better than us. Whether we get stale performing Dvořák's American Quartet or Bartók's Fifth String Quartet for the 250th time is a legitimate question, but with music of this caliber, it is quite impossible for our interpretations to settle into a static mode.

A quartet must play the backbone of the literature, but if Beethoven, Brahms, and Bartók were not composers but corporations, anti-trust action could be considered. It is unfair to blame them for their genius, but those nine composers do hog the marketplace, and they needn't. A string quartet is surrounded by riches of every imaginable shape and size. Our regular reading sessions are expeditions in which we search for the exotic and unusual as well as deciding which of the eighty-three Haydn quartets we might next choose.

One such work, the emotional and unabashedly autobiographical Smetana Quartet No. 1, "From My Life," captivated us in our very first year. In a letter dated April 12, 1878, the composer explained its significance:

> *The First Movement* depicts Smetana's love of Art in his youth, his search for the imaginary, and the premonition of his approaching illness.
>
> *The Second Movement*, "Quasi Polka," refers to the carefree days of his youth and his passionate love for dancing at the period when he composed many dances.
>
> *The Third Movement*, "Largo Sostenuto," portrays his idyllic love for a young girl who later became his wife.
>
> *The Fourth Movement* pictures the composer rejoicing over the recognition attained by Bohemian National Music and its achieved success. A sudden high E indicates the noise in the composer's ears prior to his deafness. Then follows a painful recollection of his youthful days, a ray of hope against hope which gives way to resignation before the inevitable destiny.

The interruption of the last movement's joyous dance by a shuddering chord and the unwanted, uncalled-for appearance of a high, sustained E played by the first violin is one of the most bizarre and heart-wrenching moments in music. The relentless and unwavering E, an unfeeling and foreign object, bears no relationship to the music it has just displaced, giving a chilling impression of what Smetana himself must have experienced when he first heard the ringing in his ears. In fact, the pitch was an early sign of the illness that was eventually to lead him to madness and death. The high E is followed by a fragment of the first movement, but its youthful ardor has been transformed into melancholy. It fades away gradually and finishes with three pizzicato notes, three heartbeats that seem to mark the end of his life.

It is futile to try to describe music's beauty, and doubly so about the end of the Smetana, which overwhelms the listener both as music and as a personal story ending in tragedy. But we were not tongue-tied in talking about the quartet's programming difficulty. Where do you place a piece that finishes so quietly? Such a heart-on-the-sleeve work traditionally ends a concert, but the audience might be uncomfortable, leaving the concert hall with a sense of gloom hanging over them. On the other hand, putting the quartet earlier on the program meant that the spell Smetana so artfully cast would be broken by the work following. There seemed no other solution than to end the concert quietly and run the risk of laying an egg in front of an audience that expected fireworks before going home. At our first performance of the Smetana, the three closing notes were followed by total silence. Not even coughs and shuffling. Either the hall was empty or the entire audience had spontaneously decided to stop breathing for a moment. Applause finally began to break out in little pockets, slowly gathered mo-

mentum, and finally erupted into an ovation laced with bravos. The Smetana was a magnificent program ender.

Anton von Webern's Five Pieces offered an entirely different world conceived in miniature. The movements themselves are short, over almost before they begin, and the
phrases often amount to little more than gestures—quick
outbursts, sighs, exclamations. Webern loved the world of
quietness. He would indicate *piano, pianissimo, pianississimo*,
and then, in his own German, *kaum hörbar*, barely audible.
Doling out sound in dropperfuls rather than buckets was a
challenge to us. "Shh!" was the comment heard most often
in rehearsal.

We entered Webern's world with the same excitement
that Alice in Wonderland must have felt going from large
to small. And audiences seemed to be drawn to this music—
which might have its visual counterpart in the squiggles,
curlicues, and bursts of light in a Miró painting—that is,
they seemed to until we played it once in Harvard's Sanders
Theatre. The second movement had just gotten under way,
a series of murmurs and sighs that require the utmost attention from the listener, when the Cambridge fire department,
situated next door, was summoned into action. The fire en-
gines, sirens screaming, rolled past Sanders Theatre. Onstage
at that moment, four musicians could be seen moving their
bows and fingers uselessly, for not a sound could be heard
over the din.

⌐•

WITH AN ALMOST inexhaustible supply of stimulating music
such as the Smetana and Webern quartets to choose from,
we looked forward to our reading sessions throughout the
season. The Guarneris are "in residence" at the University
of Maryland in College Park, Maryland. Each of our eight
yearly visits there includes an open rehearsal for students,

faculty, and the general public. At least one of them each year is reserved for sight-reading new scores that are regularly sent to us, and established music with which we are unfamiliar. We began last year's session by reading through several works that had been sent to us unsolicited. It was impossible to predict what these would sound like. One seemed static and unimaginative, the next energetic but without a sense of formal compositional skill. Both were voted down. But sometimes I worry about our ability to absorb new works. Would we recognize a masterpiece written in a new language that we could relate to only upon repeated hearing? It is so easy to pass judgment from our established position, to roll our eyes a few minutes into a new work, shake heads in distaste a few pages later, and finally put the instruments down in exasperation. Was the young composer's new quartet truly bad, or were we overlooking a diamond in the rough?

In the case of the next piece on our list, Shostakovich's Third Quartet, his style was too well known to require familiarization, but because of our ambivalence about his music, we had performed only two of his quartets. This one came highly recommended by Shmuel Ashkenasi of the Vermeer Quartet. Only a minute into the piece, David began to mutter, "This is crap. Ridiculous." Michael immediately came to Shostakovich's defense. "Come on, Dave. It's very strong music." They kept up a running argument as we waded through the five movements. John joined David's camp, his face looking pinched when a passage particularly displeased him. I sat on the fence, admittedly less than enchanted with some of Shostakovich's clichés—wicked, biting humor in a circus-like atmosphere, for one. Then came what I considered a moving and lovely fourth movement. Michael agreed. David and John, unimpressed, had little comment. When we finished the last movement, Shostakovich's Third Quartet floated in limbo with one vote for, two vociferously against, and one uncommitted. Whatever interest any of us had in the work had to be weighed against the fact that, if picked as part of next year's repertoire, it might be performed as much as thirty times. If a work was to undergo the incessant glare of the concert stage, one had better like it a lot. The quartet was shelved.

Our open rehearsals are followed by a question-and-answer period. I asked the audience to raise hands if they liked the Shostakovich. Hands shot up everywhere. If the decision had been left to them, next year's programs would include the Shostakovich Third String Quartet.

This year we would take a look at Janáček's First Quartet, the Kreutzer, inspired by Tolstoy's novel. A wife's adultery and subsequent murder by her jealous husband was the subject, and for those with a taste for the lurid, certain basic aspects of the plot can be followed in the music, including the murder itself. This gruesome fact notwithstanding, the Janáček had caught our attention. The wildness and tenderness, the spasmodic stops and starts of its musical syntax, fully evident in both of his string quartets, intrigued us. It resembled, at times, the feverish but truncated speech of a person with too much to express at once. According to the composer Josef Suk, a member of the Bohemian Quartet who gave the first performance of this work, Janáček wanted to make this a moral protest against men's despotic attitude toward women.

I also planned to bring the Kreisler quartet to our next reading session once again, although it was doubtful the guys would like it any better this year than in the past. Maybe I still smarted from the last experience. Granted, we were not weighing the merits of a work in the Beethoven quartet class here, but the Kreisler had charm, wit, and lightness. It hurt me that my colleagues were closed off to its allure. Maybe I could bribe them into playing it, discreetly leaving greenbacks on their music stands.

These were some of the thoughts in my mind as we drove through Haworth, New Jersey, en route to John's house. It wouldn't be the end of the world if the Kreisler didn't fly—we had so many other works to look at. Besides the Janáček, Michael had brought along several contemporary string quartets, some by well-known composers that we had heard about through the musical grapevine or in concert, and others with the print hardly dry.

We arrived at John's house and walked up the path, past the lawn bordered by well-tended shrubs and mixed flowers. I suspected that this read-through would have its share of dissension from a familiar quarter. John was sure to bring up the Sibelius quartet again. Last time, we had been tied, two for and two against, but he had not mentioned it again during the ensuing year. It would have been so easy for him to lobby for the work a bit while we sat in some airport. "Guys, you really should listen to the Sibelius again. It's such a lovely work." I might have done just that to give Kreisler a little help, but not John. There was no editorializing with him.

We had very different ways of expressing our opinions. If at this rehearsal we were to read through a work by a mythical composer—let us call him Tibor Shmeggegi—I can easily imagine the following conversation:

DAVID: I *hate* that Shmeggegi quartet. [David is openly opinionated.]
MICHAEL: Yes, but his mother adored it. [Michael probably agrees with David's assessment but wants to soften the verdict somehow.]
ARNOLD: Do you realize the horrible childhood Shmeggegi had in war-torn Lower Slobovia? I don't like the quartet,

but under the circumstances it's a miracle he could write at all. [I, on the other hand, have the unfortunate tendency to want to see the good in everything.]

JOHN:

MICHAEL: John?

DAVID: What did you think of the Shmeggegi, John?

JOHN: I don't care for it. [Succinct is what I would call John.]

John opened the front door and we made our way to the rehearsal space, a small television room lined with bookcases. "There's coffee and bagels for everyone except Michael on the kitchen table," John announced. "Michael, you can only have coffee." This was a running joke that went back to a time when the visits to John's house had included only coffee. "John," Michael had said then, in mock embarrassment, "you wouldn't have anything to go with the coffee, would you? It doesn't have to be much. Just a plain piece of bread will do. Coffee needs something, don't you think?" David would pretend to get mad when this happened. "Michael, you schnorrer, you mooch," he hollered.

While this drama was going on, John set up the folding stands and placed the parts for the Sibelius quartet on them. It was inevitable. "Ah, the Sibelius," David said cheerfully. "This is a very, very good work," he confirmed quietly, almost as if talking to himself. Michael and I waved eyebrows at one another, helpless in the face of intractable disagreement. Our read-through would be followed by some preaching to the converted. David would tell John how much he loved the quartet, I would tell Michael how much I disliked it, and we would have the same impasse as the last time, but there was no getting out of it. We played the quartet.

The first violin has the opening phrase of the Sibelius, and the cello answers. Their plaintive single voices might be two close friends expressing the sadness of their parting. The first violin repeats his figure with an additional embellishment, as if to say that this separation will be especially painful. The cello again responds, agreeing, but Sibelius has cut his dynamic in half, making the answer sound distant. The friend has already started on his journey and is calling back one last time from afar. Then the four instruments join quietly in a unison chord that swells and leads into the main body of the movement: they could be the chorus that has witnessed this sad event and then elaborates on it for the duration of the movement.

This time, I found myself touched by the opening and swept along by the music's agitation. That momentum, once established, carried me through all five movements. The part of me that had disliked this work lost substance and then, like any respectable ghost, disappeared into thin air. I loved the Sibelius, and as if that wasn't enough of a surprise, Michael had also changed his mind. In the course of twenty-five minutes, all four of us unexpectedly found our opinions realigned and unanimous.

We all know people whose indifferent and unpleasant qualities, with the passing of time or an intervening event, are reshuffled in our minds and mysteriously reemerge as positively attractive. This had *undoubtedly* happened to Michael and me with the Sibelius quartet, but the process eludes easy explanation. The Sibelius remains an outsider to the standard repertoire, even though, when the work is placed at the end of a concert, the bristling energy of its last movement never fails to bring down the house. Do string quartets not play it because John Dalley is not a member of them, or does every quartet have its equivalent—a hothouse plant that can be grown only in a specific, rarefied soil while remaining misunderstood or ignored by the rest of us?

If Rudolf Serkin had been privy to the process we had just

undergone, he would have smiled. The pianist Lydia Artymiw told me that several years ago two musicians in a group slated to play a Benjamin Britten string quartet at the Marlboro Music Festival came to Serkin with a problem: one loved the Britten, the other hated it, and they hoped that Serkin would give them guidance. "Always trust the opinion of someone who loves a work," he advised. "The person who dislikes it has simply not yet been open to its beauty. That will come." And it had. Next year we would be touring with the Sibelius quartet.

As I feared, the Kreisler quartet was again voted down. Perhaps my colleagues were unaware of Serkin's dictum about time's ultimate unmasking of beauty, but Mr. Kreisler's future in this group looked bleak. I would probably have to play the quartet in my dotage, or perhaps in heaven itself. Imagine Fritz Kreisler showing up and inviting me to play the quartet with him and his cronies. That would be the ultimate revenge on John, Michael, and David, those unbelievers! They would refuse Kreisler himself if he asked them to play his quartet in heaven's great concert hall. "I'm sorry, Mr. Kreisler, we feel it's too weak to play in public."

.⌣.

LEAVE, RETURN, LEAVE, return. Like a piece of wood bobbing in the water, continually swept away and then drawn back to shore by the tide, this is the story of a musician's life. Accustomed as we were to the coming and going, it was still no easier either on us or on our wives, who regularly became temporary widows while their husbands went on tour. As professional musicians themselves, Nancy Dalley and Janet Soyer had personal experience of a musician's itinerant ways, but that didn't make repeated separations any easier. On rare occasions, my wife, Dorothea, went out on a photographic assignment and I was the one who stayed at home. So this is what our wives experienced! It was different to be left rather than to leave oneself, when one's departure is always eased by the concrete urgency of the tasks at hand. But when I was the one staying at home, Dorothea's exit gave me a pang and made me feel as if the bonds of the family unit had been threatened. David's children were grown, but the rest of us had young ones, and they, too, had to adapt. My children's tearful goodbyes would be erased by the joy and excitement when I returned: "Daddy, did you bring me anything?" But after a particularly long trip I often felt like a visitor in my own house: my family had grudgingly learned to live without me, and this necessitated a certain reentry period before the old rhythms could be reestablished.

Going on tour had become something of a routine. Travel arrangements and hotels were discussed and decided on with our travel agent long in advance. The day before departure, I would call a limousine service to pick me up at my apartment building; with an instrument and luggage, this was much easier and no more expensive than flagging down a taxi in competition with a million other New Yorkers. Then I would pick up David and Michael or head out to the airport alone. One morning, the driver came for me in a Lincoln Town Car. Even half asleep, I noticed its smooth ride and luxurious appointments. The radio was playing and I heard an advertisement for the very car in which I was riding. "The new Lincoln Town Car is so spacious it deserves its own zip code." This broke through my early-morning stupor and coaxed a smile out of me, until I learned that the shuttle was delayed because of rain.

Since we arrived at and left cities so quickly, the cities themselves receded in importance. The concerts and the preparations were the thing. I once had a dream in which I arrived late at an airport, knowing only the flight number and the gate, but not my destination. Breathlessly, I sank into my seat as the doors closed and the plane taxied out to the runway. Once we were airborne, the pilot made his usual announcement: "Good morning, and welcome to United Airlines flight number 723. Flying time to the moon will be two days five hours and twenty-five minutes. Please sit back, relax, enjoy the flight, and thank you for flying United Airlines." To the moon? This was most aggravating. I knew I should have paid more attention. I had boarded the plane wearing my concert shirt, and it would be grubby by the time we arrived. The moon itself had no special significance in the dream—it was just another concert destination; what mattered was the condition of my white shirt after days in space. But there was a way out of this unpleasant situation. I went to the lavatory, took off my shirt and washed it, and hung it up to dry on the window by my seat. For the duration of the flight I sat in my undershirt, the spectacular approach to the moon blocked by my cotton-and-Dacron-blend shirt (35 percent, 65 percent) as it dried for the next two days. But I was happy: I would be wearing a clean shirt for our lunar concert. Important things first.

Touring life has a dream-like if not downright surreal aspect to it. Once, changing planes en route to Louisville, Kentucky, I saw a familiar coffee bar. I had had a good espresso and a sticky bun there earlier that week. I even remembered where the seating area was, around the corner. The experience was now repeated. Only, as I sat sipping, chewing, and reading *The New York Times*, I suddenly felt disoriented. Where was I? For the life of me, I didn't know what city I was in, only that I was sitting on the very same stool and clutching a *New York Times* with a different date on it. "The cities are all interchangeable for you, aren't they?" a friend threw accusingly at me when I related this incident. "All you know is the plane flight, the hotel, and the concert hall!" I had no rebuttal. Touring musicians live in a dimension in which normal life is set apart, seen through glass, from the windows of airports, taxis, and hotel rooms. Even the concert audience is quarantined from us by the footlights. The human beings we do see are a select group: taxi drivers, airline reps, stewardesses, waitresses, concert organizers, and a few well-wishers backstage. Besides that brilliantly lit two hours onstage, life on the road for us is probably not much different from that of a salesman for electrical wire.

If you tended to be negative, every aspect of touring life would involve a potential mishap or disaster. The taxi to the airport could have a flat, the flight be delayed indefinitely, the hotel reservation lost. And the luggage! A whole book could be written on this subject. In the early years, we checked our bags at the airline counter and innocently watched them disappear down the conveyor belt, secure in the knowledge that they would arrive safely. But many misplaced and lost bags later, all of us have taken a more realistic view. In Cleveland, Ohio, we once arrived at the airport whereas David's luggage did not. Although the airline promised it in two hours, his suitcase never arrived. That night, three dark suits and one tweed jacket with slacks walked onto the stage of a packed Fairmount Temple. David announced to the audience, "U.S. Air didn't want me to shave or wear a suit," and promptly sat down. There is an old joke about a customer who requests reservations for a trip: "I'd like to go from Boston to Bangkok to Salt Lake City to Tokyo to Atlanta to Singapore, please." "I'm sorry, sir," says the airline rep, "but we don't fly to those cities." "That's funny," the customer replies. "You flew my luggage to all those places last week."

David was also the one who mistakenly took a look-alike bag from the baggage carousel. When he opened what he thought was his bag at the hotel, a pistol was lying on top of a stranger's neatly packed clothes. David returned to the airport and exchanged bags quickly and quietly. These unfortunate experiences might explain the idea he has for a play: Passengers are waiting for their luggage. The baggage carousel begins to move and the pieces of luggage move along the conveyor belt. Suddenly a corpse appears on the belt, with a luggage tag, like all the other pieces. Two men in blue suits and dark sunglasses pick up the body and bring it to the baggage checker, who, without batting an eye, pulls the ticket off the corpse and waves the men through. David says he hasn't been able to get any further with the plot.

We crossed our fingers about the accommodations awaiting us on the road. Travel agents and promoters had our instructions that, regardless of cost, we wanted to stay in the best hotel any city could offer. It was hard enough to be away from home, enduring the wear and tear of constant travel. At the very least we could indulge ourselves in pleasing surroundings and good food at a fine hotel. Also, we were traveling with priceless instruments and, presumably, a good hotel cast a more watchful eye on its guests' valuables. By the time we were in our teens as a quartet, the collective age of our instruments was some nine hundred years and their worth substantial. Any one of them could buy you a respectable house. They were insured, of course, but the loss of an instrument would be devastating. My violin was not simply a tool of the trade; I had cultivated a relationship with it over many years. How could I enjoy my peas and carrots if I left my beloved violin unguarded in room ten of a Motel Eleven?

Insisting on good accommodations did not necessarily guarantee them, however. In fact, the quality of life on tour careened from glamour to gloom, from comfort to combat, from cuisine to queasy. One winter night we stayed, pampered in luxury, in a converted castle outside of Dublin, but just across the Irish Sea in Rhyl, Wales, my room had no heat and neither did the concert hall we played in. The audience sat dourly in their overcoats as we tried to play, four space heaters placed near enough to warm us somewhat but not close enough to set us on fire. Chattering from cold in my hotel room later that night, I briefly entertained the notion of sleeping in my concert tails. But when I did dive under the covers, I involuntarily cried out. There was a small, warm animal in my bed, or at least that is what it felt like. In trepidation, I lifted the covers and found a green hot-water bottle!

In Atlanta, Georgia, we often stayed in a deluxe hotel that boasted an indoor swimming pool and sauna, but once we opted for a place outside the city, conveniently located next to Agnes Scott College, where we were playing. The Heart of Dekatur motel was a basic place, but it offered something unique. Unbeknownst to us, it was situated by the railroad tracks. Much later that evening, the nightly freight train roared by, blowing its whistle as it passed the rooms of the Guarneri Quartet, perhaps in acknowledgment of our shared musical abilities. I sat bolt upright in bed, realizing in terror that the end had come. There are so many ways to die. Mine was to be mowed down by a train while in bed.

There were other unexpected aspects of hotel life. In Memphis, Tennessee, ducks were splashing around in the lobby's fountain as we checked into the Peabody Hotel. Every afternoon at five, a red carpet is laid out from the fountain to the elevator, and accompanied by solemn march music, the mallards, four females and one male, climb out of the fountain, down steps onto the carpet, and waddle into the elevator, escorted by a uniformed employee. The sight of the elevator doors closing on five ducks on the way to their penthouse night quarters was unforgettable. And in Levens Hall, somewhere in the heart of England, we were put up in the ancient manor house where our concert was to take place. Later that evening, our host wished us good night and, almost as an afterthought, warned us about the ghosts. Ghosts? Yes, there were three of them that appeared occasionally in the middle of the night. One played the harpsichord, a little white dog snapped at your heels, and a gypsy woman put a curse on you if you passed too close on the stairs.

The food on the road was equally unpredictable. In general, anything served in private homes was on a very high level. People take pride in their cooking and they would feature their favorite recipes in the after-concert parties they gave for us. Restaurants were riskier. When we started to travel in the 1960s, it was possible to find mom-and-pop restaurants that would serve home-made vegetable soup, a hearty main dish, and a memorable fruit pie whose recipe might have been in the family since the Civil War. Once discovered, these were places we treasured and remembered. I daresay that even at this date, some twenty years after it closed, if I mention a certain restaurant in Duanesburg, New York, at the intersection of routes 7 and 20, John will talk glowingly about their sticky buns. For years, we looked forward to our Salt Lake City visits, not just for the concerts, the appreciative audiences, the friends we had cultivated there, and the magical mountains surrounding the city, but also for the buckwheat pancakes served in the downtown hotel where we stayed. They were made from scratch and from a superb recipe. John and I spoke reverently of these wonderful pancakes, especially when we were reduced to eating lackluster substitutes elsewhere in the world. One year, the buckwheat pancakes in Salt Lake City were tasteless. I approached John, who was seated at another table with a half-eaten plate of pancakes before him, and gestured toward them. "Are they—" A shake of his head interrupted my sentence. "I just asked," he said, looking as if he had lost a loved one. "The hotel has changed hands. These are made from a mix." Salt Lake City has never been quite the same.

The spreading convenience of cheeseburgers and french fries in twenty seconds went a long way toward eliminating the prospects for hearty home-cooked soups away from home. But in reaction to the new order of fast-food chains, upscale restaurants didn't seem to get better, just snootier. Places with names like Ye Olde Fox and Hounds, or Chez Moi et Toi et Vous et Nous, began to appear. "Would you care for a frosted fork with your salad?" a waiter dressed in a red-and-black costume out of another century asked me solicitously. The frosted fork, cool as it felt in the hand, was unable to resuscitate wilted lettuce drowned in dressing.

A certain sameness often characterized the food, no matter where we ate it. I began to suspect that all chicken à la Kiev was made and frozen in a Midwestern processing plant and shipped to restaurants around the country—price to be determined by location and ambience. This was halfway to Andy Warhol's prediction that restaurants of the future would provide only atmosphere. You would pick which setting to dine in, French, Italian, or Ethiopian, say, and bring your own food.

ARNOLD: I'm home, dear. [My wife and I embrace.]

DOROTHEA: Oh joy! You're back. You must be exhausted!

ARNOLD: I'm fine, but last night after the concert we were served ham that was so dry I couldn't touch it. Listen to this, though. The host announced that the quartet has been reengaged and, since nobody had eaten the ham, he was freezing it to serve at next year's party. Can you believe it? So we get in the car and go to Kansas City for ribs. You know, of course, that Kansas City is famous for its ribs. They cure them with hickory smoke for over

twenty-four hours. Best ribs I ever ate. There was a
guy in the men's room who wanted to play three-card
monte with me on the floor, but that's another story. Anyway, this morning I had a wonderful breakfast with the
Berkowitzes. They served bagels every bit as good as
New York's and with a special cream-cheese-and-scallion
spread. Delicious!

DOROTHEA: Nice, but how were the concerts?

ARNOLD: What?

DOROTHEA: The concerts. How did they go?

ARNOLD: Oh, the concerts. They were okay.

Life is surprisingly spartan away from home. No family,
friends, or the mundane aspects of life such as paying bills
and taking out garbage. The enduring staples of this existence are the traveling itself, the practicing, performing,
sleeping, and eating. Then the quality of the food—whether
Kansas City ribs, the fresh buffalo mozzarella cheese in Naples, or Indonesian rijstafel in Amsterdam—becomes a pri-
ority item. And it is so much easier to talk about food than
about music when you get home. How can I describe to my
wife the magic of the Debussy String Quartet in performance? It was Felix Mendelssohn who purportedly said that
music is too specific to be described in words. And to tell
her of our triumphs! Boasting is a sin, and besides, tales of
conquest are usually boring. No, it was definitely better and
easier to describe those smoky ribs, how surprisingly lean
they were, the oh-so-tangy flavor of the sauce, and how generous were the portions served in Kansas City.

Years later, an outstanding dish became a handy mne-
monic device for summoning other features from past tours.
When Michael wondered when we had last played in Rome,
I could say definitely that it was two years ago. I knew because, following that Rome concert, I had reveled in a mem-

orable plate of gnocchi with Gorgonzola sauce, a dish I have not had the good fortune to encounter before or since.

People are generally curious about life in a string quartet, and now that the Guarneri Quartet was in middle age, our answers were expected to reveal the wisdom of experience. But the questions asked by professional interviewers on assignment from newspapers, radio, and television were surprisingly similar. Marc Gottlieb, first violinist of the Claremont String Quartet, once mimicked their predictability at a party. "Tell me, Mr. Steinhardt," he asked with mock formality, swiveling around to face me on the couch on which we were both seated. "How many concerts a year does the quartet play? How many hours a day do you practice? How do you decide on the repertoire? Do you fight? Is there a boss in the group? Do you get stale? Do your interpretations change? Do your wives travel with you? How have you managed to stay together so long?" True, interviewers asked us and every other quartet these questions over and over again, but if not these questions, what should they ask?

Another frequently repeated group of questions had to do with our instruments: How old are they? How valuable? Do you all play Guarneris? Do you have a matched set of instruments? The last was at the heart of a misconception that instruments can be replicated like washing machines or television sets, and that players respond to all instruments alike. In fact, two violins made by the same maker in the same year with wood from the same tree, and even with exactly the same dimensions, will often sound quite different; and because we all have different bodies and minds, we need different kinds of instruments to carry out our musical intentions. When John and I play the same violin one after another, the instrumental timbre changes significantly. The weight and length of our arms alone are significant factors.

The maker, the piece of wood used, and the player are living and therefore variable. Seeking out the right instrument is as difficult and elusive as finding a mate. Is the sound generous enough? Is the instrument comfortable to play? And, most important, does it have a quality of sound that can be the servant or even the partner that enables your musical ideas to take wing? And, as with a life's partner, where, when, and how love arrives in the form of an instrument is unpredictable.

Several years ago, the Corcoran Gallery in Washington, D.C., offered us the extended use of their quartet of Stradivarius instruments. The value of this offer was enormous. The golden tone and exquisite workmanship of Stradivarius instruments are the standard by which all others are measured, and their numbers are finite. There are approximately five hundred violins, fifty cellos, and a mere ten violas in the world made by the great master from Cremona, Italy, who lived to be ninety-three and worked to the very end. A museum curator brought the instruments with great fanfare and no small amount of trepidation to one of our rehearsals for us to try. At the time, David was playing an Andrea Guarnerius cello made in Cremona in 1669, Michael a 1750 viola by Dominicus Busan of Venice, John an 1810 violin by Nicolas Lupot, and I a late-eighteenth-century violin by Lorenzo Storioni. The craftsmanship, choice of wood, varnish, and substantial age of each of our instruments had come together to create a sound of warmth and complexity that enticed and then seduced each of us, and although their collective worth was perhaps only a tenth of that of the Stradivaris, which were valued in the millions of dollars, we turned down the Cremonese master's instruments with little discussion. David has since changed cellos again, but John, Michael, and I will probably remain with our present instruments for the rest of our lives. After much trial and error, each of us has found what could aptly be called his musical soul mate.

Even more elusive, but of vital importance, are the bows we use. The uninitiated might ask why the fuss over a long, curved wooden stick with horsehair attached to both ends. Made by artisans from Brazilian pernambuco wood, each bow varies in thickness, weight, and elasticity. A bow that works for one violinist may be out of the question for another. The bow has to match not just the player but his instrument as well. A lightweight, supple bow fits one instrument; a heavy, stiff one, another. String players can talk for hours about bows, whose effect is so intangible—their playing qualities, the difference between the great makers, what is for sale, where, and for how much. At this writing, some bows sell for upwards of $100,000. Could I hear the difference between the Mendelssohn Violin Concerto played on a Dominique Peccatte or a Xavier Tourte bow? Probably not, but in a way that doesn't really matter. If the performer finds a bow comfortable and responsive, then that's the one for him.

What kind of a person makes bows? Someone with an extraordinary eye and the precision needed to calibrate the weight, balance, camber, and elasticity of a piece of wood so that it is miraculously transformed into a "great playing stick." Whom do I know personally who makes such bows? Sitting next to me in our very own quartet, John Dalley. Over the years, John has made dozens of fine bows. I have recently acquired one, which I use with great pleasure. It is responsive, draws a healthy sound, and has an attractive look and feel. John has the eye. He is the kind of guy who will walk into a post-concert party with the quartet, and while the rest of us are shaking hands and making small talk, he will unobtrusively lift the corner of an Oriental rug to examine its nap appreciatively.

It is appealing to talk about our relationship with the instruments we play in terms of a love affair, but we are also their temporary caretakers. These are instruments that were being played for centuries before we arrived and will be around long after we've gone. If my violin could only talk, what places, performances, and violinists would it describe in the two hundred years since it was made in Cremona? Not long ago, the quartet played in Reggio Emilia, a city not more than an hour or two from my Storioni's birthplace. I wondered whether, in all of the violin's travels, it had ever returned home, the prodigal son, to be fêted and, yes, played.

At least some of our instruments' history is known. My Storioni was brought into the Budapest String Quartet by its original first violinist, Emil Hauser, who when he left sold it to his replacement, Joseph Roisman, and Roisman played it until the quartet disbanded. Including the time spent in our group, the Storioni has been in a professional string quartet for almost three quarters of a century. Michael's viola shares a similar background, having been played by Denés Koromzay in the Hungarian Quartet before he acquired it. Michael and I have a little secret: we don't need to practice, since our instruments have been playing quartets for so long. John, sadly, knows nothing about his Lupot violin except the name of the man who sold it to him, but David can trace his Guarneri back to the last century. The cello was in the possession of the Italian violinmaker Leandro Bisiac and other members of his family for one hundred years before it immigrated to America.

Two of our instruments have undergone major surgery. When Michael's Busan left the Hungarian Quartet, its enormous eighteen-inch body length was considered so awkward for most players that a decision was made to shorten it before offering it again for sale. René Morel, a master instrument-maker and craftsman, cut off portions of the top and bottom so gracefully that he had to produce the scraps of cut wood before people would believe what he had done. René's artistry is so complete that he once defied me to find the spot on the maple back of a Guarneri viola where he had replaced wormwood, even after he pointed out the exact area. For an entire year, René had searched up and down the East Coast for the right wood with the right grain for the job—a piece of wood that needed to be no more than a square inch. In the back of a Salvation Army store, he finally spied an old chair with a twisted maple leg and the perfect grain. He paid fifty dollars for the chair and told the storekeeper to keep it for him while he got something from his car. In a moment he was back with a saw, quickly cut a small section out of the leg, and handed the rest of the chair back to the astonished man. "This is all I need," he said, waving the small piece of wood triumphantly. "You can sell the chair again if you want." Try as I might, I was unable to locate the newly grafted piece of wood, the place where the Salvation Army and Cremona had unexpectedly met on the back of this rare viola.

My Storioni has also undergone surgery. When I purchased the violin, the rare-instrument dealer Jacques Français told me that the scroll was made by another master, in his opinion none other than the great Guarneri del Gesù. As fate would have it, Jacques had a del Gesù without a scroll and a Storioni viola scroll without an instrument. The scroll, although oversized, was a perfect color and match for my instrument, and Jacques sketched an unlikely but believable scenario. According to him, both instruments and the decapitated scroll had at one time all passed through the shop of a dealer with an unsavory reputation for dismembering instruments and unscrupulously recombining them for profit—a kind of chop shop for string instruments. It was entirely possible, Jacques maintained, that the Storioni scroll originally belonged to my very instrument. But how could a viola scroll match a violin? Jacques then divulged something even more astonishing: my violin was originally a small viola that had at some point in history been cut down and made into a violin. Perhaps that is why the Storioni's lower register has a throaty roar not unlike the sound of a viola. I consented to having the scrolls exchanged, possibly bringing the original parts of my violin-viola together again and enacting an instrumental approximation of the Tristan and Isolde myth. In any case, the Storioni was that rare case, an instrument that had undergone a sex-change operation.

By far the most asked question, and one that has taken on additional meaning as the years tick away, was how we had managed to stay together so long. The answers we gave in interviews became as predictable as the question: We still love what we are doing, we continue to be stimulated by the exalted repertoire, and we still get along. Reasonable as these answers are, they are not necessarily the only ones. It could be argued that we had gotten too old to start new careers, or were prisoners of our own success, unwilling or unable to kill the golden goose. But if this pessimistic view bore any truth, either it would have been expressed immediately or the dissatisfaction would circuitously have worked its way into the open. It is very difficult to hide in a string quartet, and anger or bitterness or indeed any deep feelings are bound to surface during the rough transactions of daily rehearsal. But the only signs we saw were the ones reflected in those answers we kept giving interviewers: we did get along, we did love our work, and playing a late Beethoven quartet was still an adventure to cherish.

There was an additional reason for our longevity as a group: a sense of humor, of proportion, of lightness in dealing with our very weighty and demanding profession. When I struggled with a particularly troublesome passage, John sometimes suggested, "Bring it in again next week, please," as if he were my junior-high-school violin teacher. When we were in the throes of a particularly difficult tour, David would assume some vaguely Slavic accent and mutter, "I rub horsehair across cat gut. Make many zloties." When we sat in some faceless airport, I might tell them my latest dream, a dream in which a psychiatrist shows me a giant plastic model of a strawberry and asks me what key it is in. (I say A flat, he insists A.) Michael would tell the latest viola joke on himself.

The mirth sometimes spreads backstage. Standing in the wings before a concert in Miami, Florida, the concert organizer, Julian Kreeger, told us that he had a *short* public announcement to make. "A likely story," said John. "No jokes," Dave warned, "this is going to be like following Jolson." I groaned. Sure enough, our worst fears were confirmed: Julian went on and on. His pitch finally at an end, we heard him making his way toward the stage door we stood behind. But Michael had a glint in his eye. He pulled the door shut just as Julian tried to open it stage-side. We heard the audience laughing at poor Julian's predicament. Finally, Michael relented. Framed in the doorway, with the stage lights bathing him ghoulishly from behind, Julian threatened not to take us to the Versailles restaurant after the concert. Such a threat could not be taken lightly! This traditional Cuban restaurant was a favorite post-concert stop for Julian and the Guarneris. The laughter subsided and we walked onstage.

The fun often followed us onto the stage itself. Michael came on with the wrong glasses, went off again and returned with the right ones, then said to the audience, "*Now* you're going to hear something." John, once plagued by a squeaky chair, asked a listener in one of the stage seats to exchange it with him. As each settled into his new chair,

John wheeled around and barked at the accommodating fellow, "I don't want any more trouble out of you!" Once, an E string on my violin snapped in two only inches from my eye, and I feigned blindness. And when a crucial baseball game was being played simultaneously with a concert at the Kennedy Center, in Washington, D.C., David waited for the applause to die down after intermission and announced, "Bottom of the fourth. Yankees are winning three to one." The audience adores it when things like this happen. The formal concert ritual has been broken and the four priests of art are suddenly revealed as ordinary human beings. Perhaps this was the truest of the truths, the mother of all reasons the Guarneri String Quartet was still together. We were having fun along the treacherous path that a string quartet follows.

Our continued success also encouraged the four priests to relax their vows of quartet celibacy and perform as soloists. We played solo recitals frequently, and sometimes, before our concerts, I would hear the telltale signs of a future solo date with an orchestra: the strains of a violin, viola, or cello concerto mixing with the quartet repertoire being practiced backstage. Harry Beall began booking occasional orchestra engagements for us, in which we would split up to play, for example, Mozart's Sinfonia Concertante or the Brahms Double Concerto. The finely calibrated pianos and pianissimos that are the mark of a good string quartet gave way to a different work ethic: a powerful tone called upon time and again by the soloist to climb above the sheer mass of orchestral sound. It was refreshing, freeing, even instructive to break our string-quartet shackles and perform with an orchestra; for John, David, Michael, and me to become every now and again Mischa, Jascha, Toscha, and Sascha.

·◊·

MY DREAM from childhood was to be a successful musical performer. If a little fame, fortune, and adoration followed, all the better. But I was completely unprepared for the awards, prizes, and invitations to social functions that the Guarneri Quartet began to receive as we became established. Several years after we had left Harpur College to join the faculty of the Curtis Institute of Music, our old school (now part of the State University of New York) bestowed honorary doctorates on us all. At the outdoor ceremony, we sat before faculty, students, and the friends we had made during our time in Binghamton, and adorned with the mortarboards and hoods that signified our new status, we listened to the university president's warm words about us. This was no meaningless gesture. Our years at Harpur had been important for us, the college, and the community. The next day I paraded briefly around my apartment in my full doctoral regalia for the amusement of my young daughter, but also to hold on to the special feeling that yesterday's ceremony had engendered. "Daddy, are you a real doctor now?" she wanted to know as I hung the hood in my closet, where it remains to this day. I tried to explain that, although she could now call me Dr. Steinhardt, I could not take out her appendix.

More honors followed: another honorary doctorate from the University of South Florida, where we had appeared dozens of times; the New York City Seal of Recognition presented to us by the then mayor, Ed Koch, in 1982; the Smetana Medal from the city of Prague; and the Esther Award, conferred on us by a little old man backstage after a concert in Los Angeles, California. "I hereby present to you the Esther Award," he said, handing us a scroll bound with a red ribbon. The handwritten document, which the gentleman then unfurled with a flourish, extolled the virtues of our playing. "Why is it called the Esther Award?" Michael wanted to know. "Esther, may she rest in peace, was my wife. A wonderful woman. A queen like in the Bible," he said, visibly moved. "Such a woman must be remembered, and I am doing this by handing out Esther Awards—not to every Tom, Dick, and Harry, mind you—just for somebody special, like you." He eventually left the green room, and we smiled as we packed up our instruments. There was something touching about the gesture. Was it so different from the Nobel Prize or the Légion d'Honneur?

Books and even a film about us appeared. A *New Yorker* magazine profile by Helen Drees Ruttencutter was the basis for a lively book, *Quartet*, detailing our professional lives, and an excellent book for the devoted music lover appeared shortly thereafter, *The Art of String Quartet Playing: The Guarneri in Conversation with David Blum*. An outstanding full-length documentary film, *High Fidelity: The Adventures of the Guarneri String Quartet,* directed by Allan Miller and produced by Walter Scheuer, provides an in-depth look at the quartet from home to hotel to concert stage. The books and film are entertaining, stimulating, and probing; the publicity, priceless.

Not long before the *New Yorker* profile appeared, Harry Beall called to say that he had been contacted by the White House. Would we play there if invited? (At this point they were only inquiring, not yet inviting.) It was the height of the Vietnam War, and many artists had publicly refused President Lyndon Johnson's invitations to appear at the White House. Johnson tried to avoid further political humiliation by asking members of America's cultural community surreptitiously. It was both comical and sad. What if I had asked for my wife's hand in marriage that way? "Darling, mind you, I'm not asking you to marry me, but if I were to ask, would you?" We refused President Johnson's curious non-invitation.

Presidents changed. Now Jimmy Carter was in office. Again, Harry was called by the White House. Would we play for a state dinner honoring Menachem Begin, Prime Minister of Israel? It was, of course, an honor to be invited to the White House, and this time we gladly accepted. But five minutes later Harry was back on the phone. "They're happy you will play, but there's no room for you to sit with the invited guests in the State Dining Room. You'll have to eat elsewhere, with the White House personnel." It was the old Fritz Kreisler story all over again. Kreisler was invited by a New York society lady to play a concert in her home. The fee was to be $5,000. "You understand, Mr. Kreisler, that you are to use the servants' entrance both before and after the concert," she instructed him. Kreisler was reported to have said, "In that case, madam, my fee is only $3,000." In this case, Uncle Sam wasn't even paying us! We instructed Harry to refuse.

Our track record with the White House was dismal. My mind wandered. Maybe the IRS would find out about this little brouhaha, take it personally, and begin to scrutinize my yearly tax returns. The phone rang again. "They've managed to find places for you at the state dinner," Harry said, chortling. "You're playing at the White House on April 15, a week from Saturday."

When I informed my wife that the President of the United States had invited us to a state dinner, she made an observation: "I need a new dress and you need a new suit." The part about the suit was certainly true. The threadbare condition of my present one was not particularly noticeable from the audience, but when I shook hands with President Carter, he was bound to notice the shine on my left lapel, polished from the constant rubbing where my violin and shoulder meet.

It was only in the middle of the following week that I

managed to get to Saks Fifth Avenue for the new suit. "Looks really good on you," said the tailor as he finished marking and pinning the sleeves and cuffs. "We'll have it ready in two weeks." "Two weeks?" I was aghast. "That's impossible. I need it in two days!" The tailor smiled smugly. "You don't seem to realize, sir, that here at Saks we have an enormous backlog of gentlemen's attire to alter. Two days is out of the question." Thinking about my old shiny suit being reviewed by the President and the First Lady of the United States brought beads of perspiration to my brow. "Look," I said in something of a state, "I have to perform for the President of the United States at the White House this coming Saturday. This suit must be ready." The small group of salesmen who had gathered to see what the ruckus was about fell silent and the tailor's face suddenly had a new look. "Mr. Steinhardt, if you have to play for the President, we'll have the suit ready in two days."

Security is necessarily tight at the President's residence, but especially so for four men carrying instrument cases. Ever since *The Lavender Hill Mob* was released, the 1951 film about gangsters concealing their weapons in such cases, the public has been convinced that instrument cases have a dual purpose. Hardly a month goes by without someone in a crowded elevator asking me if I'm carrying a machine gun. The White House security force at the East Gate seemed unconcerned, however, as our names were checked on a list, and we were passed through without inspection.

The White House might not be the kind of place that you and I would live in, but it has the character of a lived-in house. All ten of us—naturally, our wives were there, and so were Harry Beall and his wife, Mary—found it appealing. Michael Tree's wife, Jani, who was born in Czechoslovakia and raised in Austria, found the atmosphere especially attractive. She comes from a part of the world where official functions are held in palaces or government buildings designed on a grand, formal scale. The White House had a more democratic and accessible feel to it, reflecting the warmth and informality of the American people themselves.

When dinner with its speeches by President Carter and Prime Minister Begin were over, the guests moved to the East Room for the concert. A raised platform with four chairs and four stands had been set up for us at one end of the room. We had decided to play Dvořák's American Quartet. Dvořák had come to America in 1892 to head the newly created National Conservatory in New York, and he took his American visit very much to heart, even making sketches for a new anthem for our country while in New York City. President Carter introduced us and the music we were to play. "I told Mr. Begin that he and I could make beautiful music together. The last time we had dinner together, we heard Itzhak Perlman and Pinchas Zukerman, and Mr. Begin told me in advance that they were the greatest." The President laughed, and added, "I chose not to argue with him. Tonight I'm offering Mr. Begin something that *I* call the greatest, and I don't think he'll argue with me." He spoke at some length about the growth of chamber music in America, the new abundance of American quartets, and in some detail about the many ways in which the Guarneri Quartet was unique. And then he said, "A Beethoven recording of theirs is on Voyager 2, launched in August 1977, and tonight it is somewhere between Jupiter and Saturn. After it passes Saturn, it will go into interstellar space . . . Ten million years from now, if it's recovered by some remote galactic body, the Guarneri Quartet will still be making beautiful music, as they will for us tonight." (This part of the President's speech was especially exciting. Only later did we learn that the President and our publicity machine had both erred. NASA actually chose the Budapest Quartet to represent mankind in outer space.)

The President concluded, "They are performing for us just one major piece and that is the Dvořák number. He came here, as you know, in 1892. He was a Bohemian. He went to a little place called Spillville, Iowa, and he located there because there was a fairly substantial Bohemian community. And while he was there he was able to listen to a lot of American performers. One of those performing groups was a group of Iroquois Indians who came and put on a musical drama, and from that Dvořák derived several pieces of music—the most famous of which is the one they will perform tonight. It doesn't have the same rhythm as Indian music, but the style and the mood and the emotion of it will be apparent to all of you."

I listened in amazement. The President of the United States was speaking extemporaneously and knowledgeably about chamber music, about string quartets, about Dvořák, and about us! Who was the last President who knew something about string quartets? Jefferson played the violin. Perhaps he knew some ensemble music of his day. In any case, *our* President most certainly did.

President Carter came to the end of his introduction. "It's a great pleasure to introduce to you the Guarneri String Quartet—I think the finest in the world—playing Dvořák's wonderful piece, the American Quartet." Flanked by Gilbert Stuart's outsized portraits of George and Martha Washington, we played. At the end, the audience gave us a standing ovation, and only moments later we stood before the President and the First Lady. In the instant in which I shook the hand of our President, there was no time to thank him for his loving appreciation of our work, but none of us would ever forget his words and the tone he had set that evening.

The rarefied world that string-quartet players inhabit, a small circle of interest within the barely larger one of classical music as a whole, was being celebrated that night on the highest official level.

Later, in my room at the Hay-Adams Hotel directly across from the White House, I was too excited to fall asleep. Tossing and turning, I imagined a conversation the Presidential couple might be having as they prepared for bed just a few hundred yards away. Rosalynn asks Jimmy what he thought about the Guarneri's performance. The President ponders the question and finally speaks. "They play well, but why was the second theme of the first movement so slow? Dvořák indicated no tempo change." The First Lady yawns. "Oh, well. Just curious. Good night, Jimmy." "Good night, Roz."

~

WHEN A STRING QUARTET plays year after year, it is cause for celebration. When that quartet persists decade after decade, and without any change in personnel, it becomes a phenomenon to muse and wonder over. Having been in existence for more than twenty years, the Guarneri Quartet fell into a blissful routine. Every year brought new repertoire and a different list of concerts, but the mold of the season, of rehearsal, travel, and performance, remained unbroken. If the leaves were beginning to turn, touched by the cool nights of late summer, then it was almost time for us to come together for another season. The regular and repetitive motion of this yearly event lulled me into thinking that we might go on forever.

Indeed, there had never been a reason to think otherwise. Our health, which was generally good, had almost never been a reason to cancel a concert. John had once been out for a week with a pulled tendon, Michael came down once or twice with a high fever, and David had gotten his finger pinched in a door when the wind unexpectedly slammed it shut. But in almost all cases the quartet managed to salvage the concerts by playing duos, trios, or piano quartets instead of the scheduled program. We missed an astonishingly small number of concerts in all these years, and they were almost all weather-related.

But trouble was brewing. Years earlier, I had begun to experience an odd sensation in the little finger of my left hand, which felt weak when I played. In normal times, I had never even thought about fingers. They were my servants, always on call to do my bidding effortlessly, but now I had to plan the use of a finger which only reluctantly came down on the string. My doctor ordered an electrical-conduction study in the hope that it might reveal any abnormality in the nerves that relay information to the muscles of the left hand. The test proved negative. The specialist doing the test told me that my condition would have to worsen before the cause could be detected. And over several years, it did just that. My whole hand was now weaker, requiring me to change finger patterns when the old ones no longer worked. I could still play, but by the end of our twenty-third season, it was an enormous effort. The summer vacation I had looked forward to was filled with a round of doctors and tests. Conduction studies now showed an entrapment of the ulnar nerve at the elbow that probably would continue to worsen.

There was a sliver of good news, however, in this dismal situation. An operation for this surprisingly common condition might release the pressure by moving the nerve to a new location, but for at least two or three months I would be unable to play, and surgical success, although likely, was not guaranteed. By the time I had gotten a second opinion and decided to have the operation, the summer was almost over. One, possibly two months of the coming season would be lost to us. I dreaded phoning the guys, blissfully ensconced in their summer retreats, to tell them the news. In our seemingly secure world, I was presenting Michael, John, and David with a plateful of uncertainties. Yet they said: Take as long as you need, we'll manage.

What a load off my chest to hear those words! But what did "We'll manage" mean? This wasn't a job in which, with one person sick, you simply call the musicians' union for a substitute. Even if an experienced violinist with a compatible musical temperament could be found—no small task—it would take months for the new group to jell. And it wouldn't sound like the Guarneri Quartet. Our audiences had come to expect "our interpretation." The replacement of any member of the quartet would automatically neutralize the web of connections that gave color and personality to the group.

There was also the issue of loyalty. After so much time spent together, we had become irreplaceable to each other. Some years earlier, Alexander Schneider insisted impulsively on taking John's place for one movement of a composition we played at a benefit concert in New York City. It was all in fun, the audience undoubtedly loved it, and John himself seemed genuinely amused. But I felt uncomfortable: for those few moments, the invisible bonds that held us together were broken and four individual musicians were playing in place of the Guarneri Quartet. When the violist of the Amadeus Quartet, Peter Schidlof, died, the remaining members were asked whether they were going to continue as a group. The Amadeus had been together in their original configuration for thirty-nine years, a record that is unlikely to be broken any time soon. Their answer was that it was impossible to continue. There was nothing written for two violins and cello.

The quartet aside, I was facing a personal crisis. What if the operation failed and I was left unable to play the violin?

It had happened to other musicians and they had gone on, but at what personal cost? At least there was another possible life in music for me to consider: I could expand the teaching that had been part of my professional life since the quartet's beginning. I had also written a couple of articles for music publications and even conducted the Curtis Institute of Music orchestra in concert. These might be the seeds of future activity. But it was hard for me to dwell on "what if" situations. At the core, I was a violinist, a performing musician, and to stop playing would be tantamount to wrenching my beating heart from my body. In a long, probing conversation with my old friend Shmuel Ashkenasi, I discussed the relationship a musician has with his instrument. Shmuel reflected, "If you think you're nothing without the violin, then you're nothing with the violin." I could never forget this remark. But how could you separate a musician's personal identity from his instrument? It wasn't a career choice I had made as an adult. I had started playing the violin at the age of six. It was imprinted on every cell of my being like a genetic code.

I had more immediate concerns, however. A string quartet is like Siamese quadruplets as far as concerts are concerned. When Michael had a high fever, in effect so did I. When David pinched his finger, we all felt it. And now that I had hand problems, so did the rest of the quartet. A short-term plan was devised: until I was out of the woods, Michael, John, and David would play concerts without me but with a pianist. Two programs of string trios and piano quartets were offered to all the presenters who had booked us as a string quartet. A surprising number accepted. Steven De Groote and Seymour Lipkin were the pianists for two separate tours.

Through all my pre-operation procedures, I had been in touch regularly with the guys. They had their own burdens to shoulder because of my disability—learning two difficult programs in a hurry, for one—but at no point did they communicate to me the stress of their work or the worries they might have about their own futures. They were shielding me from that world so that I could better deal with the surgery to come.

The morning of the operation, Dorothea stood by me as I was shifted onto the gurney to be taken to the operating room for what surgeons call their controlled mayhem. A knife was about to cut through the flesh-and-muscle tissue with which I had played the violin all my life. It was not a pleasant thought. The phone by my bed rang and the attendant who was about to push off with his patient looked up questioningly. On an impulse I reached over and picked up the phone. It was Isaac Stern. He had heard about the operation and had somehow tracked me down to wish me good luck. I was overwhelmed. Isaac, who is justly revered as a great musician, violinist, and tireless crusader in the cause of music and young musicians in this country, has become the unofficial spokesperson for music in America. Lying on my back in a hospital gown and with a name tag on my wrist, I held the phone with the hand and arm about to have mayhem committed on it. Isaac's message was a personal one, from his heart to mine, one musician reaching out to another in need—but I had the feeling that he was also speaking for the whole musical community when he wished me well.

I survived the operation and began the slow healing process. The cast finally came off. I was not allowed to play the violin yet, but occasionally, while doing basic muscle exercises, I would eye the instrument case in the corner of the room. It was not easy to understand my relationship to this piece of wood with four strings. In one sense, I was happy to be rid of it. The violin is such a jealous mistress: one day without practicing and the fingers become fuzzy and unsteady. The violin is so difficult that sometimes I felt I was not playing it but at war with it. With my arm healing, I didn't have to play, *couldn't* play the violin. What a relief!

But I missed it. I missed that sound—as agile as quicksilver, as sweetly piercing as Cupid's arrow—and I missed the violin itself, its feel, its lightness, the pressure of the bow hard on the string and right up close to the bridge when I drew a sound that almost roared from the G string, or the feel of it under my fingers when I stroked it with the delicacy needed to spin a golden thread from its upper registers. When I finally opened the case five weeks after the operation and looked at my violin, it lay mute as always, looking back up at me, but the silence felt different. There would have to be a new understanding between us. I would have to start as a beginner again, and my violin, spoiled on a diet of masterpieces from the solo and chamber-music repertoire, would be obliged to put up with the most basic sounds for a while.

As I picked up the violin and bow, they were totally familiar yet, parodoxically, limp in my hands. Perhaps these two inanimate objects were trying to tell me something: You walk out on us, without a word, and two months later expect to start up this relationship where you left off? Not so fast! The first few notes surprised me. Although my fingers were rubbery and weak, the neural and muscular connections were still in place. I could play the violin.

The only other time I had been away from the violin for so long was during my two months of basic training for military service. The cheap violin I had sent to the base when I was finally allowed to practice caused a stir when it arrived. It had been insured for one thousand dollars, a pittance for a violin, but probably the most expensive item ever to have been sent to a soldier in Fort Knox up to that time. I heard over the intercom: Steinhardt to base headquarters, on the double. Flinty, no-nonsense Sergeant Stevens was waiting for me when I arrived.

SERGEANT STEVENS: Steinhardt, what the hell is in that package that's worth a thousand bucks?

PRIVATE STEINHARDT: A violin, sergeant.

SERGEANT STEVENS: (*long low whistle*) A thousand bucks for a violin. Wow. Is it a Stradimawhoosis?

PRIVATE STEINHARDT: No, Sergeant, it's not.

Stevens leaned back in his chair and placed his booted feet conspicuously on the desk in front of him. Then his usually dour face turned mischievous.

SERGEANT STEVENS: You want to take that fiddle outta here, Steinhardt, you play me "Flight of the Bumble Bee."

PRIVATE STEINHARDT: I can't do that, sergeant. It's got a million notes and I haven't played in two months.

SERGEANT STEVENS: Look, no ticket, no laundry. Either you play or the fiddle is mine. You can't cut the "Bumble Bee," then at least play me "Fascination."

"Fascination" was a tune that had been featured in a recent popular film. Even I knew it, but would my fingers, unaccustomed to any motion in basic training other than firing, dismantling, and cleaning an M1 rifle? From the dreamy look on Stevens' face, I must have played the lilting waltz well enough, for at its finish he gave me the green light to leave with my violin.

"You sure know how to play that thing, Steinhardt." To this day, I have received no higher compliment.

It was one thing to regain instrumental muscle tone when I was a healthy young guy in my twenties, but recovering the ability to play some thirty years later, using the very arm that was healing from surgery, was a long and uncomfortable process. As bad luck would have it, the first operation was unsuccessful and had to be redone. Bertrand Jacobs, a psychiatrist and amateur violinist, generously applied his two fields of expertise to help me sift through a new round of doctors before the second operation. I am forever grateful to him. His efforts eventually led me to Dr. Michael Charness, a neurologist who has dealt with hundreds of musicians in trouble, and who also has a foot in each of the connected worlds of medicine and music: he is a fine amateur pianist. Charness masterminded the second operation and spent countless hours overseeing my recovery. His was an expenditure of time and expert care that is almost unknown in these days of cost cutting and patients as profit units. Michael has my heartfelt thanks, along with those of the hundreds of other musicians he has advised and treated.

While I sat at home nursing my wounds, I received a regular paycheck from the quartet. No disability-insurance policy was involved. We had decided long ago to split all expenses and all fees in the event of illness, and our guest pianists graciously went along. So I paid a fifth of all travel expenses and collected a fifth of our fees. The Guarneri Quartet was not a Communist organization or a welfare state, but simply four devoted people—a family, in effect, taking care of each other. During two separate stretches in the working year, Michael, David, and John stoically and without complaining played our concerts without me. Later, when I tried to thank them, the words came out awkwardly. They had done far too much for mere words.

It was difficult to get back into shape. The muscles in my hand and arm regained their strength very slowly after the pain and tenderness subsided. The violin looks as if only a feather is needed to coax a sound from it, but in truth it requires substantial muscle, and the first-violin repertoire presents every possible difficulty a violinist can imagine. But there was a way for me to make the return to playing easier. John and I began occasionally to switch parts, he playing first, I playing second. In a true republic of equals, this was an instinctive and natural move, and we had never been a group in which first and second meant better and worse. Indeed, there was a bonus to the switch: what a pleasure for us both to be wearing new musical hats.

As I stood bowing with my colleagues at the end of the concert in South Mountain, Massachusetts, that was our first performance after my second (this time successful) operation, tears welled up in my eyes. I was finally a musician again, and we were still the Guarneri String Quartet.

⌒

WHEN THE GUARNERI Quartet became twenty-five years old, we rejoiced. It was no longer possible to cultivate the illusion that we would go on forever. But the number 25, the silver anniversary, is auspicious, and I dare wager that a greater percentage of married couples reach the mark than do string quartets. It was an occasion to celebrate. Harry Beall, still our manager after all these years, arranged a meeting with one of the most successful and well-known public-relations agents in music. We had never bothered much with PR; our one year dabbling in it had been unproductive. The agent was unimpressed with our silver anniversary as a marketing tool. "Do you men fight a lot? Has there been some kind of juicy controversy? Have you commissioned some wild or spectacular composition? These are the things I can get into the media. Twenty-five years together? It's just an okay kind of story." We looked at one another, four graying, balding men. Perhaps he was right. We were not the stuff for a brilliant marquee, gossip tabloid, or outdoor arena.

Just how important was our work, and for whom? The Guarneri Quartet trudged onstage a hundred times a year and played music of the gods for a passionate and intensely involved audience. Not much to write about there, but good enough to keep playing.

Diary. Tuesday, March 4, 1997. It happens again in tonight's open rehearsal at the University of Maryland. For at least twenty minutes, we argue about a dot. This particular dot occurs over the second of two tied notes in Alban Berg's Quartet, Opus 3. We actually pass the dot and go on to the next passage when, almost as an afterthought, I mention to Michael that the dotted figure sounds clipped.

MICHAEL: *There is a dot over the note, which means it should be shorter.*

DAVID: *But it sounds better without the dot. I try to sustain the same figure when I play it just before you.*

MICHAEL: *Berg wrote the dot and he must have meant something by it. Why not cavalierly get rid of every composer's direction that doesn't please you?*

JOHN: *Michael, you follow David, and if he plays without a dot, then you must do the same. There has to be some consistency.*

MICHAEL: *I happen to think the passage is characterless without the dot.*

The audience sits mutely by while the four of us discuss (sometimes heatedly) the pros and cons of a little black speck on the music, as if the fate of the world rests on its outcome. In the final vote, the dot stays in but in a longer, more singing manner. We have put the matter to rest, but only until the next Berg performance, when the ominous specter of a dot will again loom over the proceedings.

11

"Death and the Maiden"

FOR THE LONGEST time, I harbored the illusion that the Guarneri Quartet was still young. Even when the quartet was twenty years old and I was forty-seven, I continued to think of us as Young Turks swashbuckling our way across the concert circuit. As human failings go, the refusal to believe you are getting older is commonplace, if not quite admirable. What middle-aged woman doesn't like to imagine that her skin is still alabaster, and her male counterpart is convinced he can run a mile in a respectable time, as he did in the good old days. Certainly, I rationalized, the audience was too far away to see the touches of gray hair and the crow's feet around the eyes. But the most persuasive reason for our feeling young was that we were behaving as if we were—rehearsing seriously, playing a hundred concerts a year, continuing to make records.

Signs of advancing age became unavoidable, however.

Harry Beall, with us from the cradle of our career, finally retired. Harry, who had booked the concerts, negotiated the fees, advised us on countless details of quartet policy, was the indispensable fifth member of our four-man group. If he could leave, then nothing was forever. The ten of us, Harry, John, Michael, David, and I, together with our wives Mary, Nancy, Jani, Janet, and Dorothea, gathered for a farewell dinner at an Italian restaurant on the Upper West Side of Manhattan. The last time we had all been together like this was probably in the van driving to the White House several years earlier. On the surface, the meal was upbeat, with jokes and recollections of past experiences, but the departure of Harry, a man with a big heart and a sense for the concert business, was a sad event for us. Our new management, Herbert Barrett, and our new personal manager, Nancy Wellman, looked very promising, but we would miss Harry. There was an unsettling undercurrent to the round of toasts for Harry and Mary, and their new life in retirement. With Harry's departure, an invisible but protective membrane surrounding the quartet had just burst.

There were other, smaller but no less significant signs of age. After a recent concert, a young, attractive woman looked brightly into my eyes and confessed that her mother used to have a crush on me. And in Berlin's Kempinski Hotel a portly man recognized us as we checked in. "You're the Guarneri Quartet, aren't you? I knew you thirty-five pounds ago."

The aging process has many numbers attached to it other than years. Riding from the airport to the city, someone in the group asks how many times we have played there before. If "there" is Ann Arbor, Michigan; Tampa, Florida; Albuquerque, New Mexico; Palo Alto, California; or New York's Rockefeller University, the answer is probably thirty or forty times. Across town from the Rockefeller at Lincoln Center's

Alice Tully Hall, the number hovers around one hundred, and in Grace Rainey Rogers Auditorium at the Metropolitan Museum of Art, we have played easily close to two hundred concerts.

On a recent tour through Europe, I bumped into Michael in the hotel lobby. He waved a fax at me that had just arrived from Sonia Simmenauer, our European manager, who wanted to know if we were willing to play the Brahms Piano Quintet with Elisabeth Leonskaja in Israel next May. Of course we were. It is a magnificent quintet and she is a great pianist. I wondered out loud, "How many pianists has the Guarneri Quartet played with in thirty-three years?" Creasing his brow, Michael pondered the question. "I would have to say fifty." I objected. "That's impossible. You're prone to exaggeration, Michael. No more than thirty pianists."

We headed for breakfast. David was already there, reading a newspaper over a cup of coffee. I asked him the p question. He put down his paper, intrigued. "We would have to start with Rudolf Serkin and Arthur Rubinstein. And Mieczyslaw Horszowski, Richard Goode, Leon Fleisher, and Daniel Barenboim," he added. Michael could hardly contain himself, but I begged him to wait with his own list until I fished out a pencil and a piece of paper. "All right, go!" He began to blurt out names as they came to him and we continued to interrupt with our own. There was no rhyme or reason to the order: Rudolf Firkusny, Peter Serkin, András Schiff, Mitchell Andrews, Alicia de Larrocha, Jorge Bolet, William Doppmann, Victor Steinhardt, Cecile Licad, Lee Luvisi, Murray Perahia, Lilian Kallir, Claude Frank, Christian Zacharias, Elisabeth Leonskaja, Patricia Parr, David Burge, Horacio Gutiérrez. "I've counted twenty-four and the end isn't anywhere in sight," I volunteered.

"Gary Graffman," Michael announced triumphantly. "How could we forget him?"

"Well, you also forgot Emanuel Ax, Garrick Ohlsson, Philippe Entremont, John Browning, Joseph Kalichstein, Menahem Pressler, Misha Dichter, Seymour Lipkin, Eugene Istomin, Ruth Laredo, Malcom Bilson, and Anton Kuerti," David countered.

"That makes thirty-seven," I announced. More stream of consciousness followed. Lydia Artymiw, Cynthia Raim, Mikail Rudy, André-Michel Schub, Anne-Marie McDermott, Steven De Groote, Bradford Gowen, Ena Bronstein, Reiko Aizawa, Vincent Persichetti, Santiago Rodriguez, Bernice Silk, Ward Davenny, Arthur Loesser, David Golub, and Jean-Bernard Pommier.

"Michael, I owe you an apology," I said sheepishly, completely swept up in our numbers game. "I count fifty-three pianists and there are certainly more."

David had another line of thought. "What about Russian-speaking pianists?" We came up with Nikita Magaloff, Vladimir Feltsman, Yefim Bronfman, and Bella Davidovich.

That night, before the concert, I confronted John in his dressing room with my list. He was amused. "Do you have Gaby Casadesus, Jean Casadesus, Alexis Weissenberg, Stephanie Brown, Adolph Baller, Leonard Shure, and Malcolm Frager on your list?" I counted again. Sixty-four.

We were still caught up in the list while we waited in the wings for the second half of the concert to begin. Another name came to me as I walked onstage, and between movements of "Death and the Maiden" I saw that Michael had a faraway look in his eyes. The concert finished. We bowed and walked into the wings. "Tamás Vásáry!" Michael cried. "Grant Johannesen," I counterpunched. Sixty-six pianists, sixty-six collaborations, sixty-six performances. I have my suspicions that the list is not yet complete.

As time passes, the Guarneri Quartet carries the increasingly heavy baggage of memory—memories of concerts, people, adventures and misadventures. These days, any detail of our life is a trigger for a flood of recollections. Bad weather at an airport: "Remember when we made that scary landing in Vienna during a snowstorm?" A broken string onstage will get Michael talking about the time his viola's tailpiece collapsed during a performance in Los Angeles and Hans Weisshaar, a well-known rare-instrument dealer and repairman, stood up in the audience and announced, "I can repair the viola and the concert will go on if you give me thirty minutes." And a traffic jam will remind us of Naples, Italy, and the beautiful baroque theater in which a surreal incident occurred. As we arose to accept the applause after finishing Berg's First Quartet, the stage doors burst open and two men dressed bizarrely in strange uniforms and massive boots rushed to the front of the stage with a great deal of noise, brushing us aside, and began hollering at the audience in Italian. My heart was beating wildly and I felt my knees wobble. Were these mental patients who had just escaped from an insane asylum? The public, far from being frightened, as we were by this inexplicable outburst, regarded the two madmen coolly, almost sullenly, as their frenzied oration played itself out. The two left as they had come and we wandered, shaken, off the stage. The organizer then told us what had happened: a fire had broken out in a house nearby and the fire trucks' access was blocked by someone parked illegally behind the theater. The two wild men were firemen in traditional Neapolitan uniform who hoped the culprit was in the audience and might identify himself and remove his car. "Well?" we asked the manager eagerly. "Oh, don't worry about it," he said with a wave of a hand. "The house burned down." Some time later, Michael told the story to an Italian musician of our acquaintance. "Yes, yes, I know the story. By the way, the theater burned down too, a year later." We have enough stories to pass around for another thirty-three years. Suddenly, although not that suddenly, we have gone from being the young kids on the block to the wise old men—"a piece of stubborn antiquity," to borrow Charles Lamb's phrase.

Although the Guarneri Quartet has undoubtedly more years behind it than ahead, we seem to be comfortable wearing the mantle of our age. Sooner or later, we will step aside for the next generation of string quartets, but if there is any sense of loss when that happens, it will be tempered by the knowledge that those younger groups will have a large component of musicians we have taught or influenced indirectly through performances and recordings.

We teach in various combinations at the Curtis Institute of Music, the University of Maryland, Rutgers University, and the Manhattan School of Music. And we teach with the perspective that our chamber-music career has given us. It is a goal for every musician to hear the whole of which he is a part, but it is impossible to play quartets while focusing exclusively on your own voice. If a student who must play the first half of a two-measure ritard slows down too much, what is his poor friend to do who follows with the second half? We try to open their eyes to a broader view of music. Felix Kuhner, second violinist of the renowned Kolisch String Quartet, which always performed by memory, was once asked how he could play their vast repertoire by heart. His answer: "I play the part that I don't hear." The rest of us, professionals and students who play with music on the stands, must also hear all four voices as we play our assigned one.

We ask the same profoundly basic questions of our students that we ask of ourselves: What does the music have to say, and how will we say it? How should a note be fashioned? What is its place in a phrase? And the phrase's function in the context of an entire work? As if this weren't hard enough, how do you teach a young group to make these decisions in committee? for that is what a string quartet is. But now that we are gradually aging and ripening into elder statesmen, we can offer ourselves as a bridge connecting different ways of thinking about music, and even different centuries. Our teachers and mentors—Efrem Zimbalist, Ivan Galamian, Josef Szigeti, Diran Alexanian, Pablo Casals, Rudolf Serkin, Arthur Rubinstein, and Alexander Schneider—were all born in or espoused the humanity of the nineteenth century. Their playing was personal, detailed, instantly recognizable. But styles of performance change as inevitably as hemlines. Our students, raised in a late-twentieth-century world of smooth surfaces, clean lines, and emotions under wraps, listen to the connections we make with the nineteenth century and our world of the twentieth. I hope that the wealth of interpretations available in performance and on recording doesn't confuse and paralyze young musicians into safe but sterile playing. I often find it difficult to identify string players these days when listening to them on the radio. This could not be said fifty years ago when the reigning performers were cellists like Casals and Gregor Piatigorsky, the violist William Primrose, and violinists like Kreisler, Heifetz, Szigeti, Mischa Elman, Yehudi Menuhin, and the young Isaac Stern. A handful of notes from any one of them and the cat was out of the bag—playing as certifiably unique as their voices, their strides, their fingerprints. Perhaps young musicians are at odds with our more emotional approach to music, but they will listen to us, choose from the array of ideas offered them, and slowly evolve into musicians for the twenty-first century.

In my own formative years, encounters with three musicians from older generations—Isaac Stern, Pablo Casals, and Arthur Loesser—illuminated my journey. Curiously, all three experiences involved the music of Johann Sebastian Bach, and although Bach wrote nothing for the string quartet, his music establishes a valuable internal compass for one's guidance in all of music-making, including quartets.

When I was a student at Meadowmount, Isaac Stern came to give a class on Bach's celebrated Chaconne. To begin with, Stern took the Chaconne apart the way a mechanic would disassemble a gas engine. He showed us how the ever-present "ground bass" served as a basis for a series of variations, the bass's different guises, how Bach grouped variations together in a subplot to the overall text, and how at the end of one variation he sometimes tipped his hand to give us a preview of what the next variation had in store. When the analysis came to an end, Stern put all the pieces back together. He played the Chaconne stunningly, weaving coherence and feeling into a sublime artistic whole: the textbook and the concert hall had been seamlessly joined.

Several summers later, in a Marlboro master class, I played Bach's G minor Solo Sonata for Pablo Casals. When I finished the first movement, Casals held up his hand for silence. "Very well played," he said after a moment's thought. "But let me tell you a story. Alfred Cortot, Jacques Thibaud, and I were on tour and had just finished a trio concert in Budapest. We were hungry and asked our manager to recommend a good restaurant. He told us that the greatest gypsy violinist of the era was playing in a restaurant across town. Of course, that is where we went. When we entered the restaurant, the gypsy recognized us and immediately ordered his band to stop. In our honor, he played before our table the very same Bach adagio that you have just played. It was the most fiery, the freest Bach I have ever heard. Also the best. This gypsy had none of our fears and inhibitions about what to do or not do in Bach. He played uncensored, from the heart; and that is what I encourage you to do—put aside convention and play as I believe Bach himself played, with great freedom."

The last of my Bach encounters was with the pianist and scholar Arthur Loesser. Loesser, the brother of the Broadway musical composer Frank Loesser, had a broad-ranging intellect coupled with a playful curiosity. Still insecure about my own interpretation of Bach, I arranged to play the D minor Partita for him in his home. The slight, elderly Loesser listened at his piano while I played, and when I finished he arose from his piano bench. "Do you know how to dance the movements of this partita, Arnold?" I certainly did not. "It might help you to understand each movement's character if you did. Let me demonstrate." Looking quite frail and with his glasses hanging from a string around his neck, Loesser gracefully danced the D minor Partita for me in his living room; the allemande, the courante, the sarabande, the gigue, and finally the lusty chaconne. The old dance forms came to life.

Isaac Stern, Pablo Casals, and Arthur Loesser wanted to pass on vital elements in the music they loved, elements that would enable a young performer coming of age to play with the structural vision of an architect, the abandon of a free spirit, and the grace of a dancer. I try to hand these elements on to my own students.

♫

ALTHOUGH TEACHING IS important, the heart of our career remains our performances as a string quartet, but with our average age already in the sixties, how long can we continue? Three possibilities occur to me: until no one hires us anymore, until the audience begins throwing yesterday's fruit at us, or until we decide of our own volition to retire. Herbert Barrett and Nancy Wellman have been skillful in getting us all the concerts we want; and our audience, many of whom have followed our career since the beginning, still clap, still ask for encores, and still make us feel appreciated. Hanging up the horsehair and catgut is a complex business for a string quartet. Those of us who play instruments tucked under our chins must do so with hand and arm positions that become more difficult with age; and violinists, violists, and cellists alike must execute precise, exact motions at considerable speed. String players are especially vulnerable to aging. As the hands become less steady, control of the bow and intonation become more difficult. Unlike pianists, who often play into their eighties (Serkin, Arrau, Kempff, and Richter), nineties (Rubinstein), and even hundreds (Horszowski), the elderly performing string player is a rare phenomenon. The cellist Pablo Casals, who played into his nineties, was a remarkable exception, as was the violinist Nathan Milstein, still concertizing in his early eighties. A newspaper reporter who was interviewing Milstein was so taken by his age that she would not leave the subject alone. Milstein lost his patience: "Look, it's not my fault I'm eighty-one."

A performer is part artist, part athlete. As I have gathered the strength of my musical convictions and focused and distilled whatever creative spark I might possess, my body has slowly but inexorably been losing its resilience. Fingers that were so effortlessly nimble in my youth now have to be coaxed a little to do their job, and muscles show their displeasure more actively when an extra hour is added to a rehearsal. Instead of despairing, I choose to believe that this inevitable deterioration will take decades rather than years. If I can no longer play the violin when I'm ninety-six, then so be it, but for the moment I believe I am getting smarter as I get weaker. If a passage doesn't come off satisfactorily, I look for creative solutions—an alternate way of practicing, a new fingering, a different part of the bow. If my muscles ache, I pace myself a little more slowly. Youthful impatience would have limited these variations earlier. The building that is my body will eventually collapse, but I can successfully patch the small fissures that now and then appear.

All four members of our quartet undoubtedly operate under the same laws of nature, but we have never called an emergency meeting accompanied by our gerontologists to discuss our aging bodies and what to do about them. Changes in the body are often so slow that adjustments are instinctive. As card-carrying pragmatists, we do whatever is necessary to play our best.

But when an aging quartet does play its best, is that good enough? We would not like to be taunted with, "Old quartets never die, they just play that way." At the age of seventy-one, Franz Joseph Haydn, the father of the string quartet, could go on no longer. He placed at the end of his last and incomplete quartet the inscription: "All my strength is gone. I am old and weak." Sooner or later, our music will cease, but for the moment, the forces of age and wisdom seem to be at a standoff. The vibratos have become a little slower, tempos sometimes more reflective, and bringing a new work in the repertoire to performance level takes us longer, but I hope that at today's concert our playing has more understanding and nuance than at yesterday's. Each performance being the sum total of all others means that a listener now hears the Guarneri Quartet playing Schubert's "Death and the Maiden" in the ripeness and detail that we have developed over the two hundred performances that preceded this one. As matters now stand, we are aged but not cured.

In June 1996, we recorded "Death and the Maiden" (for Arabesque Records). Adam Abeshouse was both engineer and producer. It was the second time we had recorded the work, some twenty years after the first (for RCA Records).

And for the next season we again chose "Death and the Maiden" for one of our three touring programs. In the hands of a quartet in the autumn of its professional life, how much might the Schubert still evolve over the course of a season? A pertinent question, but not one I planned to dwell on during our upcoming summer vacation.

Yet the Schubert did gently intrude on a late-summer afternoon, with the arrival in the mail of the collected works of the eighteenth-century German writer Matthias Claudius. It had been sent by an acquaintance in response to my curiosity about a lovely children's song, "Der Mond ist Aufgegangen" ("The Moon Has Risen"), that my German-born wife, Dorothea, had sung to our children when they were young, the lyrics of which were written by Claudius. After reading the seven verses of the poem, I thumbed idly through the volume, and my eyes fell upon "Der Tod und das Mädchen." I had completely forgotten that Claudius wrote the poem that inspired Schubert's song in 1817 and, in turn, the D minor String Quartet in 1824. The terrified young woman's entreaty to Death and Death's reply cast a chill on that carefree summer day:

> The Maiden:
> Pass me by, o pass me by,
> Go, wild skeleton!
> I am still young: go, dear one,
> And touch me not!
>
> Death:
> Give me your hand, o fair and tender form!
> I am your friend; I do not come to punish.
> Be of good cheer! I am not wild,
> You shall sleep softly in my arms.

What had drawn the twenty-year-old Schubert to the subjects of this poem? Or to that of Goethe's great poem "Erl-könig," in which a child's life is taken by the Erl-king even as the father holds his son helplessly in his arms? Perhaps it was simply part of his general attitude toward life as well as death. Schubert is reputed to have asked, "Do you know any *really* cheerful music? I do not know any." It was tempting to read into this young man's morbid interests a premonition of the struggle he himself was to have with death only a few years later.

I looked at Schubert's song "Death and the Maiden," which differs strikingly from its counterpart in the quartet. It is concise and almost plain in comparison with the more developed, expanded version he used as a theme and five variations in the quartet's second movement. Between the earlier song and the later work that evolved from it, Schubert had contracted syphilis, which would cut his life short and change the scope and nature of his creative output. In a letter to his friend the painter Leopold Kupelwieser on March 31, 1824, he wrote, "In a word, I feel myself to be the most unhappy and wretched creature in the world. Imagine a man whose health will never be right again, and who in sheer despair over this ever makes things worse and worse, instead of better and better; imagine a man, I say, whose most brilliant hopes have perished, to whom the felicity of love and friendship have nothing to offer but love and pain."

Schubert learned only months before he composed "Death and the Maiden" that he had contracted the disease. There is no longer room for speculation. Death is front and center in every movement, each in a minor key, each grappling with the forces that were eventually to snuff out his life: the first movement's fearful opening chords announcing its verdict of doom, the dirge-like second movement in which Death speaks to the young woman, the manic and menacing scherzo of the third movement, and the fourth movement's Tarantella of Death.

In the heat of that lazy day laden with the sounds of insects and of wind gently rustling through the leaves, I had violated one of the Guarneri Quartet's unwritten commandments: Thou shalt have nothing to do with string quartets during summer vacation. Instead of gardening or throwing a Frisbee on the front lawn, I had spent time thinking about the evolution of a poem into a song and a song into a quartet—a quartet that we weren't going to play for another month. Perhaps John, David, and Michael would forgive my transgression when we gathered for the first concert of the season on September 15. At that South Mountain concert in the Berkshires, "Death and the Maiden" was to end the program.

There was really nothing for the guys to forgive, and there was nothing to talk about. What possible bearing could my unstructured musings on the Dead Maid have on our performance of the work, anyway? They would have as dubious an effect as those art-appreciation classes given by museums for viewers bent on understanding the Mona Lisa. If there is a key to the Schubert, it is embedded in the genetic code of every note and phrase and of the work's overarching structure, waiting passively on the printed page for performers and listeners to unlock with the sensibilities each has at hand.

But reading about "Death and the Maiden" had to alter one's perceptions somehow. Knowing that Mozart was writing the Requiem for himself changes forever how you listen to the first bars of the Lachrymae (the last notes from his pen), and once you are aware that the high E ringing in Smetana's ear was a manifestation of his terminal illness, the appearance of that pitch in the waning moments of his first string quartet has to pierce the heart. And the Schubert! Reading his letter to Kupelwieser and the grim words of solace proffered to the young maiden etched the quartet ever more clearly on the senses.

·∾·

THIS VACATION, LIKE all others, has slipped by too quickly, and the Guarneri Quartet now stands backstage, relaxed, somewhat tanned, ready to play the first concert of its new season. The four of us, four beings separated by a world of biological and experiential differences, are again ready to throw the creative life lines from one to another that will make this performance possible. I have noticed that married couples after a certain amount of time together pick up each other's traits—a laugh, a turn of phrase, a gesture. But there is no evidence that I am beginning to sound like John, he like Michael, or Michael like David. Even after all these years, each of us probably harbors a secret conviction: the right way is my way! The group can vote on musical issues all it wants, but the core of our personality as a quartet still comes from the inside out. That is one of the unnerving things about playing in a quartet that does not abate with the years—you are you, they are they, and the ability to come together successfully remains tenuous.

The program ends with "Death and the Maiden." Our interpretation has moved a degree or two from the performances we gave last season. Some tempos are brisker and yet there seems to be more spaciousness in the phrasing. If this is a result of vacation, perhaps we should do without rehearsals entirely. Ensemble and intonation are also tighter. Could it be that the intense and withering scrutiny of our recording sessions last June remained with us over the summer?

The fruit of that recording session is waiting for us when we return to New York City. I listen to it, and then I pull our first recording off the shelf, curious to hear the effect of twenty years of playing on our interpretation. Glancing at the timing of each, I become momentarily confused. The lengths of the first and last movements of both recordings are exactly the same, down to the second, 11:26 and 8:35, and the inner movements differ only by a total of 21 seconds. The unsettling suspicion enters my head that we have simply stood still while playing the piece dozens of times in the intervening years. Listening to the first recording, I am somewhat reassured—we sound like the Guarneri Quartet I know and occasionally love—but this older rendition is nonetheless vaguely dissatisfying. Like a face that is too young and unweathered to have acquired significant character, our first "Death and the Maiden" lacks the conviction, coherence, and overview that age has brought, in my opinion, to the second recording. Now the musical phrases are more sharply defined, and above all, I feel the urgency and heart of the theme: time has applied some measure of patina and understanding to our playing.

As the season progresses, our performances of Schubert's "Death and the Maiden" continue to evolve. From one night to another there are, inevitably, impulsive little alterations in phrasing that can't be planned or known beforehand. And glacial changes arching over longer periods of time take place that sometimes become apparent only after many performances. After South Mountain, the Guarneri Quartet has nineteen more performances of "Death and the Maiden"—in Pittsburgh, Pennsylvania; Cleveland, Ohio; New Albany, Indiana; Miami, Florida; Philadelphia, Pennsylvania; West Palm Beach, Florida; Bologna and Rome, Italy; Tübingen and Rolandseck, Germany; Alicante, Spain; Tully Hall, People's Symphony Concerts, and Rockefeller University, New York City; Prague, Czech Republic; Kempen, Austria; Ludwigsburg, Germany; Jerusalem, Israel; and Albuquerque, New Mexico.

Before the concert in Pittsburgh, Michael comes into my dressing room. "I just listened to our new recording. Don't you think the middle of the third movement sounds too slow, too unrelated to the rest?" I disagree, but as we perform the movement that evening, I realize Michael has a point. We may be breaking the continuity between the movement's outer and middle sections by a too sudden change of tempo. At our next Schubert performance, in Cleveland, the third movement's differences of tempo realign themselves more convincingly.

Fine-tuning of the Schubert continues throughout the season, but before the concert in Jerusalem on June 4, 1997, we call a "dry" rehearsal for the work. When we have gathered in one of our dressing rooms, Michael suggests that the *entire* third movement be played more slowly. With repetition, the tempo has gradually become somewhat breathless and out of control. We all agree. John suggests that we also play the last movement slower, so that there is more of a contrast with the final coda, in its headlong rush to the end. Again, everyone agrees. The Schubert that finishes our program tonight in Crown Center is appreciably better with these changes. Is it encouraging that after so many performances we are still improving, or is it depressing that we have played for so long without hearing something so obvious as the right tempi? Perhaps today's tempo is possible only because it is an outgrowth of every single one that preceded it.

In Albuquerque on June 13, we play "Death and the Maiden" for the last time this season. I feel an extra heaviness in the air before the performance. Perhaps it is the heaviness of our age, the perception of time itself diminishing and pressing in on us. How many more seasons does the Guarneri Quartet have ahead; how many more performances of this glorious music? Since we reschedule any given work only every few years, this performance in Woodward Hall may very well be our last "Death and the Maiden" ever.

We enter stage left, we bow, we take our seats, and we assume our expected roles in the drama that will unfold in the next forty minutes. Last performance? At this point it matters not. Several hundred people in the hall are awaiting the Schubert, and so for this moment there is no last performance, only the one before us. We begin—one long powerful chord followed by four short, hammered strokes. Judgment Day has arrived. The opening movement runs its dark and troubled course, finally yielding to the centerpiece of this tragedy, the second movement, "Death and the Maiden" itself.

Give a good lead, Arnold—distinct but soft—so that we can start together and set the stage for Death's words to the Maiden:

> Give me your hand, o fair and tender form!
> I am your friend; I do not come to punish.

In four-part harmony we begin the solemn theme softly. Decent blend. Together. Good. John and Michael now have the moving voices. Watch John's fingers. Eat them, as Sascha Schneider once advised us. We repeat the first eight bars. Not the same, but not too different, either! David's bow floats more this time. Nice. Match that sound. We move into the theme's second part, cautiously measuring our crescendo from pianissimo to forte together. A diminished chord brings us for the first time into a major key. It must be so soft, so gentle. Again I hear Death's words:

> Be of good cheer! I am not wild,
> You shall sleep softly in my arms.

Repeat. We feel each other's rising volume. The crescendo is fiercer, our vibratos more intense, and now for the final bars in E flat major, we recede—barely audible. Softer than usual. John waits an instant extra for the aura of the theme's end to dissipate before he leads the beginning of the first variation. He has the melody, in triplets, as I weave an obbligato a register above him, seeded with pairs of sixteenth notes. They tug, clutch, plead. It is the Maiden speaking:

> Pass me by, o pass me by,
> Go, wild skeleton!

More bow, less sound on the sixteenth notes. It is the heart speaking, not the violin notes. We take courage in the variation's second half, roaring to a forte and then subsiding, but my last notes are too free. John has to stand on his head to follow me. Sorry, John. Thanks, John. The cello variation is upon us. Don't follow David's lead, instead watch his third finger, which lifts up for an instant before he puts it down to play. Imagine that! We're with him. No time for self-congratulations. David is now the rhapsodic soloist, we the little wheels and springs of a fine watch that must be perfectly timed to him. Tonight David ignores our plight and goes on a flight of fancy. How are we supposed to follow him and play together at the same time? David's free flight is impressive and we somehow manage to hang on, but it scares me every time. The four horsemen (Death's henchmen?) gather for the "rider" variation. John leads the eighth- and two sixteenth-note pattern that is our gallop across the heavens. We dig roughly into the strings. These riders are up to no good. Sweat is streaming down Michael's red face, and he is bobbing and weaving excitedly. Is his horse giving him more trouble than ours? Michael and John's gait drops quietly to piano, muffled by winsome voices from David and me:

> I am still young: go, dear one,
> And touch me not!

The music bursts suddenly into fortissimo at the second half of the variation. David and I trade off quarter notes slurred into chords. We are angry gods hurling thunderbolts across the sky at one another. But David's thunderbolts are different every night, and since he throws first, I must be prepared for anything. Tonight he sweeps the chord with a little extra length. When David sweeps, I sweep. We all come together for the last three notes, which ring in unison, and as the dust settles, John flips his page over. How does he do it so fast? The minor key is cast aside for the first time in the next variation. Perhaps the Maiden has already left our world. In the ethereal key of G major, our four voices weave together, with mine providing a filigree wandering up and down the scale. Whose voice is more important, John's or mine? We sleepwalk through it, letting our subconscious do the work. Watch out for that arpeggio in the second half! Ah. At least, better than Jerusalem last week. But they loved us in Jerusalem. We had to play an encore. Will we have to play one here in Albuquerque? Stop it, you idiot. Your mind is wandering. A woman is grappling with Death and you're thinking about encores. All right, all right. Where was I? Oh yes, my triplets. I love the way they end this fourth variation breathlessly and are taken up by David in the beginning of the fifth, transformed from the tranquillity of major to trouble brewing in minor. The storm threatens with our crescendo, but it is only playing with us this first time around. I almost lose my way as David's triplets, bearing down oppressively with a single C in broken octaves, momentarily disappear in the mass of sound. We repeat, David reappears menacingly, and the crescendo is now in earnest, gathering in power as it careens into the second half. Michael, John, and I flail away at the sixteenth notes in triple fortissimo, but we still hold something back: we must sound violent but, paradoxically, transparent, for it is David's great moment in a melodic line of varied rhythms and bizarre leaps of pitch. This E flat section, always quiet in the preceding variations, is now wild and desperate. David leans forward into the cello to extract every last ounce of sound from his instrument. One last time the Maiden cries, to no avail:

> Pass me by, o pass me by,
> Go, wild skeleton!

The dynamic suddenly drops to mezzoforte and fades into the repeat of the second part of the variation, now quiet and with entirely different notes. A profound transformation is taking place, an easing, a letting go, as the diminished chord takes us for the last time into E flat major. Michael's repeated B flats are the bells that toll for the Maiden, who has finally left us. David, John, and I, voices in the choir, must mesh perfectly with him. In profoundly peaceful four-part harmony, the opening dirge is sounded for the last time, and now in major.

> Be of good cheer! I am not wild,
> You shall sleep softly in my arms.

We follow John's motion, eating his fingers again. One last crescendo tries to take wing, cannot, and then the final chord of the movement fades away. I give the cue that brings all our bows gently to a halt. There is the silence of being too filled with something. Schubert's grip on us slackens, and we are gradually restored to this world.

The faces of David, Michael, and John come back into focus. We four are in the midst of a great and wonderful journey.

ACKNOWLEDGMENTS

WRITING ABOUT THE LIFE and work of a string quartet might have remained only an intriguing idea but for my old friend Jill Kneerim, who first encouraged me to write, then counseled me about my first efforts, and ultimately became my literary agent. I am greatly indebted to her. Loving thanks to my wife, Dorothea, who provided unflagging support as the book progressed and astute observations from her vantage point outside the music profession. In addition, her gift of a lap-top computer enabled me to put to good use the enormous amount of time that a concertizing musician spends in trains, planes, and hotel rooms. Working with my editor, Elisabeth Sifton, at Farrar, Straus and Giroux has been an unalloyed joy. Elisabeth has just the right touch with a neophyte writer forever in the midst of a hectic concert schedule—gently but firmly coaxing words from a mind and heart filled with music. I cannot thank her enough. My children, Natasha and Alexander, gave me extremely helpful criticism, and Michael Batshaw provided surprisingly useful background material. Alan Alda's wise remarks about writing in general proved most useful in particular, and Arlene Alda's specific comments about the story line were much appreciated. Richard Uviller spent a generous amount of time reading through my tale from the perspective of an amateur chamber musician, and I am especially grateful for his many valuable comments. Lincoln Mayorga supplied both pertinent and colorful technical information about the recording process, and Max Wilcox helped rekindle the memories of our many experiences in the recording studio. Hiroshi Iisuka illuminated the three-century-old violin-maker's craft for me, and Daniel Fallon served up delicious anecdotes about Mozart. The excellent Carmen Gomezplata helped to clean up my grammar and to clarify material.

Lastly, I want to thank my colleagues in the Guarneri String Quartet for the astonishingly long-lived adventure we have shared together (our thirty-fifth season begins this fall), and also for their forbearance with my story. A string quartet, given its different members with their different opinions and memories, can prove the old adage that there is no such thing as history, only historians. David, John, and Michael might easily have said about any number of details in my book, "That's not how it happened. You've gotten the facts all wrong!" Ideally, they should all write their own versions of our life and work together—a book we could still call *Indivisible by Four*, but divided into four volumes.